The Enigma of Presidential Power

With gridlock, presidents increasingly rely on unilateral actions – means not requiring legislative statutes – which many view as tantamount to exercising power. Using a variety of approaches, Chiou and Rothenberg show that this need not be the case as, under many conditions, the chief executive's employment of such tools is constrained. Rather, presidents contemplating issuing executive orders are often constrained by worries about challenging the legislature and the courts. Most notably, the ability of Congress to employ extra-statutory means, involving efforts by legislators and their parties that don't require the passing of a law, limits how presidents utilize their discretion in this regard. Additionally, key features of the legislative process, such as agenda-setting, impact presidential power in a variety of ways. Political parties also play key roles in the exercise of presidential discretion and in how Congress impacts the choices a president makes. Nor are all presidential actions equal: the authors show that the policy area and the importance of a particular action both matter.

Fang-Yi Chiou is Full Research Fellow at the Institute of Political Science at Academia Sinica in Taipei. He has published on a variety of subjects in major political science journals such as the *Journal of Politics* and the *American Journal of Political Science*. He was selected to be a member of the Global Young Academy (2010–2016), was the recipient of the Elinor Ostrom Prize and has received five prestigious Taiwanese national research awards.

Lawrence S. Rothenberg is the Corrigan–Minehan Professor of Political Science and the Director of the W. Allen Wallis Institute of Political Economy at the University of Rochester. He is the author of four books and numerous journal articles, and was recently a co-principal investigator for a multimillion dollar IGERT grant for research and training in energy.

The Enigma of Presidential Power

Parties, Policies and Strategic Uses of Unilateral Action

FANG-YI CHIOU
Academia Sinica

LAWRENCE S. ROTHENBERG
University of Rochester

CAMBRIDGE
UNIVERSITY PRESS

CAMBRIDGE
UNIVERSITY PRESS

University Printing House, Cambridge CB2 8BS, United Kingdom

One Liberty Plaza, 20th Floor, New York, NY 10006, USA

477 Williamstown Road, Port Melbourne, VIC 3207, Australia

4843/24, 2nd Floor, Ansari Road, Daryaganj, Delhi – 110002, India

79 Anson Road, #06–04/06, Singapore 079906

Cambridge University Press is part of the University of Cambridge.

It furthers the University's mission by disseminating knowledge in the pursuit of education, learning, and research at the highest international levels of excellence.

www.cambridge.org
Information on this title: www.cambridge.org/9781107191501
DOI: 10.1017/9781108123556

© Fang-Yi Chiou and Lawrence S. Rothenberg 2017

First published 2017

Printed in the United States of America by Sheridan Books, Inc.

A catalogue record for this publication is available from the British Library.

ISBN 978-1-107-19150-1 Hardback
ISBN 978-1-316-64211-5 Paperback

Contents

Figures

Tables

Preface

This document represents the culmination of roughly a decade's worth of research on unilateral actions (presidential choices made prior to congressional legislating) – sometimes interrupted by a variety of work and life obligations – and an even longer collaboration. In 2001, we began our initial research together, focusing on exploring how legislative institutions, preferences and parties jointly shape legislative gridlock and productivity. After some initial success, and with a continuing interest in exploring legislative-executive bargaining, we decided to focus more centrally on presidential choices and how they reflect inter-branch forces, legislative dynamics and political parties. This led us to author a paper about presidential appointments to the bureaucracy that was published in the *Journal of Theoretical Politics* (Chiou and Rothenberg 2014) and, to a far greater degree, to concentrate on presidential unilateral actions.

Regarding the latter, we began thinking about unilateral action in 2006. Larry, having returned to the friendly confines of a Political Science department, invited Fang-Yi – having relocated from New Jersey to Taiwan – to escape the humidity of Taipei for the more favorable climate (at least in the summer) of upstate New York by visiting the University of Rochester's Wallis Institute of Political Economy, a practice which we have continued ever since. Our first several years principally focused on striving toward beginning to establish a theoretical apparatus that would help generate the kinds of insights in which we were interested. After examining some of the empirical implications stemming from our theoretical work with data generously furnished by other scholars, we came to the difficult conclusion that, for our purposes, more empirical heavy lifting was needed. Most notably, we realized how important it would be to develop a means of measuring the significance of a given unilateral action, in light of the substantial variance in importance of these presidential choices, ideally measured continuously and with a strong statistical foundation. This required many eye-straining hours in front of computer screens, not to mention the mastering of both complex statistical models and C programming. We also became increasingly committed to a belief in the importance of developing competing theoretical models that lent themselves to direct statistical comparison.

Since then, to our amazement (and sometimes to our dismay), our joint research interests have taken us through the second half of the following decade. During this time we have published articles in the *American Journal of Political Science* and *Public Choice*. Some of the materials presented here are expanded and revised materials from those pieces.

In the arduous process of preparing this book manuscript, we have incurred a multitude of professional debts. Thanks go to William Howell and Adam Warber for generously furnishing data. Much gratitude is also due to participants and discussants at the International Conferences of Positive Political Economy on Political Institutions, where parts of our project were presented and where we received valuable feedback, particularly from Craig Volden, in the springs of 2011 and 2014. We owe a considerable debt to the Institute of Political Science at Academia Sinica in Taipei, Taiwan for organizing these conferences.

Also, we would like to single out two colleagues and friends, Nolan McCarty of Princeton and David Lewis of Vanderbilt, each of whom crossed the ocean to visit Academia Sinica in 2013 and 2014, respectively, and discussed earlier drafts of the book. We are very grateful and thankful that Academia Sinica funded Nolan's visit and that Taiwan's National Science Council (NSC) provided support for David's travel. Nolan was especially magnanimous in his help, given that his principal reason for visiting Taiwan was to give several research lectures at Academia Sinica. The chapter-by-chapter comments that we received from both Nolan and David had substantial impacts on our revisions and additions and, whatever the final product's weaknesses, it is certainly much better for the input of these two fine scholars of political institutions and the presidency. We also want to recognize Professor Lewis for continuing to be a sounding board and a source of helpful advice as the manuscript wound its way toward completion.

As mentioned, much of the research for this project occurred in Rochester in the cozy confines of Harkness Hall. Many thanks to the University of Rochester's Wallis Institute of Political Economy for facilitating Fang-Yi's summer visits – especially John Duggan, Terry Fisher and Christine Massarro – and for providing a stimulating environment for productively completing this endeavor. Fang-Yi received great support from, and would like to express extreme gratitude to, his home Institute, and particularly to its former Chair, Dr. Yu-Shan Wu, for both making his academic visits possible and offering much encouragement and valuable advice throughout the course of this project, and to Taiwan's NSC and Ministry of Sciences and Technology (MOST, of which the NSC is now a constituent part) for their financial support for most of these trips. Fang-Yi's research was also aided by a generous grant from Taiwan's Foundation for the Advancement of Outstanding Scholarship. Fang-Yi would like to express his deep thanks to his colleagues at Academia Sinica for the friendly, intellectually-engaging, environment which they jointly create and to acknowledge the longstanding mentorship of Dr. Jih-wen Lin. Fang-Yi also wants to thank Larry for his hospitality during his summers in Rochester and for his accommodating nature and patience during the writing process; Larry wants to acknowledge the extraordinary sacrifices that Fang-Yi has made in uprooting himself during these summers and his commitment to mastering the many technical tools needed to bring the book to fruition.

We would also like to thank Cambridge University Press for steering this project to completion. Robert Dreesen has been unfailingly encouraging and working with him and his staff has been a delight.

On a personal note, Fang-Yi wants to thank his parents for their wonderful love, care and accommodating nature, and for their lasting support for his academic career in Taiwan. While relocating from the US to Taiwan has provided Fang-Yi many more opportunities to visit his parents regularly, they furnished the maximum flexibility and room for Fang-Yi's developing academic career in Taiwan. When plans for visiting them would be interrupted, they were always willing to adjust without complaint, consistently urging Fang-Yi to prioritize his work. What is a great pity is that Fang-Yi had planned to present this book as a gift to his mom in appreciation of her long and deep love but had no chance to do so, as she recently passed away just as the final draft was nearing completion. Regardless, Fang-Yi dedicates this book to his parents, whom he loves so much.

Larry would like to acknowledge his children – Daniel (who often told his father to get the book done, in not-so-subtle tones) and Sarah – who have grown into adults during the writing of this manuscript, and to Irina, who entered late in the process but has taken on a very large role in a very short time. He looks forward to many shared experiences with her, in many different places and continents, in the years to come. He dedicates this book to her and to their future together.

I

Introduction

Unilateral actions by the chief executive – directives not requiring statutory authorization but which may move policy – are often done quietly and receive little fanfare from those who lack strong vested interests. Hence, all of the details of what is occurring may be difficult to discern, meaning that drawing important insights from the underlying processes at work can be problematic.

However, this is not always the case. Consider two contrasting situations where such actions (in one instance, a failure to act on a matter that was clearly under consideration) did receive substantial attention.

In September 1991, a group of military leaders overturned the government of Jean Bertrand Aristide, the first democratically elected president in Haitian history. The new regime became known for treating its population brutally, leading the US government to slap economic sanctions on the country. This brutality also helped induce large numbers of Haitians to attempt to flee to the United States, often in unseaworthy boats. Traditionally, American policy would have involved interdicting these refugees and screening them (e.g., regarding eligibility for political asylum, which roughly one-third of those picked up were receiving) on Coast Guard cutters. However, when the flow of Haitians became too great, the Department of Defense established temporary facilities for screening at the United States Naval Base in Guantanamo, Cuba. Very soon, though, Guantanamo could no longer handle the large numbers either.

In response to this state of affairs, on May 24, 1992, President George Bush issued Executive Order (EO) 12807, which became widely known as the "Kennebunkport Order." Relying on the Refugee Act of 1980, legislation designed to set up systematic procedures for dealing with immigration on humanitarian grounds, the EO stipulated that the Coast Guard pick up the

Haitian refugees and return them directly, without screening, to the mercies of the military government.[1]

Human rights leaders plead with the Democratic Congress to act, even claiming that the President had violated international law by returning those fleeing back to their persecutors. But efforts by the Democratic House majority never got past the committee stage, and the Senate did not move on proposed legislation (leaders of the opposition to the new policy included House Democrat Stephen Solarz of New York – a key member of the House Foreign Affairs Committee – liberal Massachusetts Democratic Senator Edward Kennedy and the Congressional Black Caucus). The Bush rules that were set forth in the EO, which seemingly moved policy to the ideological right against the wishes of a Democratic legislature, remained the status quo.[2]

Five years after the Bush order, at a meeting of the AFL-CIO in February 1997, Vice President Al Gore publically promised that the Clinton administration would issue an executive order requiring that federal agencies employ project labor agreements, negotiated before construction projects commence, which would establish wage and work rules. Requiring such covenants was clearly understood as heavily favoring union contractors. As such, the pledged EO would be considered extremely pro-Democratic, given the party's tight alliance with unions, and would be quite contrary to the wishes of the Republican-controlled 105th Congress.

Regarding the latter, for example, the House Republican Conference, led by Ohio Representative John Boehner, developed a series of talking points for party members about how to fight the proposed EO. Among other things, these instructions for the rank and file depicted the order as the "giving of $200 billion in federal contracts to the AFL-CIO in exchange for organized labor's $100 million in Democrat campaign contributions – both legal and illegal – during the 1996 elections."[3]

However, as the Republicans clearly knew, such vitriolic claims need not have stopped Clinton if the President was determined to act. Most notably, Senate Democrats could have easily stopped legislation rolling back an EO, once issued, via the use of the chamber's filibuster rule requiring 60 votes in favor of a policy change.

In response to this seemingly poor strategic position, Republicans in the US Senate did not sit idly by, but instead enlarged the scope of conflict.

---

[1] Actually, the executive order (EO), titled "Interdiction of Illegal Aliens," did not specifically mention Haiti; this was done in a subsequent press release (Dodds 2006). Also, although not part of the EO, Bush did establish a means for allowing Haitians to apply for political asylum from the country's capital, Port-au-Prince.

[2] There were also efforts initiated by pro-immigration forces in the courts, but the Bush EO was eventually upheld by the Supreme Court (*Sale* v. *Haitian Centers Council, Inc.*, 509 U.S. 155 (1993); see Wasitis (1993–94)).

[3] See http://thetruthaboutplas.com/wp-content/uploads/2009/06/house-republican-conference-talking-points-on-clinton-payoff-to-union-bosses-pla-issue-0423971.pdf.

Specifically, they responded to the threat of the EO by holding up Bill Clinton's appointment for Secretary of Labor, Alexis Herman. In May 1997, an "exasperated" (Baker 1997, p. A10) Clinton first publicly condemned Republicans and then relented by agreeing not to issue the EO in question as a *quid pro quo* for Herman's [successful] confirmation vote (Kosterlitz 1997, Wells 1997). Put differently, the Republican gambit worked, with Clinton deciding that the importance of placating labor via the EO was less valuable than was securing Herman's appointment.

In short, in the case of project labor agreements, the chamber median/ Republican Party seemingly prevailed when Clinton wanted to adjust the policy status quo in a direction contrary to their wishes – even though it was extremely unlikely that Congress could have directly overturned the President's change statutorily. The President and the legislative majority party negotiated, and an accord was reached.

The Haitian EO and the unissued labor EO reflect two possible perspectives – which, combined, epitomize what we will call the *enigma of presidential power* – about how presidential unilateral action operates in general. In one, the President is able to move policy away from the dominant forces in the legislature and win the day. In the other, the chief executive must negotiate and receive acquiescence or agreement, or no change in policy will be forthcoming.

The matter of distinguishing which viewpoint is most apt, or under what conditions this is the case, is at the heart of what we wish to understand. As we will elaborate, a presidential ability to move policy contrary to dominant legislative interests can be viewed as the ultimate exercise of political power. Alternatively, if policy requires tacit agreement from other political actors, power is more constrained. The untangling of whether the President is positioned to exercise either type of power via unilateral action, and the specification of conditions under which there is and is not a need for acquiescence, is at the heart of our effort to make the understanding of power clear rather than enigmatic.

UNILATERAL ACTION AS PART OF THE PRESIDENTIAL REPERTOIRE

"Stroke of the pen," "Law of the land. Kind of cool."
Clinton Presidential Advisor Paul Begalia, as cited in Bennet (1998)

Of course, these stories of potentially difficult-to-reconcile presidential actions are not unique. Rather, they represent examples – perhaps not completely representative, given their seemingly high profiles – of how unilateral executive action has become a standard tool that the chief executive employs as part of his or her repertoire to achieve policy success. Indeed, despite many such decisions being of minor policy relevance (and hence falling under the radar of all but the most interested and dedicated of observers), the importance of these choices is increasingly recognized by not only scholars (whose perspectives we will turn to in the next section) but by the media as well.

Such increased popular and journalistic attention has been particularly notable during the last few presidential administrations, where the chief executive has frequently confronted legislative gridlock (the extent to which, due to varied preferences and congressional structure, that Congress is unlikely to be able to produce new legislation).[4] For example, Bill Clinton was attacked, principally by those on the right, for his abuse of executive orders after the Democrats lost the House in the 1994 elections. Illustratively, just after the Clinton administration ended (February 2001), Todd Graziano of the conservative Heritage Foundation decried that

Clinton proudly publicized his use of executive decrees in situations where he failed to achieve a legislative objective. Moreover, he repeatedly flaunted his executive order power to curry favor with narrow or partisan special interests. If this were not enough, Clinton's top White House political advisers made public statements about his use of executive decrees that were designed to incite a partisan response.[5]

From most popular accounts, as the President struggled to produce a legislative record consistent with his stated policy goals, his focus seemed to move increasingly to what could be done with the proverbial stroke of a pen, as referenced by the often-cited quip of his aide Begalia, above.

George W. Bush, also seen as facing difficulty in producing statutes to his liking, was subject to similar accusations. For example, somewhat ironically as it would turn out, candidate Barack Obama publicly proclaimed in March of 2008 that

I taught constitutional law for 10 years. I take the Constitution very seriously. The biggest problems that we're facing right now have to do with George Bush trying to bring more and more power into the executive branch and not go through Congress at all. And that is what I intend to reverse when I become President of the United States.[6]

Yet Obama, too, has found himself seeming to follow the same strategy shared by his predecessors, even augmented at times by the identical set of advisors.[7] This, naturally, led to condemnation of the President by those on the right and encouragement of the President by those leaning left.

[4] This should not be construed as a claim that earlier presidents were never accused of overstepping their executive authority – just that this assertion seems to be more prevalent than in the past. An example of a well-known overreach in earlier times was Harry Truman's 1952 seizure of steel plants, which created one of the greater furors every associated with a unilateral action and was eventually overturned by the Supreme Court (Marcus and Fisher 1994).
[5] Quote from www.heritage.org/research/reports/2001/02/the-use-and-abuse-of-executive-orders-and-other-presidential-directives.
[6] Quote from http://abcnews.go.com/blogs/politics/2014/02/obamas-long-lost-campaign-promise/.
[7] For example, John Podesta, who was considered a champion of the use of executive orders during the Clinton administration and publicly advocated their usage by Obama, was brought back

For example, David Davenport (2013) of *Forbes* has lamented that

Frustrated by his inability to work with Congress, Obama seems willing to do more and more unilaterally, to the ultimate detriment of the republic. It's hard to overlook the irony that part of his brief against his Republican predecessor was George W. Bush's willingness to stretch presidential power... But Obama himself is taking presidential power to new heights.

Consider his use of executive orders. There's no real Constitutional authority for these, but presidents have long allowed themselves this privilege... What's new is Obama's use of executive orders to initiate action where, in his view, Congress is moving too slowly, rather than to execute laws Congress has already passed... [With regard to gun control] Rather than working things through the Congress, he could throw down the gauntlet, saying here's a series of reforms I will do by executive order, deal with it![8]

For a view emanating more from Obama's allies on the left, consider the following interchange between the *New Republic's* Chris Hughes (2013) and Obama himself:

HUGHES: It seems as if you're relying more on executive orders to get around these problems. You've done it for gun control, for immigration. Has your view on executive authority changed now that you've been President for four years?

OBAMA: I don't think it's changed. I continue to believe that whenever we can codify something through legislation, it is on firmer ground. It's not going to be reversed by a future President. It is something that will be long lasting and sturdier and more stable... But what I do see is that there are certain issues where a judicious use of executive power can move the argument forward or solve problems that are of immediate-enough import that we can't afford not to do it.[9]

AN OVERVIEW OF UNILATERAL ACTION

Having provided initial motivations for why we are interested in understanding unilateral action, it is helpful to furnish a bit more of a systematic overview on the subject (for more detailed discussions, see Relyea 2008, Cooper 2002, Dodds 2013). Essentially, as constitutional head of the executive branch and as commander-in-chief of the armed forces, the President possesses a degree of authority to direct the bureaucracy (including the military and the national security apparatus) with respect to how it should carry out its responsibilities. From this, in a nutshell, comes unilateral action.

In other words, at its root, presidential unilateral action has two sources: the Constitution (specifically, Article II) and delegation from Congress associated

---

during Obama's second term, seemingly to work on such efforts with the current President (Holland 2014).

[8] Quote from www.forbes.com/sites/daviddavenport/2013/01/16/president-obamas-executive-power-end-run-around-the-constitution/.

[9] Quote from www.newrepublic.com/article/112190/obama-interview-2013-sit-down-president#.

with the passage of statutes. The constitutional source of this authority is intuitive. The President is the titular boss of the US bureaucracy, including the military. As such, there is an implicit amount of presidential discretion implied in the Constitution if the President is to carry out his or her varied tasks. The most obvious involves the President's role as commander-in-chief of the military (e.g., it is up to the President to determine what constitutes an offense that is subject to a court-martial, a not-infrequent subject of formal presidential unilateral action), but the same applies to other domestic and international considerations (everything from whether bureaucrats should recycle to whether Iran's assets might be seized in the face of foreign conflict). With regard to delegation, when legislation is enacted, it can rarely if ever be so specific that there is no room for executive branch interpretation. As such, there is typically a level of discretion – sometimes greater and sometimes lesser – assigned to the bureaucracy headed by the chief executive to carry out the law. This discretion may be very clearly delineated in statutory language or be left quite obtuse.

Not surprisingly, with the great expansion of government in its size, reach and complexity in the years after the New Deal, the relevance of presidential unilateral action has risen greatly. Over this time, chief executives have utilized unilateral action for important social and economic issues, such as whether stem cell research should be permitted or whether wage and price controls ought to be put into effect, as well as concerns about how government should function and how international affairs should be carried out. Consequently, no understanding of the modern presidency in terms of its operation or its power can take place without sensitivity to the role that unilateral action plays.

Corresponding to the sources of this authority to act unilaterally, if the President should overstep his or her boundaries there are two *direct means* through which he or she can be reined in.[10] First, the courts can overrule the President's action on the grounds that he or she lacks the constitutional or legislative rights to have done what, in fact, he or she did. Put differently, if the President oversteps the boundaries of discretion, the courts retain the right to invalidate the action. Perhaps the most famous example of this occurring involves the 1952 *Youngstown Steel* case, which followed the previously mentioned decision by President Harry Truman to seize control of steel plants in the wake of labor unrest and to the consternation of the steel firm owners. In the aftermath of this executive order, Truman was called to task by the Supreme Court in a 6–3 decision. According to the Court majority, Congress had already elaborated where the President's discretionary authority began and ended over such labor disputes and, in light of this specific legislative delineation, Truman had substantially exceeded his discretion.

---

[10] We will discuss indirect vehicles, such as legislative punishments inflicted on the chief executive by members of Congress for engaging in an unwanted unilateral action, shortly.

Second, the legislature itself can directly overrule the unilateral action by passing a subsequent statute. If the President initially acts in a manner that those in the legislature find inappropriate for whatever reason (i.e., not necessarily a violation of delegated discretion but simply by producing a policy that is viewed negatively), Congress can respond by enacting a law that trumps the unilateral action. In doing so, Congress can either reinstate the *ex ante* policy by invalidating the unilateral action or choose a new *ex post* policy of its own that it prefers over both the previous status quo that the President altered and the policy that the chief executive has put into place. As part of this action, Congress can also redefine the discretion allocated to the President.

Although we will focus in our empirical analysis on executive orders (while our theoretical approach fits unilateral actions generically), which are the most prominent of presidential unilateral actions and which have typically been thought of as having the most policy content, there are actually myriad alternative means that the chief executive can decide to utilize.[11] Formally, a presidential executive order is issued to federal agencies, department heads, or other federal employees by the President, given his or her interpretation of the President's statutory or constitutional powers. An EO takes effect 30 days subsequent to its publication in the *Federal Register*. In reality, an EO, as is presumably the case for other unilateral actions, is frequently a function of bargaining and persuasion within a presidential administration and with the larger bureaucracy (e.g., Rudalevige 2002, 2012) and may involve reaching out to Congress as well (e.g., Boyle 2007). Put differently, the chief executive's creation of an EO may come with considerable transaction costs in terms of requisite time and effort expended.

While we will not survey all other forms of unilateral action in detail, a number of such actions deserve special mention as they have gotten the most academic attention and may serve as substitutes for executive orders under some circumstances. Presidential proclamations are also issued by the President, but have tended more toward the ceremonial (but with notable exceptions, such as Lincoln's Emancipation Proclamation). For example, Bill Clinton's five initial proclamations when assuming office in 1993 were the National Day of Fellowship and Hope, recognition of the death of Thurgood Marshall, National Women and Girls in Sports Day, American Heart Month

---

[11] For example, Relyea (2008) includes administrative orders, certificates, designations of officials, executive orders, general licenses, homeland security presidential directives, interpretations, letters on tariffs and international trade, military orders, presidential announcements, presidential findings, presidential reorganization plans, proclamations, regulations (which are typically not thought of as presidential directives) and eight different national security instruments. There are other types of actions, such as executive agreements with other countries and executive rules proposed by agencies (which follow formalized rule-making procedures), which might also be lumped into a very expansive view of unilateral action, but which proceed under institutional rules that differ markedly from unilateral actions and, hence, no model of unilateral action would apply to them.

and National Visiting Nurse Associations Week. Presidential memoranda have traditionally been thought of as similar to executive orders, in that they are designed to govern the actions and behaviors of executive agencies and departments, but to be of generally lesser importance (but see, e.g., Lowande 2014; for a discussion of their joint use with EOs, see Cooper 2001).

Finally, although not formally a unilateral action in that they are *ex post* to a legislative enactment while unilateral actions are *ex ante*,[12] scholars increasingly pay attention to presidential signing statements. Such actions are written statements by the chief executive when formally signing legislation, and have seemingly been employed more in recent years in ways that have policy content (e.g., Rodriguez, Stiglitz and Weingast 2016). To reiterate, however, they would seem not to serve well as substitutes for *ex post* unilateral actions such as EOs, as they will be a function of the Congress's initial choices.

Before turning to broader scholarly assessments, we should note that, while there is a great deal to be learned about how constrained or unconstrained presidents are in issuing EOs, we do know quite a bit about the correlates of when EOs and unilateral actions take place.[13] Scholars began to take greater notice of EOs in the 1980s (for a comprehensive survey, see Cooper 1986) and, especially, the 1990s – not surprisingly, given that increasing polarization in American politics was drawing attention to presidents' utilization of alternative means of influencing policy (e.g., Ronald Reagan's efforts to restrict the bureaucracy through a series of EOs in 1981 and 1984 [Orders 12291 and 12498, respectively] were early efforts in this vein).

A number of initial studies conceptualized the production of EOs as not being particularly related to the relationship between the President and Congress (e.g., Morgan 1970, Light 1982, King and Ragsdale 1988, Wigton 1996), often focusing on features such as the lack of an issue's salience, the problem's complexity and the desire to make only incremental changes. Later analyses tended more toward quantitatively estimating and examining separation-of-powers features in greater depth (see Gleiber and Shull 1992, Shull and Gomez 1997, for two of the earliest analyses examining the effects of partisan majorities and legislative success on EO production), as well as a few other intuitive predictors of action.

Over time, for instance, a variety of measures were adopted to capture congressional fragmentation. For example, Krause and Cohen (1997) employed presidential majorities in the House and Senate, and found conflicting results across chambers. Deering and Maltzman (1999) used

---

[12] This distinction between *ex post* and *ex ante* is quite important both for the technical exercise of mathematical modeling and for assessing whether the presidential action corresponds to chief executive influence.

[13] We will leave in-depth coverage of the formal theoretical models used in a number of works (Deering and Maltzman 1999, Moe and Howell 1999a, Howell 2003) for the next chapter.

comparable measures and again uncovered contrary results by chamber; they also found that when presidents face a Congress with both an ideologically opposed median and override pivot, they are more likely to issue EOs. As we will discuss in greater depth in the next chapter, Howell (2003) utilized majority party size and a variant that incorporates party cohesion, and produced support that fragmentation matters.

Another feature that scholars have examined is public opinion, typically on the grounds that it should impact the ability to push legislation through the legislature (e.g., high public opinion can make EOs less necessary, everything else being equal). In one of the earlier efforts, Krause and Cohen (1997) discovered that public opinion does not matter; two years later, both Mayer (1999; see also Mayer 2002, Mayer and Price 2002) and Deering and Maltzman (1999) came to the contrary conclusion, asserting that unpopular presidents are more likely to promulgate EOs.

Similarly, the contrast between unified and divided government has been accorded considerable attention. In general, there has been a belief that significant executive orders are more likely to be produced when there is a partisan division between the legislature and the chief executive, presumably because the lawmaking branch will have greater difficulties both in overruling the chief executive and in producing legislation on the President's agenda.[14] However, empirical evidence for this supposition has been mixed, e.g., it was insignificant in Deering and Maltzman (1999) and for some of the presidencies studied by Mayer (e.g., 2002), but was significant in Howell (2003; see also Fine and Warber 2012).

Also, not surprisingly, executive orders tend to be issued at different times in a President's term. Cooper (2001), for example, noted that Bill Clinton acted quickly to make an imprint once he got into office, while Howell (2003) showed that, in general, presidents moved to act in their first year in office. This is somewhat intuitive, as a new chief executive may desire to put his or her own imprint quickly on politics and the bureaucracy, particularly if he or she is from a different party than his or her predecessor, or otherwise contrasts considerably in preferences from the person he or she succeeds. Conversely, Howell and Mayer (2005) found that the chief executive tends also to move late in the presidential term.

SCHOLARLY ASSESSMENTS OF UNILATERAL ACTION

Having laid out what unilateral actions are and the correlates of their issuance, we can now turn to broader issues that concern scholars. As indicated by the discussion above, heightened popular and journalistic scrutiny of unilateral

---

[14] There is an alternative "evasion hypothesis" (Martin 2000, 2005) that predicts that the chief executive will act more given unified government in an effort to move before Congress does. However, this prediction has generally not received much support.

action as part of the presidential repertoire has been paralleled by increasing scholarly attention to such actions (for reviews, see Howell 2005, Mayer 2009, Waterman 2009). Such academic efforts reflect the belief that the ability of presidents to move on their own without formal statutory authority has been understudied and underappreciated.

This does not mean that scholars agree in assessing such choices. Rather, in the spirit of our claim about presidential power being enigmatic, there is considerable debate among social scientists about what effect unilateral actions have on the political system in general and on the specific public policy outcomes that are generated.

Additionally, as we will elaborate in more detail, important issues remain unsettled and need refinement. There are both theoretical and empirical concerns requiring considerable further development (e.g., Mayer 2009). Most notably, the linkage between unilateralism on the one hand and presidential power on the other has too often remained unexamined or somewhat arbitrarily assumed, without careful scrutiny and attention to what might affect this association. In particular, we believe that the key to understanding this relationship is integration of unilateral action as part of the President's overall bargaining relationship with Congress as well as the formal constitutional arrangements involving the President, the Congress and the Judiciary. This involves building new models and, with great attention to measurement, taking them to data. Failure to integrate unilateral action and to build and test the appropriate models can lead to incorrect inferences about the balance of power between the competing political institutions.

Regardless, many scholars assert that unilateral action considerably impacts the political system. In this spirit, for example, one long-standing claim, which has a strong normative flavor, involves accusing presidents of undermining the system of checks and balances by acting unilaterally. This belief was stated most forcibly by Schlesinger (1973), who asserted an "imperial presidency," where the chief executive takes policy into his or her own hands without the checks that would otherwise be applied by the legislature or the courts. In more recent years, prominent legal scholars have vigorously debated whether presidential control of the sort being discussed is a good or bad thing, most notably in assessments of the "unitary executive theory" (see, most importantly, Calabresi and Yoo 2008; for additional discussions, see the symposium edited by Yoo 2010), which was wielded by George W. Bush's administration to justify the expansion of presidential unilateralism (e.g., Cooper 2005, Singh 2009, Bjerre-Poulsen 2012), such as its response to the terrorist attacks of 9/11. Stated succinctly, some legal scholars advance the notion that the President must have authority to control completely all government officials who implement the laws, claiming a foundation in the Constitution, while others maintain that this authority should be shared to a considerable degree with Congress (for a clear statement, see Lessig and Sunstein 1994).

More contemporary work by political scientists, which is of the greatest relevance for our study, has been almost exclusively focused on positive analysis, trying to understand what determines presidential choices, but it, too, tends to emphasize the importance of unilateral action for the political system.[15] Like the case of Bush and Haiti in our introductory discussion, some note specific instances where presidents are able to win the day despite potential opposition. For example, Lewis and Moe (2010) cite George W. Bush's ability to unravel unilaterally provisions in the Detainee Treatment Act that might otherwise limit his ability to deal with captured terrorists in his most preferred manner;[16] in the same vein, Mayer (2009) notes how much Bush employed his executive authority in myriad other ways in the aftermath of 9/11. More commonly, analysis is quantitative and occasionally formal and theoretical.

Regardless, and as we now detail in more depth, political scientists to-date have emphasized the possibilities for unilateral action (or what we also call *unilateralism*) to move policy and initiate an end-run around the legislature's formal ability to respond in a statutory way.[17] Principally, scholars differ in their assessments of the extent of presidential aggressiveness and in their beliefs of how the underlying process functions. Some maintain that presidents push forcefully and the impediments from other institutional forces are not comparable; others argue that the chief executive is more restrained.

Analyses Emphasizing Statutory Constraints

In all of the previous theoretical developments of unilateral action (i.e., Moe and Howell 1999a, b, Deering and Maltzman 1999, Howell 2003), the President is posited to move first in the sense of deciding whether or not to issue a directive to alter the status quo. This step is succeeded by Congress's collective choice as to whether or not to respond directly by passing a law on the same subject, essentially overriding the unilateral action. As mentioned, the legislature can either return policy to the initial status quo or change it to some alternative that it prefers over that created through the unilateral action. Differences in these theoretical developments, which we will detail in greater depth in the next chapter, rest on how the law-making process is conceptualized.

---

[15] As Mayer puts it (2002, p. 223), "The importance of the legal construction of the executive has not been matched by a commensurate level of attention, at least among political scientists, to the empirical, historical or normative aspects of the question."

[16] The Act actually amended a supplemental defense spending bill in late 2005 that detailed specific provisions regarding the treatment of detainees being held in Guantanamo Bay, Cuba.

[17] Courts have been recognized as potentially important but attention has, for the most part, been focused on direct statutory action.

In all such analyses, the President is considered to have a first-mover advantage, stemming from his or her having taken control of the agenda by moving the status quo. This is in contrast to the passage of new legislation, where Congress must formally initiate the process (perhaps, but not necessarily, in response to a presidential request). In the context of unilateral action, Congress is placed in the role of possibly checking the President's power through its ability to pass new laws to override or to amend any unilateral action.[18] As is standard in strategic models of this sort, in contemplating whether to issue an EO, the President anticipates whether the legislature will, indeed, pass a law to reverse the presidential unilateral action, and integrates this into how and whether he or she acts. Such a possible congressional response constitutes an important, and certainly the most clearly recognized, constraint on presidential action.

By standard logic, the President will generally not act unilaterally if he or she knows that a given choice will be overturned by the legislature. Put differently, assuming that the chief executive anticipates that the action will be reversed, Congress will not need to override presidential unilateral action very often. Rather, the chief executive will refrain from taking the requisite first step if he or she knows it will be to no avail. So, while we rarely witness reversal of presidential actions, this fact neither indicates that the threat of statutory reversion is or is not consequential.

We should recognize that (perhaps because the President is not sure whether the Congress will act to reverse, or for other idiosyncratic reasons, such as an intent of the chief executive to try to embarrass legislative opponents or to polish his or her image with external constituencies) there are a very few instances when we have seen statutory reversion. For example, Howell (2003) found that only four bills were reversed between 1945 and 1998, several of these repealing actions that had been taken by presidents many years before. One of the few reasonably contemporaneous reversals occurred in 1973 when Congress overturned a Nixon EO designed to link government pay to industry standards. Nonetheless, direct statutory overrides are a rarity, to say the least.

While the lack of frequent statutory reversals does not negate their possible importance because of the logic of anticipation, some have questioned the possible effectiveness of real or potential overrides on limiting presidential unilateral action. There are two, not mutually inconsistent, reasons for such wariness. The first involves collective action problems in the chamber

[18] This process of passing a law initiated by the legislature has been typically captured by the well-known pivotal politics framework (Krehbiel 1998), which we will formally overview in the next chapter but whose insights we will use throughout our discussion here. This framework highlights the importance of recognizing that congressional action requires the assent of multiple internal veto players. These veto players consist of legislators who can determine whether statutory attempts to change the status quo go forward or are abandoned, and are defined by the rules of the institution and the Constitution.

as a whole – difficulties associated with members of the legislature coordinating their activities, given their own interests and given demands on their time – within Congress. Moe and Wilson (1994) and Moe and Howell (1999a, b) have argued that such obstacles often stymie the ability and willingness of legislators to respond jointly to presidential unilateral action.[19] As such, the kind of direct statutory responses, real or threatened, that we have discussed would be less effective than they might otherwise be if coordination were cost-free and simple.

Second, as foreshadowed above, is the sheer difficulty of getting legislation through Congress, with its labyrinthine structure and rules and with its members' widely varied preferences. As previous theoretical studies argue, Congress is not a unitary actor, comprising instead multiple veto players or pivots, whose assents are required for legislation to pass. Assuming presidential opposition such that the chief executive will not sign a bill overturning his or her own action, overriding presidential vetoes in the law-making process will require the concurrences of median legislators in each chamber, the decisive Senate pivot (e.g., the 60th most liberal or conservative Senator, depending on the context under current rules) to overcome a filibuster, and the decisive chamber pivots (using the 67th percentile in each chamber) to override an executive veto. The President can take advantage of there being so many different actors, with such potentially varying preferences, all needing to agree before a law can be passed, by moving a status quo to a place where one of the veto players will not agree that a legislative proposal is better than the new policy, so that no overriding law can pass. Given this, previous theoretical analyses highlight how legislative structure can provide the chief executive with leverage to shift policy more to his or her liking without vulnerability to statutory action. In short, congressional structure and related fragmentation undermines the potential effectiveness of direct statutory reversal as a constraint on unilateral action.

To summarize, while statutory constraints are certainly relevant, two related considerations may make this congressional constraint rather weak. The first is that legislators have to find ways of putting aside their narrow, private interests in a collective effort to overrule the President. If they cannot, then there is the possibility that the chief executive can move policies around rather freely. Second, even if the collective action problem is not substantial, the multiple veto points within the legislature open up opportunities for the President to alter a status quo without statutory consequences. Put differently, if overriding statutes are really the principal legislative

---

[19] While these scholars seemingly assume that solving collective action issues in the chamber as a whole is required to respond effectively to presidential action, as we will discuss and demonstrate in later chapters, this is unnecessary. Instead, we will show that an effective congressional response often requires that parties, particularly the majority, be able to solve their collective action problems.

constraint, the ability of Congress to check the President will be substantially limited.

Analyses Emphasizing Judicial Constraints

While most analyses by social scientists have stressed direct statutory constraints, there is common recognition that the courts are a potentially constraining force, at least in extreme instances. As we pointed out earlier, if judges decide that a presidential order exceeds presidential discretion, then they can rule the action out of bounds and reinstate the previous state of affairs.

Most studies of such constraints note that the courts are hesitant to deal such a blow to the chief executive (e.g., Moe and Howell 1999a, b, Howell 2003). One can conjure up a variety of possible reasons for this, such as the inability of the judiciary to implement its decisions and the strong desire of judges to maintain the judiciary branch's reputation.[20] Furthermore, in the spirit of transaction costs, the price of waging judicial battles may not be inconsiderable, so even when an EO might seem to exceed presidential authority, conditions may not be such that societal interests will want to take on the costs of a challenge.[21]

As mentioned before, this does not mean that the courts are irrelevant for what we witness, as the executive may anticipate how much discretion the courts will permit. And, as implied by our earlier discussion of *Youngstown Steel*, the judiciary will step forward at least in some circumstances. In that specific case, we might note that the Courts were seemingly protecting the rights of Congress, in that the legislature had spelled out rather clearly what the nature of the chief executive's discretion looked like. Whether judges are motivated to uphold the law or advance their own policy concerns, they may feel the need to protect the legislature in some circumstances.[22]

Yet, in the end, as a direct constraint to determine whether the President is overstepping his or her discretionary bounds, it would not seem like the limiting effects of the courts would produce great fear in the heart of the chief executive. Of course, the judiciary possesses the ability to decide the extent of executive discretion if societal interests protest (it can also broaden agency discretion if it wishes to avoid conflict with the executive). Further, there may be instances

[20] However, this is a bit hard to swallow, in that the judiciary has proven consistently willing to intervene on issues raised by regulatory rulemaking, for example.
[21] In other words, the courts rely on aggrieved parties with standing to appeal an action; if the redress from undoing a unilateral action, conditional on the probability of winning in the courts, is deemed too costly by those impacted, they may refrain from appealing even if there is a positive likelihood that judges will rule in their favor.
[22] More recently, although not technically involving an executive order, the courts – again consistent with majority congressional interests – invalidated President Obama's executive actions to loosen immigration rules.

where there is a belief that the President really has violated his or her legislatively or constitutionally delegated authority, and the President will need to anticipate this or face the consequences. But, typically, the courts would not seem to represent a strong, binding, constraint.

Any Other Constraints?

While the potential for Congress to strike down unilateral action directly through a new statute or for the courts to invalidate an action on constitutional or other grounds has been analyzed in considerable detail, the potential for the legislature to employ various other means to undermine unilateral action has been largely ignored as a possible constraint on the chief executive. In other words, a simplified, literal discussion detailing presidential unilateral action might focus exclusively on the possibility of Congress directly overturning a chief executive's action by statute. An EO moves a policy in a liberal or a conservative direction and the legislature – perhaps as dictated by its median members or its party leaders – either responds by moving it back to the previous status quo or toward a place more to its liking.

In truth, Congress possesses a number of what one prominent textbook calls "extra-statutory tactics [that]... often necessitates informal accommodation" (Smith, Roberts and Vander Wielen 2013, p. 312).[23] A partial list of these could include Congress's control of the legislative agenda and calendar, its involvement with the budgetary purse and its ability to include substantive restrictions in the form of riders in such allocations, and the constitutional requirement that appointments be approved by the Senate, by which the legislature might constrain the chief executive in addition to direct statutory action. While these tools are likely imperfect relative to passing a statute dealing directly with an actual or potential unilateral decision, they may nonetheless represent substantial impediments for a President with numerous legislative priorities and policy goals to move forward with EOs that are contrary to dominant preferences in Congress, at least for certain types of policies that are particularly dear to members of the legislative branch.

Put differently, the number of arrows in the proverbial quiver of the legislature that the President must anticipate before acting – and which he or she may or may not confront after acting unilaterally on some issues and deferring on others – are actually, quite likely, far greater than statutory enactment.[24] Should the President too greatly alienate the legislature by

---

[23] While we will focus on such tactics, it is possible that they could be reinforced by a judiciary that effectively checks the chief executive by enforcing legislative intent.

[24] In other words, it may again be the case that these actual actions are witnessed infrequently in terms of "off the equilibrium path" actions, i.e., when everyone is behaving according to expectations, we witness these behaviors rarely, if at all. When this does not occur and expectations are not met – for example, if the President misjudges the likelihood of a congressional reaction to undermine his action or if the legislature mistakenly believes that the President will

moving policy independently, without paying attention to legislative interests unless they can overturn his or her actions through direct statutory action, the Congress can quite conceivably respond by either instrumentally acting in ways contrary to the President's interests or, more passively, failing to do anything on concerns important to the incumbent administration.

We can imagine a number of scenarios taking place that go beyond presidents' only considering the possibilities that the legislature will overturn or that the courts may rule that the President has overstepped lawful, discretionary boundaries. Particularly in a world where Congress has myriad concerns and considerations and the legislative calendar is notoriously tight, the chief executive might find that new legislative initiatives near and dear to him or her are delayed or even dropped from congressional consideration. Appointments that are needed to keep agencies running, perhaps concerning bureaucracies whose missions are central to a President's core constituencies (e.g., the Department of Labor for Democrats or of Commerce for Republicans) may be held up as a warning against a potential unilateral action or as a retribution for one that has taken place. Or budgets that presidents have no desire to veto may be laden with provisions that either make implementation of a desired unilateral action problematic or that otherwise punish the chief executive.

We are not alone in recognizing these possibilities. Mayer (2009) argued that scholars need to consider more than the straightforward reactions of Congress and the judiciary that are reflected in the difficulty of restoring the status quo after a unilateral action. Rather, Mayer called upon us to look at the subtler kinds of forces – "checks that are far more difficult to see than the obvious and formal legislative or judicial sanctions" (p. 448) – many of which occur prior to an action taking place. Quite a bit more vigorously, Christenson and Kriner (2015, p. 897), have adopted a similar stance:

When contemplating presidential unilateral action, presidents anticipate more than whether they can defeat legislative efforts to overturn their unilateral initiatives. They also consider the politics costs of acting unilaterally and weigh them against the benefits of doing so. Paying greater attention to these political constraints on unilateral action affords a more accurate picture of the place of the unilateral presidency within our separation of powers system in the contemporary era.

As mentioned, this view of the legislature is, in fact, quite consistent with the modern textbook view of Congress, which sees the relationship between the executive and legislative branches as far more complex and nuanced than a stripped-down version, where Congress either does or does not legislate on the issue at hand (e.g., Smith, Roberts and Vander Wielen 2013). Even in today's extremely polarized world, Presidents need to bargain and establish good will with their counterparts in the legislative branch rather than focus

---

back down in the face of certain costs that it imposes but the President nevertheless moves – we can observe these actions in practice.

myopically on a single issue. Otherwise, the chief executive may lack congressional support or cooperation and may find Congress using all sorts of mechanisms to undermine the administration. Although this does not mean that what we are calling extra-statutory constraints – legislative actions other than direct statutory changes to the concern of a unilateral action that are still germane – are sure to effect presidential unilateralism, it does seem more than sufficient to suggest that the possibility that they do so under some conditions deserves careful examination.

What instruments does Congress possess that are likely to induce a President to either seek tacit legislative approval or perhaps not act, even if direct statutory action might not be feasible? While this is almost certainly not a comprehensive list, we focus on three such potential, related mechanisms: (1) control of the legislative schedule, (2) the appointments process and (3) budgets and legislative riders.

Control of the legislative schedule. Non-scholars and scholars alike often think of presidents as having a legislative agenda (e.g., Beckmann 2010). Yet, from a constitutional standpoint, the chief executive possess no formal ability to shape the congressional agenda except to the extent that the possibility of a successful executive veto is considered by representatives or that nominees sent up to the Senate are actually considered by the upper chamber. Rather, the litany of legislation that presidents need to consider is subject to the whims of those in charge of gatekeeping for the plenary agenda (on gatekeeping, see, e.g., Crombez, Groseclose and Krehbiel 2006) and the associated rules that govern them.[25] While chief executives can employ a number of strategies to try and pressure the legislature to bring issues to the forefront, such as the so-called *bully pulpit* (and popular presidents may be listened to more carefully than those who are thought poorly of by the public), or can try and employ various inducements (such as influencing how bureaucrats allocate government monies, creating a so-called presidential pork barrel (e.g., McCarty 2000b, Hudak 2014), ultimately the matter of whether their concerns make it onto the congressional agenda in a timely fashion is up to those who control the process within the legislature. This includes not just scheduling statutory proposals to change policy to go forward, but, as mentioned, and as we will discuss again shortly, bringing up appointments to a vote in the Senate and the passage of budgets.

Issues of calendar control *per se* are particularly important in the contemporary Congress because of its crowded legislative agenda.[26] Modern legislatures are extremely busy places, and the amount of plenary time is finite

---

[25] Although distinctions are made between the two, for our purposes here we will often talk of legislative scheduling in terms of gatekeeping, by which some items are allowed on the plenary agenda and others are kept off by some political decision-maker(s).

[26] Of course, even if calendar space were not being jockeyed for, legislators could still decide to keep a consideration of interest to the chief executive off of the legislative floor.

relative to potential demands, and the US Congress is no different (Cox 2006, Cox and McCubbins 2011). What this means is that those who control plenary time – the legislators who set the calendars by which some issues are considered while others are left off – could impose costs on the President if they so wished. Schedulers could simply substitute other matters of interest to members on the legislative agenda rather than include something that the President wants, as a cost that the chief executive pays for unwanted action. Hence, while the legislature could just abstain from considering presidentially desired proposals even if hours were not at a premium, trade-offs created by tight plenary time accentuate the importance of scheduling and agenda control.

There is a considerable literature, both theoretical and empirical, on gatekeeping and agenda-setting in its broadest sense (e.g., Krehbiel 1998, Cox and McCubbins 2005, 2007). One area of considerable disagreement is principally over whether or not the process is controlled by parties and their leaders on the one hand or by the median legislators, given that Congress is constitutionally designed as a majoritarian institution, on the other. While we need not fully wade into this debate here, we will discuss the difference between focusing on chamber and party medians throughout our analysis of unilateral action (although we might note that, in practice, it is typically the majority party leadership that is viewed as directly responsible for what goes on the agenda, although it may be deferring to the interests of the chamber medians in making those choices).

Related analyses of plenary scheduling are less plentiful, but there are a number of recent theoretical analyses. Most point to the likelihood of a single member or a specialized group of members being delegated agenda-setting powers. Cox (2006) maintained that certain universal features of modern democratic assemblies, such as specialized agenda-setting offices and parties, exist due to the scarcity of legislative plenary time, and with McCubbins (2011), pressed the case that the US Congress very much fits this view (see also Čopič and Katz 2014 for a model finding that scheduling induces the creation of parties). Patty and Penn (2008; see also Palmer 2013) specified a model of scheduling that they viewed as quite consistent with a world where either the US House Speaker or the majority of the House Rules Committee controls the agenda.

All of this implies that it is at least feasible to consider that those in control of the schedule and gatekeeping – be they party or chamber leaders – might make presidents pay a cost if they have not at least given tacit consent to an EO or other unilateral action. This does not mean that the chief executive would never issue an EO under such circumstances; it only indicates that, in expectation, there would be fewer actions because the additional cost would be integrated into the President's calculations.

While we would not typically expect to see public discussion of such anticipatory behavior, or even *ex post* costs being imposed, we have witnessed examples where threats have been made with respect to particularly high-profile actions. For example, in the fall of 2014, and with beliefs that Barack Obama would be issuing an immigration order, given that there was little hope of a new relevant statute after Republican victories in the midterm elections, House Speaker John Boehner travelled to the White House and said not only would there be no subsequent legislative cooperation with the administration on immigration in the aftermath of an EO but that any unilateral action "will also make it harder for Congress and the White House to work together successfully on *other* areas where there might otherwise be common ground (italics added)."[27] In other words, Boehner explicitly invoked the kinds of threats that we have been discussing.

Appointments process. Related to the idea that legislators whom the President would cross by acting unilaterally in an unwanted way might credibly threaten and subsequently respond to an unwanted unilateral action is the chief executive's needs and desires for appointment approval by the United States Senate. The reasons for singling out appointments are twofold. First, they are virtual "must-haves," essential for both the judicial and administrative branches to operate, and the President requires Senate cooperation. In other words, they are somewhat different from policy, because a policy is typically in place if no action is taken. Second, appointments have been the subject of enduring conflict between the chief executive and opponents in the upper chamber over the last decades, despite the chief executive's incentive to nominate those who would be agreeable to the Senate and the Senate's incentive to bring nominees up to a successful vote so that the judiciary and administrative branches are not shorthanded.

The extent of the appointment problem has been widely decried and need not be discussed here in much depth. There is little dispute that many nominations have fallen prey to battles between the President and the Senate, with the latter adhering to certain supermajoritarian rules and customs – some of which have been amended in recent years – that have routinely seemed to pit the chief executive against members of the other party even during periods of unified government.

Rather, we need to accentuate certain points. First, as just discussed, successful confirmation of judicial and executive appointments is not necessarily assured in the modern political world, with about a quarter of nominations failing (O'Connell 2015). Second, in a similar vein, even given confirmation, length of time from nomination to Senate consideration for a vote can be considerable, variable and quite costly. Third, the process from nomination to Senate consideration has been widely shown to be a strategic one, with both theoretical models and empirical estimation concluding that many factors go into the calculations of relevant political actors (e.g., McCarty

---

[27] This is the summary of what Boehner transmitted to the President as relayed to CNN by the Speaker's office (www.cnn.com/2014/11/07/politics/immigrationledeall/).

and Razaghian 1999, McCarty 2004, Chiou and Rothenberg 2014, Hollibaugh 2015).

This being said, it is not surprising that appointments may get caught up with substantive policy considerations or other partisan and political fights rather than always examined in a vacuum. Indeed, and again even though much behavior should be unobservable or anticipatory, we have witnessed various examples of this happening in different circumstances over the years. With respect to EOs, this has taken place in several ways. For example, there is the type of situation discussed earlier with respect to the appointment of Alexis Herman for Secretary of Labor, where the EO and the appointment in question had little to do with one another and the tradeoff was relatively straightforward (drop the EO to get your nominees). Other times, things are more complex. For example, a deal in which George H. W. Bush would issue an EO that would satisfy the Democratic majority in Congress in exchange for reauthorization of the 1980 Paperwork Reduction Act and Senate approval of Bush's nominee to head OIRA (the Office of Information and Regulatory Affairs), James F. Blumstein, fell apart at the end of 1990 due to chamber differences in their versions of the legislation (Blumstein withdrew and no EO was approved). Here an appointment was to be made (and legislation was to be enacted) as part of a *quid pro quo* for an EO, a bargain that collapsed, leaving the President with no impetus to issue the EO in question.

Again, the point that is being made here is that appointments, vital and important for the administrative and judicial branches, may be another currency that, at least implicitly, can be spent to induce chief executives to favor EOs that placate Congress rather than alienate it. This can be the case even if direct statutory overruling of an EO is not feasible.

Budgets and legislative riders. Two related features that the President needs to consider are legislative riders and the budget. Budgets, like appointments, are actions that are in some sense essential for the government to function. They are "must-pass," as the status quo is not simply static if appropriations are not forthcoming (indeed, we have now witnessed several instances of government shutdowns over the failure to come to budgetary agreements). Riders are provisions attached to another piece of legislation that are otherwise unrelated, most commonly added through the House Appropriations Committee; we talk about them with respect to budgets because it is common for Congress to attach them to appropriations bills that the President would not otherwise want to veto for any obvious reason (on riders as a veto-proofing strategy, see Hassell and Kernell 2016). For example, in arguing that legislative majorities have more impact on bureaucracies than typically thought, MacDonald (2010) documents the roughly 300 *limitation riders* (which restrict uses of money for the finite period of appropriations, as compared to *policy riders*, which can be included in appropriations even though they impact policy directly until the law is changed) that are attached to appropriations bills needed to fund agencies and programs every year. It is standard for a passed appropriations bill to come out with any number of riders attached so that, while many riders do fail, their possibility of inclusion needs to be viewed quite seriously by an administration in taking an action that can arouse opposition.

In short, the possibility of encountering riders, some of which fail but may be nuisances and others of which pass, in response to an unwanted unilateral action is something that an incumbent administration would have to take very seriously. Riders could undermine the actual implementation of an EO or cause other harm that would outweigh the benefits accrued from the EO itself. Per the former, for example, in 2012 a rider was successfully attached to the Commerce-Justice-Science appropriations to prevent the Obama administration's 2010 EO (13547) on ocean policy from being executed. An example where the latter may have been true took place after the issuance of an EO (12954) by Bill Clinton in March 1995 that strengthened the right to strike for workers of federal contractors. The majority-Republican House then turned around and inserted a rider in the appropriations bill for the Departments of Labor and Health and Human Services. The result was that the EO-induced rider contributed to this being the only appropriations bill not passed in the fiscal cycle and a stopgap measure, with spending far less than the Clinton White House wanted, being substituted.

Thus, as with scheduling and appointments, budgets (particularly as impacted by riders) may be a means by which a Congress that could not directly pass a statute overturning an EO could nevertheless derail an EO that was contrary to legislative wishes. To reiterate, much of such influence would be anticipatory, with an administration feeling it necessary to communicate and bargain with the legislature rather than act imperiously when direct statutory response is not feasible.

Other means. Note that there are other features that we could also highlight, such as the ability to impose costs on bureaucracies through oversight hearings and potential conditioning effects of presidential approval. We omit them for reasons of brevity. Also, it might be possible that roll-call voting itself on the floor of Congress might be impacted by alienating EOs. For example, Neustadt (1991) reported that John F. Kennedy held off on issuing his EO on non-discrimination in federal housing for two years because he needed Southern Democratic votes on important trade and foreign aid legislation and thought pivotal votes would be changed if he issued the EO in question. Also, congressional resolutions could be employed to voice displeasure, as was the case in response to a Clinton EO on federalism in 1998 (Bailey 2000), the implementation of which was then suspended. Finally, legislative vetoes (the power of Congress to veto executive branch actions *ex post*) could be relevant. Although such provisions were ruled unconstitutional in 1983, they continue to be utilized in the form of so-called *committee vetoes* by the hundreds (see, e.g., Fisher 2005, Berry 2008).

The general point is that it is at least feasible that extra-statutory means such as these might be responsible for what one qualitative analysis (Boyle 2007, pp. 108–109) of unilateral action finds:

Executive caution and Congressional inertia probably represent something of a balancing act; a tacit understanding of the boundaries of acceptable behavior. Power struggles are avoided by a collection of unwritten rules, or norms, that are difficult for outsiders to understand, and difficult for scholars to measure.

GOING BEYOND: ASSESSING POWER

Previous work emphasizes Congress's potential (but rarely realized) use of direct statutory means (and to a lesser extent judicial limitations) for developing insights into the President's role in policy and politics with respect to unilateral action. By extension, it is assumed that the President becomes extremely powerful if these constraints are weakened by collective action problems or via the inability of Congress to agree on a statutory alternative as a consequence of its fragmented nature and as heightened by increasing legislative gridlock.

Stated differently, whether collective action problems or legislative fragmentation – which, to reiterate, are not mutually incompatible obstacles to statutory reversion being effective – are emphasized, it is essentially maintained that the President may still be able to move unilaterally even when Congress opposes the direction in which policy is being changed (e.g., Mayer 2009, Waterman 2009). This suggests that unilateral action adds considerably to the power and influence of the chief executive.

Yet, while power and influence would appear to be at the heart of the study of unilateralism, the existing literature has yet to move the issue of presidential power (especially) to the forefront. Our analysis is designed to remedy this state of affairs.

Specifically, the above discussions on possible constraints have crucial implications for this issue. If what Congress can exclusively do is to pass a new law to override presidential directives; then, the President will have quite unconstrained leverage to move policy around to achieve his or her ambitions. This can certainly raise concerns about an imperial presidency and raise doubts about the efficacy of checks and balances. However, if Congress can go beyond direct statutory response and, to varying extents, pressure the President to account for its preferences through extra-statutory means, the President, given delegated discretion, will be more cautious in moving a policy against congressional interests. In this scenario, the effects of checks and balances are considerably more in line with how it is typically thought that they should operate. In other words, if unilateral action requires more-or-less tacit approval from Congress, the President is much less powerful than would be inferred under the first scenario.

Although presidential power stemming from unilateral action has concerned most of the previous studies on this topic, with particular concerns about whether the President has faced few constraints, little work has directly addressed this central issue. As we noted, doing so involves not just integrating formal constraints but the possible implications of presidential bargaining with the legislature in more nuanced, and perhaps realistic, ways. We do just that by proposing a new theoretical framework, which can be assessed empirically, that allows us to get to the heart of presidential power via unilateral action.

To begin, and as foreshadowed earlier in our discussion, we first need to delineate what we mean by political power with respect to unilateral action. In our analysis, we propose two alternative conceptualizations, each with its pros and its cons. Happily, in the end, which conceptualization is utilized does not qualitatively change our results.

The first definition of power has roots in the so-called Dahlian (Dahl 1957) tradition. According to this view, in our context, power constitutes the ability to move a policy in a direction that is more to the President's liking, relative to the current status quo, without needing even the *tacit agreement* of other political actors (notably, the majority in Congress or those running its majority parties). If unilateral action must push policy to make such other political actors happy – perhaps because they will otherwise react by making life more difficult for the President in a host of ways (e.g., riders to budgetary appropriations or hindering political appointments) – then the President is not truly being powerful, according to this definition.

A good example of such an EO alienating congressional forces occurred in 1991 with respect to sanctions on South Africa as a result of apartheid. While many conservatives and Republicans believed that such sanctions were no longer needed in light of changes that had occurred in South Africa, liberals and Democrats tended to believe otherwise. Nonetheless, President George H. W. Bush issued EO 12769 to lift sanctions, despite the grave unhappiness expressed by Democratic leaders (Democrats had substantial majorities in both the House and the Senate), such as Edward M. Kennedy of Massachusetts and John Conyers of Michigan.

However, the above definition may seem too restrictive, since a President is better off as long as a policy change is to his or her liking. Hence, the second, broader definition of political power we adopt in this book is similar to what we can think of as akin to political influence: the ability to move policy toward one's own preference regardless of whether other political actors are opposed, indifferent or supportive. This definition closely corresponds to how much unilateral action simply works as a mechanism for the President changing policy from where it would be otherwise. As a less-restrictive definition, all actions that would constitute power in the Dahlian view would be included, but a variety of other circumstances are also incorporated. In other words, policy gains that seemingly increase presidential influence, notably those in line with congressional interests and tacitly supported by Congress, are only viewed as powerful in this second definition. For instance, in 1976, Gerald Ford issued EO

11905, which reorganized the US intelligence community for the first time since World War II. Ford went out of his way to coordinate with the post-Watergate Democratic majority. Although some of these Democrats felt that the chief executive should have gone even further in his reforms, the move was clearly toward what the legislative majority wanted. This EO would qualify as evidence of presidential power only under the latter definition.

We simultaneously adopt these two definitions for three reasons. For one, the latter conception of power has been widely subscribed to by most scholars, so it is natural to include it for the evaluation of presidential gains from unilateral action. For another, while the Dahlian definition is more restrictive than what many (or even most) people adopt, it is useful for highlighting whether and when presidential gains are tacitly approved or supported by Congress; in such instances there is ambiguity regarding whether the President simply achieves what Congress wants him or her to accomplish, as compared to persevering despite congressional opposition. Finally, our conclusions will be more robust if we can demonstrate that they largely hold, regardless of which version of power we consider more appropriate – indeed, this is what we find.

With these two definitions of power in hand, we can undertake an analysis that distinguishes when unilateral action does and does not constitute presidential power. In doing so, we must distinguish which factors condition how and when the President is powerful and, if presidential power is not being exercised, what underlying processes are at work.

As we have mentioned and will discuss further, previous models were oriented toward the occurrence of unilateral action and focused on Congress's, and to some extent the judiciary's, direct responses to such actions. While useful for understanding such phenomena, the models are not ideally designed for assessing the relationship between unilateral action and presidential power or for making distinctions between underlying processes. Consequently, we will need to specify a series of new models to meet the goals of our analysis.

Thus, we propose a research design that pays careful attention to theory and empirical issues and integrates them structurally. This represents a challenging task, as capturing the multiple possible determinants of – and constraints on – unilateral action, examining presidential power arising from such an institution and systematically accounting for the underlying complexity of observable unilateral action (e.g., particularly distinguishing significant from mundane executive actions) are difficult. However, only in doing so – supplemented with more qualitative assessments of underlying processes – can we ascertain to what extent presidential unilateral action is constrained and, ultimately, unpack the potentially nuanced relationship between unilateral action and presidential power.

Hence, we propose competing and comparable theoretical models associated with more or less presidential power, hoping to capture the possible process of presidential unilateral action behavior. We employ Howell's (2003) theoretical work as a jumping-off point to produce competing models that allow us to distinguish more or less presidential power and are amenable to empirical investigation and comparison. Note that, despite employing Howell as a starting point, our theoretical analysis is quite distinct from his: first, in that we generate otherwise-identical models while only varying directional constraints on the use of discretion; second, by distinguishing the crucial differences that each model implies for presidential power; and third, by integrating political parties in a considerably more substantial manner, both for the chief executive's decision whether to act unilaterally and for the legislature's response.

Specifically, our analysis commences with a theoretical framework, which we will present in two steps in ensuing chapters. The first step focuses heavily on how constraints on the direction of presidential discretion can impact power. Our analysis has two key advantages, relative to past work: (1) it allows for theoretical models that can be compared empirically in a direct manner and are associated with different levels of power and (2) we can employ general assumptions about features such as the distribution of status quos. However, one obvious weakness of this approach is that the role of political parties in the legislative process is assumed to be limited, whereas not only are parties potentially important, their roles can have ramifications for assessments of presidential power in general and of how, specifically, the ability of subsets of legislators to overcome collective action problems impact executive power. Hence, the second step involves the nuanced incorporation of a key player that has typically been given short-shrift in existing work – political parties – but requires somewhat more restrictive assumptions in empirical evaluation. The more encompassing framework is necessarily messier, because it involves comparing and contrasting 18 models. In other respects, however, it is more straightforward because we use a unique and novel means of comparison that complements our initial empirical work. Because each approach has corresponding advantages and disadvantages, analyzing both and comparing and contrasting our results will make our results more credible and illuminating.

More precisely, we begin our initial theoretical endeavor by developing a trio of competing models associated with different levels of presidential power, which share several features incorporated in previous models: (1) the President, given the first-mover advantage, can choose to take unilateral action with delegated discretion; (2) Congress can respond by passing a new law to reverse or revise presidential action, subject to a presidential veto and a possible override; and (3) the courts will strike down unilateral actions if the President overuses delegated discretion that Congress has not disallowed. This structure implies that how Congress can react to presidential unilateral action in the legislative process will shape the chief executive's incentives for whether, and how, to craft a presidential directive.

These alternative models are exclusively distinguished by a directional discretion assumption in the first stage that captures possible differences associated with whether the President needs to bargain or can just take the likelihood of formal statutory or judicial overturn into account. In our so-called unilateralism model, the President is assumed to be able to move the status quo through unilateral action to the ideological left or right; in the chamber-compliance model, the status quo can only be shifted in a direction consistent with the chamber median's ideal point; and, in the partisan-compliance model, the status quo can exclusively be moved in the direction of the majority party median's ideal point. Note that, in the latter two instances, the chamber as a whole or the majority party can be conceptualized as overcoming collective action's impediments to some degree.

It is important to note that, while not commonly recognized, assumptions about presidential discretion are intimately intertwined with inferences regarding presidential power. If anything, scholars have focused on the *size* of presidential discretion (how far the President can move policy in the ideological space), but not on the *direction* of discretion (whether presidents can move policy in a liberal or conservative direction, or both).[28] As we will show theoretically, direction is actually far more important than size in this context for assessing power and influence.

With this in mind, and in contrast to past work, we will integrate discretionary constraints in a manner that highlights how they are crucial for distinguishing presidential power. Specifically, each of these directional constraints on discretion has substantial, distinct implications for how much unilateral action corresponds to presidential power. Intuitively, assuming that presidents can move the status quo through unilateral action in any direction, which is what most scholars (e.g., Epstein and O'Halloran 1999) have assumed, is associated with the most power. Alternatively, assuming the additional legislative constraint (as explained above) that the President can only move the status quo toward either the congressional chamber or party median, where at least tacit acquiescence from key legislative players or their judicial surrogates (who rule whether a presidential action is beyond what is delegated by the legislature) is required, corresponds to a world where there is a less influential President and a chamber that can organize collectively as a whole or via its majority parties.[29]

---

[28] As far as we know, Howell (2003) is the only work that makes alternative directional discretion assumptions analogous to what we are proposing. However, his purpose is to provide circumstances under which varying hypotheses hold (and we do find some issues with his matching of theory and empirical hypotheses when we carefully examine his claims), while we concentrate on the profound implications that stem from *identical* models where only the direction of discretion assumption is allowed to vary. In other words, our purpose (which was not Howell's) is to generate directly comparable models that can then be contrasted empirically.

[29] Although we primarily discuss the legislature, we reiterate: restrictions can be thought to reflect judicial actions enforcing an enacting coalition's congressional will. It is possible to

Regardless of which of our two alternative definitions of power are considered, the first assumption implies a strong association between unilateral action and presidential power, while this is attenuated in the latter two. Hence, our unilateralism, chamber-compliance and partisan-compliance models – each with an associated discretion assumption – provide alternative and consistent theories of unilateral action. As we will see, we can test which if any of these models best fits data, and doing so not only tells us about power but generates new insights into the relationships that condition when it will be in the President's interest to move unilaterally. For example, we find that greater legislative fragmentation gives the President more opportunities to act unilaterally under the unilateralism and chamber-compliance models, but not under the partisan-compliance model if government is divided.

As mentioned, our second theoretical initiative involves thinking about parties to a greater extent than has been the case previously in the unilateral action literature (and, for that matter, in the literature on the institutional presidency), particularly by considering how they may impact the possibility of direct statutory override through agenda-setting or party pressure in the legislative stage. Surveying research on political institutions, and as implied by many instances where the President runs into problems over unilateral actions, the one factor that clearly needs to be considered carefully and thoughtfully is the role of political parties in the lawmaking process. Institutional literature in particular goes from claiming that parties are little more than surrogates for political preferences (Krehbiel 1993, 1998) and that they are purveyors of negative agenda-setting power by which they can hold back what choices can be considered in the statutory process (Cox and McCubbins 2007) to seeing them as active, positive agenda-setters, determining actual proposals over which choices are then made (Rohde 1991). In exercising their influence, parties are also posited to impact revealed member preferences, pressuring the rank and file to choose differently (i.e., to be more liberal or conservative) than they would in a party-free world (e.g., Snyder and Groseclose 2000, Cox and Poole 2002, Evans and Grandy 2009).

Hence, in the second step of our theory building, we expand our theoretical framework such that, in the middle of its three game stages (presidential unilateral action, the legislative process and the judicial process of ruling over presidential discretion being the three sequential stages), parties can organize collectively and play agenda-setting or member-influence roles. Additionally, parties may impact the actions of their members through (imperfect) party discipline (e.g., by changing a member's vote) so that a legislator's induced preference will replace his or her primitive preference in determining legislative policy outcomes. While adding parties into the legislative process stage comes at the expense of making some more restrictive assumptions relative to the first set

---

conceptualize judges as playing a more independent, complex, strategic game, but for our purposes it will be sufficient to assume that judges play a more muted role.

of theories that we initially examine when we turn to their empirical investigation (our ultimate purpose), making the models more encompassing in terms of the players involved is a substantial return.

Most importantly, given our goals, this framework is flexible enough to subsume different combinations of party roles at different stages, party discipline levels varying from non-existent to complete and incorporating our alternative assumptions about presidential discretion for unilateral action. As such, previous models in the literature just constitute special cases, and we will be able to examine a spectrum of models associated with more or less presidential power. Furthermore, each alternative model will have clear empirical predictions regarding the level of unilateral activity observed, if it holds.

Empirically Distinguishing Presidential Power

Empirically, solving the enigma of presidential power by distinguishing which model best matches empirical reality comes with a number of corresponding tasks. While we will leave many of the details to subsequent chapters, we wish to emphasize several elements of the empirical enterprise here.

The first is the need to measure significant unilateral actions. Even more than is the case for legislative statutes – where assessing the importance of one statute compared to another has been a concern meriting much investigation (e.g., Mayhew 2005, Clinton and Lapinski 2006) – distinguishing significant from insignificant unilateral actions is crucial. While in our analysis we will focus on executive orders, given that they are typically seen as the most prominent of the decisions falling under the rubric of presidential unilateralism, the same necessity of ascertaining an action's importance would be true of any unilateral action. When it comes to EOs, it has been recognized that many are purely symbolic (e.g., Warber 2006) and, more generally, that significant and insignificant executive actions (e.g., Cameron 2006, Mayer 2009) are intermixed. However, for understandable reasons, myriad scholars have ignored such actions' heterogeneity, and a few others (Howell 2003, Mayer and Price 2002) have developed a dichotomous significance measure, looking at whether either a single source (e.g., the *New York Times* front page) or one of a small number of sources mentions a given action – i.e., the EO is significant if it gets mentioned at least once and is insignificant if it doesn't. Either pooling all actions or separating them via a fairly simple method of distinguishing the important from the unimportant likely produces measurement shortfalls in terms of judging significance, what Cameron (2009) aptly labels the "Wheat-from-the-Chaff" problem. In turn, these measurement difficulties likely limit empirical analyses.

In our analysis, we improve EO significance measures by constructing a new means of statistical analysis that applies data from alternative sources (serving as "raters") to assess significance in continuous fashion and, unlike past work, builds-in information about rater biases.[30] Happily, electronically searchable databases and the development of new measurement techniques of this sort make addressing these difficulties possible (although still quite time consuming).[31]

Subsequently, with our superior and more flexible significance measure, we empirically test the hypotheses derived from our competing theoretical models (note that this conforms to the kind of comparative model testing for which many scholars clamor). This includes both our initial models and those where agenda-setting powers or party influence are integrated. In doing so, we will examine how our results are a function of the thresholds for determining significant EOs.

Additionally, we recognize that, despite much of our analysis involving the construction of theoretical models, measurement of underlying concepts, and statistical estimation, subtleties of unilateral actions will not be captured completely by such analyses and the kinds of processes that we are highlighting will not be fully appreciated through a reading of mathematical theory and accompanying statistical results. As such, as we have already done in our discussion in our introductory comments, we consciously look to case studies that demonstrate these processes and that, we believe, are illustrative and illuminating.

Also, with a theoretical framework designed to delineate the relationship between unilateral action and presidential power and what party roles are played, we can distinguish between different types of policies and explore whether our empirical results about the relationship between unilateral action and presidential power depend on policy type as well. To date, scholars have tended to assume that the underlying process governing unilateral action is not conditioned by policy type. Alternatively, we will investigate whether some types of policy are more susceptible to the exercise of presidential influence or power than others, given the nature of the policy-making environment and electoral incentives. Our theoretical framework provides us the opportunity to examine whether the same model or models – each associated with relatively high or low presidential power – correspond best to some policy categories as compared to others, providing a more complete picture of how unilateralism functions.

In related fashion, we are much better positioned than past analyses to reassess the seemingly unresolved debate on whether there are two presidencies: a strong, unconstrained, foreign policy President and a weaker,

---

[30] Specifically, we develop a new variant of Bayesian item response theory (IRT).

[31] Given the extensive data collection involved and the traditional preeminence of EOs as a means of unilateral action, we focus exclusively on Orders in our empirical analysis (to reiterate: our theoretical world should be applicable to actions generically). While the inclusion of other forms of unilateral action – notably, proclamations and memoranda – might be desirable in another context, the scope of the necessary data collection would be too great.

constrained domestic policy version (for the classical work, see Wildvasky 1966; for assessments, see Sigelman 1979, Fleisher and Bond 1988, Marshall and Pacelle 2005, Canes-Wrone, Howell and Lewis 2008). In turn, this will allow us to see whether power is partially contingent on this distinction and whether parties play differential roles depending upon which type of policy is being considered. If foreign and domestic EOs are characterized by distinct policy-making environments that have implications for presidential power, we will not just shed light on the two-presidencies conjecture and provide some cautionary advice to scholars pooling all executive actions together regardless of their policy arena, but will also generate insights for our ultimate goal of understanding the enigma of presidential power.

CONCLUSIONS – UNILATERALISM AND POWER

Presidential unilateral actions receive increasing popular and scholarly attention. Journalists, not surprisingly, tend to highlight the idea that they are a means of considerable presidential control of the policy process; scholars vacillate from concurring with journalists, citing a variety of presidential advantages, to emphasizing the direct legislative and judicial constraints that limit these possibilities. In almost all instances, unilateralism and power seem to be, implicitly at least, considered one and the same.

Yet, as our initial examples of the Haitian EO and the unissued labor EO illustrate, there are two possible perspectives about how presidential unilateral action operates in general. In one, the President is able to guide policy away from the dominant forces in the legislature and win the day. In the other, the chief executive must negotiate and receive acquiescence or agreement, or no change in policy will be forthcoming. From this comes the enigma of presidential power: Does (or under what conditions can) the chief executive employ unilateral actions to exercise power?

Our analysis is designed to provide an answer to this question. For one thing, we take seriously the idea that there may be constraints on the President besides those associated with direct statutory action by the legislature or judicial reversal. If this is the case, we can imagine a world where there is far more presidential-congressional back-and-forth over unilateral actions generally and executive orders specifically than is suggested if we focus exclusively on direct constraints (we would conjecture that this would empirically apply to unilateral actions in general). In doing so, we bring the idea of power, in its several manifestations, to the forefront. We also do the same for various roles of political parties, which have been widely held as a key confounding feature in legislative choice and executive-congressional relationships, and integrate them into our analysis in a systematic fashion, both in terms of impacting the President's decision to act unilaterally and his or her related interactions with the legislature. As such, our book is the first that we know of that either explores when unilateralism may or may not constitute power or models parties and presidencies to show how various party roles can condition presidential power. We also disaggregate types of policies in a variety of ways, not only systematically investigating the two presidencies, but seeing which types of policies may correspond most to presidential power and to party influence. Analogously, far more than in past research, we are able to see how sensitive analyses of power and influence are to the significance of the actions that are being investigated.

Indeed, we will show that unilateral action is far from tantamount to presidential power, and that outcomes more consistent with bargaining and tacit accords are common, especially for domestic policy. We also demonstrate that the relationship between action and power depends on the roles of parties, as well as the nature of electoral incentives and the policy-making environment, and sometimes in non-intuitive ways. For example, we provide evidence that there are a variety of circumstances where the ability of parties to overcome their collective action problems, both in impacting the direction that the President is incentivized to use his or her discretion and in influencing members through party pressure to set the agenda in the legislative arena. Thus, while Moe and Howell (1999a, b) are largely correct in saying that Congress appears to have difficulties acting collectively as a chamber, the ability of majority parties to organize collectively does, on net, reduce presidential power.[32] We also find that results vary by policy area, including in a manner consistent with the two-presidencies conjecture, by which it is posited that the chief is more powerful with respect to foreign as compared to domestic affairs; additionally, we find that results are, indeed, sensitive to the significance of actions being investigated. In short, the President's place in the world of unilateral action is, on the one hand, not that different than it is in many other arenas; but, on the other hand, it is far more nuanced than one might have thought.

As we have implied above, making such inferences involves three related efforts: (1) developing a general theoretical framework that generates hypotheses that can be used to examine which model best corresponds to data; (2) utilizing advanced measurement techniques; and (3) applying modern statistical analysis to distinguish these competing models with confidence. It also involves supplementing these analyses and illustrating key features, with careful qualitative analysis along the way.

Hence, the next chapter of our analysis presents our theoretical framework, focusing on different ways of modeling presidential discretion with respect to unilateral action. In it, we derive alternative unilateralism, chamber-compliance,

[32] Interestingly, as we will see, collective action's impact on the direction of discretion's use substantially reduces presidential power, but the ability of party leaders to pressure their members and to manage the legislative agenda *contributes* to presidential power. However, as the discretion effect is much greater, collective action by majority parties reduces the chief executive's power.

and partisan-compliance models, each associated with different levels of presidential power.

In Chapter 3, we turn to the problem that not all unilateral actions generally, or EOs specifically, are created equal. As such, counts of actions are not sufficient to answer the questions that motivate us. Alternatively, we conceptualize presidential executive orders as lying along a continuum from unimportant to important and provide a data-collection and estimation method to provide an associated measure.

With theory and data in hand, Chapter 4 empirically analyzes the three models associated with different discretion levels. We do so both for EOs generally, conditioned by significance levels, and – on the supposition that issue type might matter for underlying politics and bargaining – for different policy concerns, specifically. Out of this we can start to make the inferences about presidential power and checks and balances that are key motivators of our analysis and we can begin to make sense of the enigma of presidential power.

We then turn in Chapter 5 to the messy task of further integrating the potential roles of political parties – as agenda-setters and as influencers of legislative actions. We complicate the theoretical models initially introduced in Chapter 2 by building different roles of parties in the legislative arena into the models, which admittedly require some additional assumptions for empirical testing, and then reexamining the data for EOs generally and according to policy area and level of action significance, with the resulting predictions. This allows us not only to gauge whether parties matter in the legislative context, but also to generate additional insights into the extent of presidential power for different policies and actions and how parties play a role in reinforcing or mitigating this influence.

The last substantive chapter finishes our empirical analysis by examining differences in policies and political context via an analysis of the two-presidencies conjecture, that the President has less discretionary constraints and, consequently, more power, over foreign than over domestic policy. We utilize our theoretical, measurement and empirical approaches to analyze the two presidencies, both to add clarity to this debate and to further make sense of presidential power. We use the distinction between policy types not only to further investigate whether the chief executive behaves differently depending on what is being considered, but to consider whether the President is more constrained and less powerful for domestic issues than for foreign issues.

In the final chapter, we conclude. We recap our analysis, discuss what our findings mean for power, unilateral action and the nature of our separation-of-powers system and suggest where future research might go.

In total, our study provides a means of solving what we have labeled the enigma of presidential power. In doing so, we offer a unifying theoretical framework for conceptualizing unilateral choices where models are carefully specified and directly comparable, we provide means for rigorous measurement and we integrate the analysis of theory and data. We also incorporate multiple party roles in a manner that is largely lacking in the literature on unilateralism and link the ways in which different incentives and abilities to overcome collective problems may produce different levels of presidential power across policy types. With in-depth analyses, we are able to draw conclusions about presidential power that shed new light on the impact of the modern presidency. As a consequence, we can also take a step in addressing important normative considerations, such as those respecting the chief executive's ability to act in an unchecked and imperious manner.

2

Thinking about Power: Theoretical Model

INTRODUCTION: POWER AND THE PRESIDENCY

As our introductory chapter implies, the study of the presidency generally has been greatly impacted by the trend toward linking theory and data. For one thing, presidency scholars have increasingly recognized the importance of applying more deductive approaches toward studying the chief executive's power and the bargaining relationship between the President and Congress. Indeed, leading presidential scholar Terry Moe (2009) asserts that the study of the presidency has undergone an intellectual revolution, shifting from stressing presidential personalities and characteristics to highlighting strategic opportunities and calculations. Along the way, a number of these models have been taken to empirical data. In this manner, institutional presidency scholars have applied formal theory to the tackling of key elements of the presidency, including executive appointments (e.g., McCarty 2004, Chiou and Rothenberg 2014), presidential vetoes (e.g., Cameron 2000, McCarty 1997, 2000a, b, Cameron and McCarty 2004) and unilateral action.

While unilateral action has been the subject of formal analysis, in truth such previous studies have been sparse (Mayer 2009). Rather, the study of unilateral action has been dominated by empirical approaches that, while theoretically motivated, have lacked formal underpinnings. The lone exceptions have been Moe and Howell (1999a) and Deering and Maltzman (1999), both of which employ graphical techniques based on spatial analysis (only the latter has a corresponding empirical analysis), and Howell (2003), who presents a game-theoretic model, which he then takes to data.

These theoretical developments, which we will review shortly, greatly inform us as to how unilateral action can enhance the president's opportunity to move policy closer to what he or she prefers and how a direct statutory response by Congress can impact presidential calculations regarding whether to take unilateral action. However, they are not as well equipped to shed light on

34

whether, and to what extent, unilateral action undermines the checks and balances associated with separation of powers, an issue of great concern to many scholars. More specifically, they cannot be employed to assess whether Congress can constrain presidential unilateral action beyond direct statutory response (which, to reiterate, is quite rare in reality).

This chapter presents a theoretical setup that will allow us to ascertain to what extent unilateral action can provide the President with an advantage in the inter-branch struggle that determines policy outputs. Our framework allows us to contemplate the impact of extra-statutory mechanisms as well as direct statutory action by the legislature. Moreover, it provides a means by which to think in a precise way about power – what it means and how unilateral action might impact its allocation.

We will begin by reviewing previous theoretical efforts in detail, first briefly noting common features of unilateral action models and then turning to the pivotal politics model of legislative activity and to initial and subsequent analyses incorporating unilateral action, as this overview covers key building blocks for our theoretical setup. We then introduce our three models, which are distinguished exclusively by directional discretion assumptions that are directly comparable in a manner making it possible to evaluate whether presidential unilateral action requires tacit approval from Congress. Along the way, we derive and graphically illustrate hypotheses from each of this trilogy of models.

PREVIOUS MODELS

Several common features characterize existing unilateral action models. One is that the President is assumed to have a first-mover advantage to adjust policy through unilateral action, followed (assuming unilateral action) by a congressional option to pass a new law to reverse or to revise the presidential action (a possibility that the chief executive anticipates). Another is that, in modeling congressional response to unilateral action, various versions of pivotal politics models (Krehbiel 1998, Brady and Volden 2005) – which consider when and how an existing policy is either sustained or replaced by a new law – are built upon.

Given the latter, a prerequisite for understanding previous models is an understanding of pivotal politics. As such, before turning directly to models of unilateral action, we provide an overview of pivotal politics.

Pivotal Politics

Typically, pivotal politics models assume a single spatial dimension, invariably liberal-conservative, as illustrated by the line from liberal to conservative in Figure 2.1. This is generally consistent with Poole and Rosenthal's (1997) seminal empirical finding that American politics is largely characterized by this single dimension, with a second, civil rights dimension being intermittently relevant before 1970. Given this result and the technical complexity of

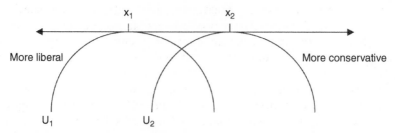

FIGURE 2.1 Single-peaked and symmetric preferences in unidimensional policy space
Note: The line indicates liberal-conservative dimension. U_1 and U_2 stand for the utility
functions of players 1 and 2, respectively, with x_1 and x_2 denoting their respective ideal
points.

utilizing multiple dimensions, there is an obvious appeal to assuming one spatial
dimension when analyzing lawmaking processes and decisions.

Pivotal politics models also typically assume that players have single-peaked,
symmetric preferences. In Figure 2.1, for instance, legislators X_1 and X_2 have utility
functions U_1 and U_2, respectively, with peaks of x_1 and x_2 as their ideal points.
Legislator X_1 is more ideologically liberal than Legislator X_2, and each legislator
prefers policies closer to rather than farther away from his or her ideal point.[1]

These models also generally assume that a chamber median, denoted as M,
sets the agenda by deciding whether to offer a proposal to change policy, with
veto decisions made by various players, notably the filibuster (F) and veto-
override (V) pivots.[2] F is the legislator (Senator, in the US context) who is
pivotal in deciding whether to pass a cloture vote in the unidimensional policy
space (allowing the floor to vote on the proposal to change the status quo), while
V is decisive in determining whether to override a presidential veto given such
action in the wake of legislation.[3]

Figure 2.2 illustrates the kind of results that are usually generated in a pivotal
politics model. Suppose that the president is a Republican. Consider all status
quo policies in this unidimensional policy space and, in equilibrium, which will
remain in place and which will be altered.[4] For any status quos between F and V,

[1] While singled-peaked preferences are key for pivotal politics models, the assumption of symmetry
is typically less important and is completely unimportant under some conditions.
[2] Note that there is no median legislator under multiple dimensions.
[3] To simplify, in our explication we assume that it takes less than a two-thirds agreement to end
a debate (i.e., to invoke cloture), an assumption consistent with the Senate's Rule 22 since 1917,
and that the legislature is unicameral. The former assumption implies that the filibuster pivot
closer to the President will either be the override pivot or will be more moderate than that pivot; in
either situation the filibuster pivot closer to the President is not relevant for determining whether
a status quo can be moved (Chiou and Rothenberg 2009). Theoretical results under bicameralism
can be found in Chiou and Rothenberg (2003).
[4] We use subgame perfect equilibrium to derive a solution to the pivotal politics game. The game
sequence starts with the chamber median's decision of which bill (including the status quo) should

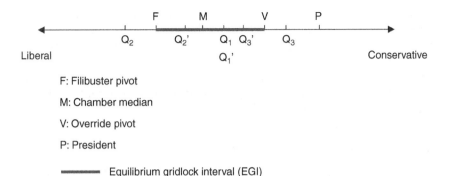

F: Filibuster pivot

M: Chamber median

V: Override pivot

P: President

━━━━━ Equilibrium gridlock interval (EGI)

FIGURE 2.2 A simple version of the pivotal politics model

say Q_1, any attempts by the chamber median to move policy will encounter opposition by either F or V such that his or her efforts will fail. Status quos to the left of F will be moved rightward. For instance, Q_2 will be moved to Q_2', the point where F is indifferent between them.[5] Given the symmetric-preferences assumption, F is located at the midpoint of Q_2 and Q_2' so that Q_2' is labeled the *reflection point* of Q_2 on F (a reflection point being the point of inversion in a spatial depiction). The new equilibrium policies (the policies chosen) with extreme-left status quos will be at the chamber median's ideal point, as they leave both F and V better off. Similarly, each of the status quos to the right of V will be moved leftward, with Q_3 moved to Q_3', making V indifferent. Extreme-right status quos will be shifted to the chamber median's ideal point.

One of the most important results in pivotal politics models is the existence of an equilibrium gridlock interval (EGI), defined as the set of status quos remaining in place in equilibrium because any attempt by the chamber median to move them fails. As shown in Figure 2.2, typically the EGI is bounded by the filibuster and the override pivots if the President is more extreme than the relevant override pivot (the scenario that is usually assumed) and by the filibuster and the President otherwise.[6] Assuming a uniform distribution of status quos (an equal likelihood of the status quo being at any point on the liberal-conservative dimension), a wider EGI produces more legislative gridlock. Various empirical studies examining this hypothesis have found strong support (Krehbiel 1998, Chiou and Rothenberg 2003, 2006, 2009).

be proposed to alter or maintain a status quo, followed by whether the filibuster pivot will veto (if not, the game ends) and whether the president chooses to veto (if not, the game ends; otherwise, the override pivot decides whether to override, and then the game ends).

[5] For innocuous reasons, in our illustration we assume that a player will not veto if he or she is indifferent about a proposed bill relative to the status quo.

[6] The same result applies with a Democratic President. See Chiou and Rothenberg (2009) for various versions of pivotal politics models and their equilibrium results.

For presidential unilateral action, perhaps the most critical implication stemming from analysis of the EGI is that the President has ample room to act by adjusting existing policies closer to his or her ideal point without concern about direct congressional statutory revision. This is the key insight in the unilateral action models developed by Moe and Howell (1999a) and Deering and Maltzman (1999), the two initial theoretical models of unilateral action, which we will now discuss.

Unilateral Action Models – Initial Efforts

As mentioned earlier, a standard assumption of unilateral action models is that the President moves first by deciding whether to take unilateral action, followed by a possible congressional attempt to pass a new law that revises where policy lies. This legislative reaction is typically captured by integrating the pivotal-politics model described above. Given the game sequence of unilateral action models, the President contemplates how Congress will respond to any unilateral choice. Congress's ability to reverse unilateral action effectively, which is largely determined by the extent of legislative gridlock, shapes presidential decisions. This implies that a President will prefer to act unilaterally if there is a policy inside the EGI which he or she favors relative to the status quo – as congressional gridlock will make statutory reversal impossible – or the President can employ unilateral action to prevent Congress from moving a status quo further away from his or her ideal point.

Figure 2.3 illustrates this dynamic, as well as the argument in Moe and Howell (1999a), where the President is hypothesized to become far more influential or powerful with the strategic use of unilateral action authority than if such authority were unavailable.[7] The players, preference configurations and the three initial status quos are identical to Figure 2.2, so we can see what the President can accomplish with unilateral action by comparing these two figures.

To begin, consider the trio of initial status quos in Figure 2.3, and how the President will act. Q_2 lies outside the EGI but to the left of the filibuster pivot. Without unilateral action, policy will be moved to Q_2', the reflection point of Q_2 on the filibuster pivot, as depicted in Figure 2.2. If the President can act unilaterally, he or she can only do better if the discretion associated with this status quo policy is quite large (i.e., greater than the distance between Q_2 and Q_2'). Otherwise, he or she will do nothing and the chamber median will shift policy to Q_2' in accordance with the pivotal-politics law-making process.

Q_3 is another status quo located outside the EGI but to the right of the override pivot's ideal point (the EGI's left boundary). As we discussed and as

---

[7] While unaccounted for in their model, recall that the authors also argue that collective action problems within Congress will further weaken its ability to respond with legislation, making the President even more powerful than what Figure 2.3 illustrates.

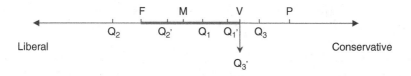

F: Filibuster pivot
M: Chamber median
V: Override pivot
P: President
━━━ Equilibrium gridlock interval (EGI)

FIGURE 2.3 The increase of presidential influence through unilateral action

we have seen in Figure 2.2, with pivotal politics and no presidential ability to act unilaterally, this status quo will be moved to its reflection point on the pivot in the legislative process. However, with possible unilateral action, the President can preempt Congress by shifting the status quo to the override pivot's ideal point, so that the legislature cannot move it further away from the President. In other words, the President will benefit from unilateral action by moving the status quo further from his or her ideal point but not as far as Congress would move policy. Preempting Congress is the main motive for presidential unilateral action, in this instance.

Finally, when a status quo, such as Q_1, lies inside the EGI, the President can benefit even more substantially from unilateral action. As shown in Figure 2.3, the President can essentially move this status quo wherever he or she wants, as long as it remains inside the EGI and within the limit of his or her discretion (the extent to which he or she can shift policy on the spatial dimension as a function of his or her delegated authority). This is true for any status quos within the EGI. This particular status quo, Q_1, will be moved to Q_1', as the distance between them is the upper bound of the President's discretion. Here, legislative gridlock is the main cause for presidential unilateral action.

Deering and Maltzman (1999) employed a similar modeling setup to Moe and Howell (1999a) and argued that unilateral action will be more frequent when the President anticipates a lower likelihood that his or her unilateral action will be overturned by legislation. Assuming that the President will tend to move status quos to his or her ideal point, they hypothesized that the more centrally the President is located within the EGI, the more likely he or she is to act, as Congress will have more difficulties successfully passing laws, particularly over presidential vetoes. While this result is not formally derived, and there is room for improving its theoretical foundation (as we will later note in deriving formal results, presidential centrality within the EGI is not key), Deering and Maltzman's approach highlights the strategic nature of unilateral action and points out how specifying formal models to advance our theoretical understanding of unilateral action can be profitably employed.

Three common features in Moe and Howell (1999a) and Deering and Maltzman (1999) deserve acknowledgment. First, both argued that unilateral action greatly contributes to presidential power. Moe and Howell (1999a) went as far as suggesting the existence of presidential imperialism by virtue of additional collective action problems that impede the ability of Congress to act either by issuing a statutory response, even when the model suggests it should be able to do so, or by other means. However, unless we specify otherwise, when we discuss collective action problems with respect to Moe and Howell we will be referring to how collective action problems either impede the use of extra-statutory mechanisms or, in Chapter 5, various forms of party influence in what we will call the legislative stage of our game. We will not focus on the notion of collective action being so debilitating that legislators just cannot organize themselves to offer an alternative to the status quo and vote, despite the lack of other impediments (e.g., party control of the agenda).

Second, they assumed that the President can use his or her delegated discretion to shift an existing status quo rightward or leftward in a unidimensional policy space. Congress, regardless of its chamber median and majority party medians, cannot influence or constrain the directional use of discretion. While this assumption is consistent with the bulk of previous studies on delegation (see, e.g., Epstein and O'Halloran 1999 for the canonical work), as Howell (2003) suggested, other alternative assumptions may be reasonable. However, how appropriate each alternative assumption is for unilateral politics has been largely ignored; similarly, the importance of varying these assumptions has been given little attention. In fact, we will see that these alternative assumptions play key roles in the dynamics of unilateral action, and substantially impact our assessments of presidential power arising from unilateral action.

Third, while these two studies bring formal models into unilateral action studies, contributing to Moe's (2009) assessment of their being a revolution in presidency studies, they do not quite meet the standards of either those who prefer strict theoretical development of models or those who advocate tightly linking theory and empirical testing (so-call Empirical Implications of Theoretical Models, or EITM).[8] Theoretically, these works do not constitute fully specified models laying out player utility functions, game sequences and game solutions with well-defined equilibrium concepts – essential elements in producing clearly stated theoretical results and conditions. As such, deducing

---

[8] EITM is viewed as involving clearly stated premises, logically coherent theory providing an understanding of the relationship among the premises and then empirical work evaluating the expectations developed (e.g., Aldrich and Alt 2003, Aldrich, Alt and Lupia 2008). In vernacular, it means tightly linking theory, typically deductive, that generates empirically relevant hypotheses, with the testing of these hypotheses with appropriate data and methods.

clear and unambiguous hypotheses from a theory is not possible, e.g., the hypotheses in Deering and Maltzman (1999) cannot be produced from their modeling setup, even with some additional elaboration.[9]

While sharing the first feature mentioned above – maintaining that unilateral action greatly contributes to presidential power – Howell (2003) was the first work that completely formalized unilateral action and more rigorously derived hypotheses, crucial elements for developing a solid foundation for analyzing unilateral action and ascertaining its importance for the American presidency. Since we will employ this model as a jumping-off point for our theoretical framework investigating the extent of presidential power, we now review Howell's model in detail.

Later Unilateral Action Models – Howell's Approach

To introduce Howell's model, we start by describing players, utility functions, game sequence and assumptions for some parameters. Along the way, we will make explicit assumptions that are implicit in the model. Players include the President (P), the chamber median (M_c), the veto-override pivot (V), the filibuster pivot (F) and the judiciary (J), whose ideal points are respectively denoted as p, m_c, v, f and j and are located on a unidimensional policy space where ideal points are real numbers. As before, each player i is assumed to have symmetric, single-peaked preferences with ideal point x_i over policy outcome $y \in R$. Without loss of generality, assume a Republican President. For more concise results with little sacrifice of generality (as is almost always true, post-World War II), the President is assumed to be more extreme than the override pivot (i.e., $v < p$).[10]

The game sequence (Figure 2.4) has three stages: (1) presidential unilateral action, (2) a pivotal politics game (which we will also call the legislative stage) and (3) the court's override decision. Initially, *Nature* (N) randomly selects a status quo, q, and an exogenous presidential discretion level relative to it, t.[11] Discretion comes from a general-probability distribution and the values of q and t are revealed to all players before their decisions. The President moves first and possibly chooses a unilateral action from a set of policies between $q - t$ and $q + t$, subject to some additional, model-specific constraints to be specified later.

---

[9] We will expound more on this after introducing Howell's (2003) model, which is very close to the Deering and Maltzman model in spirit.

[10] Assuming presidential extremity relative to the override pivot might seem severe, but it is consistent with empirical regularities in that the President and his or her party medians are almost always more ideologically extreme than the override pivots. Moreover, theoretical and empirical results are almost identical as long as the President has an ideal point that is sufficiently close to that of the override pivot. Results remain qualitatively unaltered even when the chief executive's ideal point is quite central and not close to the filibuster and override pivots.

[11] The *Nature* stage is only implicitly assumed in Howell's model.

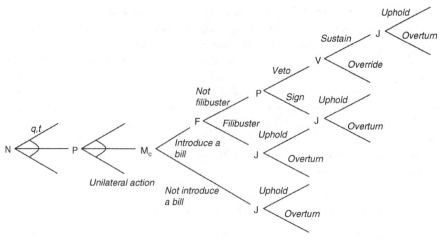

FIGURE 2.4 The game sequence

In the second stage, Congress can respond to presidential action in the pivotal-politics legislative game. Krehbiel's (1998) preference-based pivotal-politics game or a variant of this game with a majority party median as a negative agenda-setter (who is, thus, able to keep items off the legislative floor) is played, depending on whether a majority party is key for constraining unilateral action (we will be more precise about this later). Regardless of the specific pivotal-politics game, the President will take advantage of the possibility that Congress will have trouble moving some status quos at the second stage by shifting them to more favorable points within the EGI.

In the third stage, the judiciary ensures that the President's unilateral action does not overuse his or her discretion. If P moves q beyond this level, the court overrules the action and returns policy to the initial status quo.[12]

Howell explicitly derived two hypotheses from the model.[13] The first is called the fragmentation hypothesis: the President will more likely act unilaterally with a more fragmented Congress. This hypothesis stems from Howell's finding that a larger EGI will result in a higher likelihood of unilateral action under two alternative discretion assumptions – that the President can use

---

[12] While the court plays a non-strategic role here, Howell was the first to integrate it into a unilateral action model. Elsewhere in his discussion (and as mentioned in Chapter 1), he raised the possibility that judges pursue their policy preferences strategically – and demonstrated that the courts usually do seem to defer to presidential will. However, probably due to empirical feasibility, when deriving hypotheses Howell assumed that the court only ensures that the president will not overuse discretion.

[13] Howell also stated a first-term hypothesis, predicting that the President will take more unilateral actions during his first term when his predecessor is affiliated with the opposite party, which he generated informally. As we will discuss when deriving this hypothesis from our theoretical framework, its validity actually requires specific assumptions.

discretion through unilateral action in any direction or that the President can do so only in a direction advancing the chamber median's ideal point. As we will see later, this finding is not quite precise, as it depends not only on the EGI's size but also on the chamber median's ideal point relative to the EGI's boundaries. Nonetheless, in testing this hypothesis (and as mentioned in the previous chapter), Howell, instead of directly measuring EGI size, relied on partisan majority size and the "legislative potential for policy change," which combines majority party size and party cohesion (Brady, Cooper and Hurley 1979), as alternative measures for congressional fragmentation, and found strong empirical evidence for this hypothesis.

The second hypothesis was labeled the unified-government hypothesis: The President will act unilaterally more under unified government than under divided government.[14] Howell derived this hypothesis with a different discretion assumption than either of those employed in deducing the fragmentation hypothesis – that the President can move a status quo through unilateral action only in a direction consistent with the majority party median's ideal point. We should note that the unified-government hypothesis is invalid under the two alternative discretion assumptions employed for fragmentation. Regardless, while the prediction from Howell's hypothesis had been made in earlier empirical analyses that incorporated divided government (e.g., Mayer 1999, Mayer and Price 1999, Deering and Maltzman 1999), Howell was the first to lay out the theoretical foundation for why we should expect more unilateral action under unified government and, unlike previous findings, uncovered empirical support for this hypothesis.

Howell's analysis made several important contributions. For one thing, it laid out a much more precise theoretical foundation for how the President strategically interacts with Congress and, as a result, produced crucial insights into how the chief executive can take advantage of unilateral action in advancing his or her policy goals. It also demonstrated how the EITM approach can be expanded in presidency studies in an important and meaningful way.

Additionally, Howell provided a means of capturing presidential discretion through specification of a parameter; as indicated, Howell adopted different discretion assumptions in specifying this parameter at different points in his analysis. To reiterate, he proposed three alternative assumptions as to how the President can use discretion: (1) through unilateral action in any direction, (2) only in advancing the chamber median's interests and (3) only in advancing the majority party median's interests. While the first assumption has been commonly employed in the delegation literature and implicitly assumed in studying unilateral action, to our knowledge the last two are new

---

[14] As mentioned in our earlier chapter, there is a competing hypothesis, the so-called evasion hypothesis (Martin 2000, 2005), that the President will take more unilateral action under divided government than under unified government to circumvent Congress.

and novel. As also mentioned, Howell maintained that the fragmentation hypothesis only holds under the first two assumptions, with the divided-government hypothesis requiring the third.

In the broader sense, inclusion of the discretion component provided a different way of thinking about presidential opportunities via unilateral action than was found in previous models. For example, Deering and Maltzman (1999) assumed that the President can move an existing status quo to his or her ideal point, which would not always be feasible if discretion were limited. Thus Howell's analysis, although not assuming a specific discretion level but rather a parameter, underscored the difficulty that the President may have if his or her discretion is limited and how the President may need to adjust his or her strategic choices depending on his or her ideal point relative to the preference conference configuration in Congress.

More importantly, the last two discretion assumptions have completely different, and rather profound, implications for the extent to which unilateral action boosts presidential power. Note that these ramifications are not addressed in Howell (2003) but crucially underpin our analysis. Under the first discretion assumption, Howell's model implied that, by and large, the President can use unilateral action to accomplish his or her policy goals. The President's actions are only subject to the amount of discretion and the possibility of congressional direct statutory response to reverse unilateral action. This implication seems quite consistent with what most presidency and legal scholars believe, leading to concerns about the so-called imperial presidency, as congressional direct statutory response is often deemed quite ineffective because of legislative gridlock and collective action problems.

By contrast, under the last two discretion assumptions, the President, in addition to the aforementioned constraints on discretion level and the possibility of direct statutory response, cannot adjust a status quo in a manner that sabotages the interests of some key actors in Congress. This additional limitation, as we will suggest, constitutes a substantial, if not fully appreciated, constraint. If empirically borne out, it would indicate that any unilateral action requires tacit congressional approval. In turn, regardless of who is specified as the key constraining actor, and despite Congress's being a collective actor that has substantial hurdles in passing legislation that would reverse an order, the President has to take into account congressional preferences in a more nuanced way than under the unilateral discretion assumption and would be considerably incentivized to consult the legislature and anticipate more factors than its ability to produce a new statute. This, in turn, would imply that the concerns about an imperial presidency, at least via unilateral actions, are overstated, as the separation of powers provides a substantial check on the chief executive.

The key difference between the last two discretion assumptions, the actor that directionally constrains presidential uses of discretion, has profound implications for whether the legislature can resolve the collective action problems that Moe and Howell (1999a) believed undercut congressional ability to respond effectively to presidential unilateral action. Under the second discretion assumption, the chamber or its median is posited to overcome collective action problems (e.g., through exercising extra-statutory means) for the chamber as a whole, a possibility that Moe and Howell clearly dismissed, given that the Congress is composed of members with distinct and parochial preferences. However, under the third discretion assumption there is the majority party, and the members that compose it, which is assumed to overcome collective action problems by effectively exercising extra-statutory means. This possibility that an effective response to presidential action would only require that majority party members, a subset of the whole, act in tandem, was seemingly ignored in Moe and Howell (1999a). However, such an ability to overcome collective action problems by the majority party, which can then use its parliamentary resources, is very much consistent with the seminal work of Cox and McCubbins (2007; originally published in 1993). Indeed, party leaders are usually viewed as being in the thick of efforts to control the legislative calendar as a means to thwart executive initiatives – either by keeping items off or by putting them on the agenda – to manipulate the budgetary process and determine the usage of riders and other impediments to the President's getting the resources he or she desires for the executive branch, and to determine whether appointments to the bureaucracy and judiciary that the chief executive wants are brought to a successful conclusion or held in abeyance.

Which directional discretion assumption is more plausible? While the first has been the common, implicit assumption in the literature, the latter two, both essentially implying that Congress or the court can constrain the president beyond statutory means, have been little discussed vis-à-vis unilateral action. However, as indicated by our discussion in the previous chapter, the mechanisms underpinning such assumptions are certainly indicated to exist to one degree or another in broader overviews of the legislative-executive relationship. They cannot be ruled out as *prima facie* implausible.

As such, much of our analysis will concentrate on ascertaining whether one model or another using each of the three assumptions is "correct" or has stronger empirical support as a means of investigating the enigma of presidential power arising from unilateral action. As indicated, this is extremely important for determining the relationship between unilateral action and presidential power, since determining which model of the world is more consistent with reality will shape our inferences regarding the extent to which unilateral action corresponds to presidential power or influence. Accomplishing this task requires a new theoretical framework, to which we now turn.

NEW THEORETICAL FRAMEWORK

To assess the extent to which unilateral action constitutes presidential power, we go beyond previous analytic frameworks by proposing a new one employing Howell's work as a jumping-off point. Because each directional discretion assumption has substantially different implications for how unilateral action works, we will specify a theoretical framework with competing models that differ merely on their assumptions about discretion (in describing each model, we discuss the plausibility of the discretion assumption).[15] In other words, each of our three competing models varies exclusively on how it assumes the President can employ t, the exogenous discretion parameter, to shift q, the status quo: P can either move q in whichever direction he or she chooses (the *unilateralism model*), only toward the chamber median (the *chamber-compliance model*) or only toward the median of the majority party in Congress (the *partisan-compliance model*).[16] These models are directly comparable in that they only differ on this single assumption. We can, therefore, directly derive hypotheses and evaluate which of these models best corresponds to the relevant data.

Before proceeding to each of the models, it is beneficial to be more explicit regarding our assumptions about q and t. To make our models more general than their predecessors, which tend to assume a normal distribution around the chamber median (m_c), we assume that q comes from a continuous distribution whose mean is around m_c, whose support covers all real numbers and whose probability density function, $g(q)$, is weakly decreasing as q moves away from the mean (i.e., a single-peaked distribution peaking at the chamber median).[17]

To facilitate characterization of our results, as in previous delegation models (e.g., Epstein and O'Halloran 1999), we assume that the exogenous discretion level is selected from a uniform distribution between zero and $\gamma > 0$. Both to rule out any unreasonable distribution of discretion, and for parsimony, we assume that $\gamma < \bar{\gamma}$, where $\bar{\gamma}$ is twice as large as the minimized distance between the chamber median and the filibuster pivot over Congress. Allowing a slightly larger $\bar{\gamma}$ will not qualitatively change our results.

For all three models, we first solve by finding the subgame perfect equilibrium for each status quo and each possible discretion level. We then derive the

---

[15] As discussed in Chapter 1, while we first investigate the impact of varying the discretion assumption and keeping everything else constant, we will later build-in a multiplicity of partisan roles in the legislative process.

[16] We also assume in all three models that the President cannot move the status quo away from both his and the chamber median's ideal points. Given our assumption about the status quo distribution, this assumption has little impact on our theoretical results. Additionally, we assume that the President will not take unilateral action that will be overridden either by Congress (through legislation) or the courts (through judicial review). As discussed in Chapter 1, although we observe rare deviations, this assumption generally holds.

[17] Note, also, that we balance realism with clarity in dealing with bicameralism in our models. Fully incorporating bicameralism would greatly complicate our models and the exposition of key intuitions while ignoring it would run the risk of omitting a basic element of most legislative systems. Given these trade-offs, as a middle ground we focus on integrating congressional ineffectiveness resulting from bicameralism. Hence, the veto override pivot in our models is the more extreme player in the two chambers, and the chamber median is defined by the mean of the two chamber medians.

expected probability of presidential unilateral action, denoted as $\Pr(Act)$, by integrating the equilibrium presidential unilateral action over all possible status quos q and discretion levels t. Stated in simpler terms, the $\Pr(Act)$ captures the expected likelihood that the President will act unilaterally at a given game's outset before learning q and t.[18] After deriving $\Pr(Act)$ for each model, we generate corresponding hypotheses.

Figures 2.5 and 2.6 jointly illustrate how we obtain $\Pr(Act)$, and, hence our hypotheses, in two steps. First, per Figure 2.5, we generate equilibrium presidential unilateral actions for a given discretion level under various status quos (i.e., $\Pr(Act \mid q, t)$). Figure 2.6 then shows the process by which equilibrium presidential unilateral action is integrated over all possible discretion levels (i.e., $\Pr(Act \mid q)$) for each of the status quos. With these two steps, we obtain $\Pr(Act)$ by integrating $\Pr(Act \mid q)$ over all status quos.

Unilateralism Model

To reiterate, our unilateralism model is most consistent with unilateral action equaling executive power. Assuming that the President can move q both rightward and leftward, subject to the discretion constraint, implies that unilateral action is a powerful tool for setting agendas and moving status quos closer to the President's ideal point. This assumption meshes well with the viewpoint, discussed in our first chapter, that the President is greatly advantaged, given that Congress suffers from collection action problems (that make it difficult for Congress to react beyond direct statutory response) and that the judiciary is quiescent (Moe and Howell 1999a, Macey 2006). It also corresponds to assertions, which we will discuss in more detail when we distinguish between policy types, that for some policies it is difficult for Congress to respond once the President issues an EO – for instance, because it will damage national interests or be costly to reverse unilateral action. Finally, it is consistent with the standard assumption in models of legislative delegation to the bureaucracy (e.g., Epstein and O'Halloran 1999, Volden 2002) that, since determining the enacting coalition's precise will and its implications for presidential discretion is often problematic, the President can move q in either direction up to the limits of discretion.

As discussed, in general this directional discretion assumption has been widely assumed in previous unilateral action models (e.g., Moe and Howell 1999a, Deering and Maltzman 1999) and most of the literature on unilateral action. However, as shown below, even under this model the President, anticipating congressional and judicial responses and attempts to override presidential action, acts strategically by preempting them, exploiting legislative fragmentation, or being inactive and retaining the status quo. In this sense, the political environment and institutional constraints still bind

---

[18] Appendix 1 formally defines $\Pr(Act)$, states and proves all propositions.

(a) Unilateralism model
f-.5t' f m_c ν p 2ν-m_c 2ν-m_c+t' q
(b) Chamber-compliance model
f-.5t' f m_c ν p 2ν-m_c 2ν-m_c+t' q
(c) Partisan-compliance model (unified government)
f-.5t' f m_c ν m_p p 2m_p-m_c 2m_p-m_c+t' q
(d) Partisan-compliance model (divided government)
f-.5t' m_p f m_c ν p 2ν-m_c 2ν-m_c+t' q
Status quos where P will take unilateral action
Status quos where P will take no unilateral action

FIGURE 2.5 Presidential unilateral action for a given discretion level
Note: f, v, p, m_c, m_p and q denote the ideal points of the filibuster and override pivots, the President, the medians of the chamber and the majority party and the status quo, respectively. We use t' to denote a certain discretion level, which is drawn from a uniform distribution ranging between zero and γ.

presidential action, as argued by Deering and Maltzman (1999), Krause and Cohen (2000) and Howell (2003).

We solve the game by backward induction from the last move where the judge acts to derive its subgame perfect equilibrium and Pr(*Act*). To reiterate, and as seen in Figure 2.4, the game sequence is composed of three stages. The judge in the third stage ensures that the President does not overuse delegated discretion. In the second stage, M_c can essentially move the status quo previously untouched by the President or the new q established by unilateral action wherever he or she prefers, subject to the constraints imposed by F and V. The resulting EGI, bounded by the filibuster and

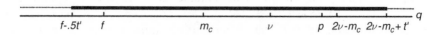

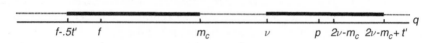

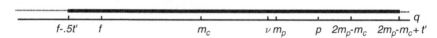

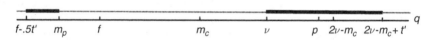

(a) Unilateralism model

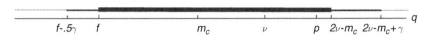

(b) Chamber-compliance model

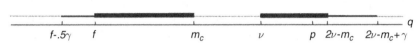

(c) Partisan-compliance model (unified government)

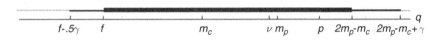

(d) Partisan-compliance model (divided government)

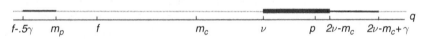

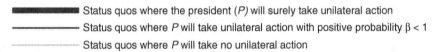

▬▬▬▬▬ Status quos where the president (P) will surely take unilateral action
———— Status quos where P will take unilateral action with positive probability β < 1
·············· Status quos where P will take no unilateral action

FIGURE 2.6 Expected presidential unilateral action
Note: f, v, p, m_c, m_p, γ and q denote the ideal points of the filibuster and override pivots, the President, the medians of the chamber and the majority party, the upper bound of the discretion distribution, and the status quo, respectively. While we determine equilibrium presidential unilateral action for a given discretion and each status quo in Figure 2.5, we integrate the expected presidential unilateral action over all possible discretion levels for each status quo in this Figure.

override pivots, consists of status quos that no players at this stage can successfully alter in equilibrium. This interval's length reflects the extent of the disadvantage that Congress, unlike the President as a unitary actor, suffers from, and the extent to which Congress is divided or fragmented.

The President's first-stage decision is key. Figure 2.5(a) graphically depicts when the President acts unilaterally in this stage for a given discretion level and for all status quos. N randomly draws a level of discretion t' between zero and γ

and q on any point on the horizontal line and reveals this information to every player. If q is interior to the EGI, P can move q anywhere within the interval, as fragmented congressional preferences will make counteracting his move impossible. Therefore, P unilaterally pushes q as close as possible to the EGI's left boundary (i.e., to v), regardless of the value of t'. In other words, the President acts unilaterally for a status quo falling inside the EGI due to the *gridlock incentive*.

If q is located between the override pivot and $2v - m_c + t'$, where $2v - m_c$ is the chamber median's reflection point on the override pivot, P adjusts policy closer to v to preempt m_c from moving q too far away from his or her ideal point.[19] In other words, the President will act, given these status quos. The reason the President has this strong *preemption incentive* for each of the status quos between the override pivot and $2v - m_c$ is that the chamber median will move them to their reflection points (i.e., to $2v - q$) by legislation, so the President can be better off by preempting even if a status quo is very close to $2v - m_c$. When the status quo is between $2v - m_c$ and $2v - m_c + t'$, the President has preemption incentives to prevent the chamber median from moving the status quo to the median's ideal point. The closer the status quo is to $2v - m_c$, the more the President can take advantage of full discretion by moving it closer to the override pivot, undermining the ability of the chamber median to move policies away from the President's ideal point. However, when the status quo is to the right of $2v - m_c + t'$, the President can no longer benefit from unilateral action even if the President uses his or her full discretion, t', because it is not possible to move the policy inside the interval between the override pivot and $2v - m_c$. In other words, if the President acts under this circumstance, the chamber median can move the new status quo established by unilateral action back to the median's ideal point.

Finally, for a status quo between the filibuster pivot and $f - .5t'$, the President has *discretion* incentives to act unilaterally. When such a status quo is drawn, if the President does not unilaterally act, it will be moved to $2f - q$, the reflection point of the status quo on the filibuster pivot. However, the President can do better by unilaterally moving the status quo to $q - t'$, which is within the EGI (i.e., the chamber median cannot alter it in the legislative stage) and closer to the President than $2f - q$. The President gains because the status quo is between the filibuster pivot and $f - .5t'$. In other words, unlike the preemption incentive where the President preempts the chamber median, here the President acts unilaterally because the chamber median cannot move policy as much as

---

[19] This result differs from Deering and Maltzman's (1999) claim that unilateral action is either unlikely or never occurs for status quos to the override pivot's right. This contrast is consequential, as in our analysis possible preemption of congressional action generates presidential incentives to unilaterally move *virtually all* status quos that lie to the override pivot's right except for very extreme ones, while in their analysis Presidents only move status quos within or close to the EGI.

the President can from using his discretion. Alternatively, when the status quo is to the left of $f - .5t'$, the President's discretion is insufficiently large to move the status quo beyond where the chamber median can move it and, therefore, the President will not act unilaterally.

A larger or smaller discretion level than t' will only affect the preemption and discretion incentives in Figure 2.5(a). With a different discretion level, the gridlock incentive remains the same, but the preemption and discretion incentives expand (or contract) with larger (or smaller) discretion levels.

In Figure 2.6, for each status quo, we integrate the equilibrium presidential unilateral action indicated in Figure 2.5 over all possible discretion levels. In Figure 2.5(a), where a given discretion level (t') is drawn, the President will take unilateral action when the status quo is between $f - .5t'$ and $2v - m_c + t'$. Varying t' will affect only presidential unilateral decisions for the status quo between $f - .5t'$ and f and between $2v - m_c$ and $2v - m_c + t'$. Whether or how likely the President is to act unilaterally does not depend on t' when the status quo is between f and $2v - m_c$. This is why the expected probability of presidential unilateral action is one for the status quo between f and $2v - m_c$ in Figure 2.6(a), when we integrate the equilibrium action over all possible discretion levels. When we integrate the equilibrium presidential action over all discretion levels for the status quo located outside this interval, the expected probability of presidential unilateral action is greater than zero and less than one for any status quo between $f - .5\gamma$ and f or between $2v - m_c$ and $2v - m_c + \gamma$, where again γ denotes the upper bound of the discretion distribution. This is because, for such a status quo, the President will prefer to act when his or her discretion is sufficiently close to γ. In fact, the expected probability monotonically decreases as the status quo moves from f to $f - .5\gamma$ or from $2v - m_c$ to $2v - m_c + \gamma$.

In terms of the various incentives discussed with reference to Figure 2.5, Figure 2.6 provides an even fuller picture for expected unilateral action. The President has the gridlock incentives for the status quo between f and v (i.e., the EGI), which is by far the most impactful incentive. This is partly because the status quo is more likely to be located inside the EGI and partly because the President will surely act in such a situation. The preemption incentive, which drives the President to act for a status quo between v and $2v - m_c + \gamma$, is less strong than the gridlock incentive. Conversely, it is clearly more impactful than the discretion incentive, resulting in possible presidential action for the status quo between f and $f - .5\gamma$.

Note that, given both the lack of correspondence between the EGI and status quos with positive probabilities of action and the different probabilities of actions, a larger EGI does not generally result in a higher *ex ante* probability of unilateral action. For instance, in Figure 2.6(a), for the same EGI length (i.e., the interval between f and v), the longer the distance is between the m_c and v, the longer the boldest line. Hence, since EGI sizes may have independent, distinct effects on $\Pr(Act)$, following past practice by employing the EGI as a predictor is

TABLE 2.1 *Hypotheses from our competing theories*

	Unilateralism model	Chamber-compliance model	Partisan-compliance model
First-term	+	+	+
Filibuster-tail EGI	+	+	
Override-tail EGI	+		
Divided government			+

Note: EGI indicates equilibrium gridlock interval; "+" indicates positive effects on unilateral action. Filibuster-tail EGI is the interval between the filibuster pivot and the midpoint of the two chambers' medians; Override-tail EGI is the interval between the override pivot and the midpoint.

misleading.[20] As such, and per Proposition 1 (stated in Appendix 1), everything else equal, unilateral action becomes more likely as the override-tail's length increases (i.e., the further v is from m_c).[21] The same relationship holds for the filibuster-tail at the left of the EGI. Effects are not constant but are always positive, since which EGI tail's effect is larger depends on q's distribution and m_c's location relative to f and v.

Based on these results, we derive the following hypotheses (summarized in Table 2.1):

> *Hypothesis A1 (first-term):* A new President whose party is different from his or her predecessor's will take more unilateral actions in his or her first term than otherwise.
> *Hypothesis A2 (filibuster-tail EGI):* The larger the distance between the chamber median and the filibuster pivot, the more likely it is that the President will act unilaterally.
> *Hypothesis A3 (override-tail EGI):* The larger the distance between the chamber median and the override pivot, the more likely it is that the President will act unilaterally.

The first hypothesis stems from the likelihood that a new President whose party differs from his or her predecessor's typically has more electoral mandates to address or needs to override EOs issued by his or her predecessors. In other words, while the distribution of status quos may remain identical, the number of relevant issues rises, increasing total expected unilateral actions. While proposed by Mayer (1999) informally and by Howell (2003) using a formal

---

[20] Whether bigger EGIs lead to more unilateral actions depend on q's distribution and m_c's location relative to f and v. This is why we earlier noted that Howell's (2003) fragmentation hypothesis needed additional conditions to hold.

[21] Recognize that we define the override-tail as the segment between the chamber median and the EGI boundary closer to the President, and the filibuster-tail as the other part of the EGI.

model, deriving this hypothesis actually requires making the assumption regarding q's distribution that we pointed out earlier.

Hypotheses A2 and A3 go beyond past research. To reiterate, EGI length captures neither additional effects of the distance between the median and the right boundary of the interval nor the subtle effects stemming from the relative locations of the chamber median and the filibuster and override pivots. Our hypotheses are a function of how each EGI side independently and distinctly impacts Pr(*Act*). From Figure 2.6(a), we can see that when the filibuster pivot moves away from the chamber median, the interval between them, constituting the set of status quos where the President will certainly unilaterally act, expands. This increases the expected probability of unilateral action, which generates Hypothesis A2. Similarly, we can see from Figure 2.6(a) that when the override pivot moves away from the chamber median, gridlock incentives (i.e., the interval between m_c to v) and preemption incentives (the interval between v and $2v - m_c$) strengthen. Although the discretion incentive is compromised (because of the lower probability density), this loss is outweighed by the substantial increases in the other two incentive types. Thus, Hypothesis A3 holds.

As an example of the kind of situation that we have in mind that will only fit unilateralism, and as foreshadowed a bit in the first chapter, one of the most obvious instances where presidents have appeared to institutionally prevail despite legislative opposition involves attempts to integrate cost–benefit assessments into regulatory analysis (for an overview, see Hahn and Sunstein 2002). In short, should a new regulation be allowed, given the associated expenses and rewards involved?

Often, answers to this question involve discussions of institutional roles – legislative versus executive – as well as of policy choices. Traditionally, building cost–benefit analysis into the assessment of regulations is a pet project of presidents generally, consistent with their emphases on factors such as economic growth and their desire to choose policies that are relatively economically efficient. Such an approach is often less popular, and typically opposed, by many members of Congress, particularly liberals and Democrats. Such congressional opposition is based both on policy grounds (cost–benefit analysis may result in certain regulations being rejected) and on institutional claims that legislative authority is being usurped by the executive.

For example, in March of 1978, Jimmy Carter issued EO 12044, which, among other things, directed agencies to begin to apply cost–benefit analysis to major proposed regulations (actions whose financial impacts were at least $100 million). His action met with a negative congressional response from the Democratic Congress and Carter – showing, as is so often the case when one examines important EOs carefully, that there is information transmission and often bargaining with legislators – agreed to exclude independent regulatory commissions (such an action might have also triggered a difficult-to-win judicial challenge for the President). Ronald Reagan, for whom implementation of Carter's EO had not been sufficiently forceful for his tastes, proceeded to revoke it with a more rigid approach (EO 12291) in early 1981, but still kept independent agencies off the table. In other words, the Reagan EO decreed that there would be much less leeway for executive agencies regarding whether a regulation would be subject to assessment. As mentioned, besides making activist regulations that much more difficult to promulgate, this action also had broader ramifications for the separation of powers: according to West and Cooper (1985, p. 207), EO 12291 "testified to the continuing, perhaps even more difficult, problems Congress faces in attempting to maintain its traditional institutional prerogatives and powers."

In a similar spirit, Ronald Reagan issued EO 12498 in January 1985, putting into place a process that Congress had refused to mandate legislatively, that the Office of Management and Budget should review agency rules before these proposals even became public. This led an exasperated John Dingell, Democratic chair of the House Energy and Commerce Committee, to proclaim that the EO "represents only the latest attempt of this administration, through the OMB, to short-circuit the fair, open and orderly regulatory process" (Burnham 1985, p. 7). Jointly, actions such as EOs 12291 and 12498 have been widely interpreted as adding to presidential power at the expense of the legislature, very much in the spirit of unilateralism (e.g., Cooper and West 1988).

Chamber-Compliance Model

As mentioned, the chamber-compliance model differs from the unilateralism model in assuming how the President can employ t to move q. It captures a world where either the courts attempt to represent contemporary legislative intent in the form of the legislative median or, per conventional wisdom, Congress has various mechanisms to impact the President and the executive branch (which have become even more prominent in the age of gridlock): among them, appropriations riders, manipulating legislative scheduling, blocking appointments and using legislative vetoes (despite their supposed illegality; see, e.g., Berry 2008). Thus, we assume that P can move q only toward m_c (which, to reiterate, is Howell's approach in generating his fragmentation hypothesis).

Put differently, this model makes the intuitive assumption that presidents may hesitate to move policy from the chamber median, usually situated in the middle of the ideological continuum, towards their own, typically more extreme, ideal points. The reason behind such executive caution is the potential for costs or actions mitigating an EO's effectiveness that is not picked up by the unilateralism model but rather by the extra-statutory means discussed at length in Chapter 1. Formally, these costs and actions are not necessarily the product of a statute moving q but are in the form of other decisions that may or may not be directly related to the policy at hand. Consequently, presidents may feel compelled to bargain with Congress and, ultimately, to adjust the policy embodied in the EO, or they may anticipate what legislative action will be and defer moving some q that would be shifted if a real-world Congress could only pass legislation. Because at least tacit approval is required, this indicates that unilateral actions provide the President with less influence than has often seemingly been suggested, but a degree of influence that is consistent with what many involved in the actual process claim to witness.[22] As reviewed earlier, this implicitly assumes that the members making up the entire chamber are able to put aside their differences in preferences and their parochial interests and act collectively.

More precisely, the difference between the unilateralism and chamber-compliance models, in terms of $\Pr(Act)$, rests on status quos where P prefers employing delegated discretion to shift policy further away from m_c in the first model. These status quos are located between m_c and v, so that P's moving policy closer to v would sabotage the median's interests, as Figure 2.5(b), which lays out the set of status quos where the President will act unilaterally under this model, given a certain discretion level t', illustrates. Since the President is worse off if he or she moves these qs in the other direction, he or she takes no unilateral action in equilibrium and, instead, maintains the status quo.

Straightforwardly following from Proposition 2 (see, again, Appendix 1), the first two hypotheses of the unilateralism model – regarding a new President's impact and the relationship between the chamber median and the filibuster pivot – still hold, as demonstrated in Table 2.1 (and, therefore, we do not repeat them here). However, in contrast to Hypothesis A3, the relationship for the chamber median/override pivot distance is indeterminate in the chamber-compliance model (we will not restate this different hypothesis while changing the expectation either). As Figures 2.5(b) and 2.6(b) show, increasing distance between m_c and v both increases the distance between v and the median's reflection point (i.e., $2v - m_c$), the segment where P surely acts unilaterally, and lowers the probability density for these status quos given our assumption about q's distribution. The former raises $\Pr(Act)$, but the latter lowers it. Hence, effects are indeterminate. They may be minimal, positive or negative – e.g.,

---

[22] We do not provide a full-blown model of extra-statutory mechanisms because it would make the analysis far too technical and tedious. Instead, our theory can be thought of as a reduced form encompassing different effects of extra-statutory mechanisms without detailing the exact processes and conditions under which such mechanisms are more or less constraining. We could think of each real or potential unilateral act as having an associated extra-statutory cost, which is a function of a variety of relevant factors, such as the importance of the issue to opponents and the ease which extra-statutory costs can be implemented. We leave the generation of such a model, however, for future work.

a status quo distribution overwhelmingly centered around m_c can result in a larger EGI override-tail that actually reduces the $\Pr(Act)$.[23] This means that the hypothesis regarding EGI for the unilateralism model no longer holds.

To see the kind of example that we have in mind that would fit the chamber-compliance model but not unilateralism, consider EO 12433, which created an explicitly bipartisan commission (the "National Bipartisan Commission on Central America") to evaluate policies on Central America, for which Ronald Reagan had come under attack.[24] This Commission would become known as the "Kissinger Commission," as former Secretary of State Henry Kissinger was named its chairman (for the Commission's report, see National Bipartisan Commission on Central America 1984).

What was notable about this Commission from our perspective is that it seemed to alienate those on both the left and right and to appeal, more or less, to the center of the legislative distribution of preferences, made up largely of Democrats. This started with the choice of Kissinger himself, whom Reagan had very publicly lambasted in earlier times as not being sufficiently conservative, and whom some liberal Democrats – naturally, given that Kissinger had previously worked for Republican Presidents Ford and Nixon – viewed as too far to the right. However, while a number of liberal Democratic critics opposed the Commission, other important mainstream party actors supported it (Broder 1983).

Put differently, the Commission was about forging a middle-of-the-road consensus. Noted *New York Times* columnist Tom Wicker stated (1983, p. A21) that the aim was "to generate for Mr. Reagan the Congressional and public support he hasn't otherwise achieved." As one scholarly analysis put it (LeoGrande 1984, p. 251) in evaluating the report, "Kissinger understood immediately the task before him: to produce a report that would preempt the unfolding national debate over the wisdom of deepening US military involvement in Central America and restore bipartisan support to the president's policies in the region."

---

[23] Figure A.1, Appendix 1, further illustrates these dynamics by showing how more-extreme veto pivots typically, but not uniformly, reduce presidential unilateral action, and how this relationship differs depending on the standard deviation of the status quo distribution.

[24] In truth, it is often difficult to pinpoint examples that clearly distinguish a model where discretion is limited by the chamber median as compared to the majority-party median (which highlights the importance of our quantitative approach for model testing). The reasons for this should be obvious (and will be that much clearer once the party-compliance model is presented). For one thing, changes may often be observationally equivalent in the sense that both the chamber and majority party medians support them. Related to this, it is much easier to distinguish the direction of change (and whether it is or is not, therefore, toward the chamber and the majority party medians) than exactly where the new status quo is located, which might help us to discern who is the dominant figure. Furthermore, materials detailing EOs almost always focus on parties and party leaders rather than the positions of chamber medians and the like.

Partisan-Compliance Model

The partisan-compliance model replaces m_c from the chamber-compliance model with the ideal point of the majority party median, denoted m_p,[25] in constraining presidential unilateral action, while the chamber median remains the legislative-stage agenda-setter.[26] The rationale for assuming that M_p, representing the majority party median, constrains discretion is analogous to that for the chamber-median assumption, i.e., the extra-statutory tactics used as checks by the legislature or, implicitly, via judicial decisions. Also, as parties become stronger, they can help overcome collective action problems pointed out in Moe and Howell (1999a) and therefore enhance the ability of Congress to initiate extra-statutory tactics to constrain how the President uses discretion. The major difference between the directional discretion assumption of this model and the previous one, consistent with parties controlling many extra-statutory mechanisms (recall Chapter 1), is that the party, not the chamber, median is the key player constraining t, which Howell (2003) assumed in deriving his divided government hypothesis. The substantive importance of substituting party for chamber median hinges on the preference difference between the two.

For consistency, we also assume that the party median exercises negative agenda-setting power in the legislative stage.[27] The resulting EGI expands and is bounded by f and m_p under unified government and by m_p and v under divided government, as the majority-party median prevents the chamber median from moving any q located between these two medians toward the latter's ideal point.

As Figures 2.5(a) and 2.5(c) display, under unified government the equilibrium presidential unilateral action in this model, given a certain discretion level, is actually quite similar to that in the unilateralism model. M_p, which now constrains how the President can use t, has an ideal point so similar to the President's that P's discretion, while bounded by Congress, is essentially unconstrained regarding which direction the status quo is moved. This is why the President's equilibrium unilateral action under the unilateralism model is almost identical to that under the partisan-compliance model with unified government. Additionally, P can take advantage of a more fragmented Congress (i.e., with an expanded EGI) by moving previously unalterable status

---

[25] As foreshadowed, bicameralism is implicitly incorporated: when the same party controls both chambers, the majority-party median is the more extreme of the two chambers' medians, and when different parties control the House and Senate there are two majority-party medians in the model. For parsimony, we only show the theoretical result under a unified Congress, while our empirical analysis also accounts for divided Congresses.

[26] While we retain this assumption to make differences between our models transparent, our results are qualitatively unchanged if the party median also sets the agenda.

[27] As such, the game tree in Figure 2.4, while representing our first two models where majority parties play no role, does not precisely capture this model because, while the chamber median still makes policy, the majority-party median exercises negative agenda power in the legislative stage and is, therefore, an added veto player.

quos. Thus, P essentially shifts q where the party median would prefer it as an agenda-setter. The same relationship holds for expected presidential unilateral action in Figures 2.6(a) and 2.6(c).

Strikingly, as Figures 2.5(d) and 2.6(d) illustrate, P is unlikely to propose unilateral action under divided government. When q is between m_p and v, the President, accounting for the majority median's preferences and opposition (or facing the court acting in this median's interest if it is interpreted as representative of the enacting coalition), will be restrained from moving q closer to P. This highlights both that unilateral action may correspond to weak presidential power and that parties, rarely explicitly addressed in the executive action literature, may be crucially important.

Two features in this model should be emphasized. Divided government's effect, displayed in Figures 2.6(c) and 2.6(d), is not driven by the majority party's negative agenda power in the legislative stage, as Deering and Maltzman (1999) implicitly argued, but by its veto or bargaining power over directional presidential discretion, the assumption distinguishing the partisan-compliance model from the first two.[28] Additionally, divided government's dramatic effect is partly triggered by the preference difference between p and m_p under unified and divided government. Presidential unilateral action serves the majority party median's interests far more when p and m_p are very similar (i.e., under unified government) than when such preferences are quite diverse (i.e., under divided government). Put differently, even when the President would greatly benefit from unilateral action, he or she must obtain the majority party median's tacit approval, as this median's welfare must increase with unilateral action.

Based on Proposition 3 (Appendix 1), we derive the following hypotheses:

Hypothesis C1: A new President whose party is different from his or her predecessor's will produce more unilateral action in his or her first term than otherwise.

Hypothesis C2: Unified government results in a larger probability of presidential unilateral action than does divided government.

Hypothesis C3: Under unified government, the greater the length of the filibuster-tail or override-tail, the more likely the President will act unilaterally.[29]

---

[28] Put differently, this is how the partisan-compliance model differs from Deering and Maltzman's (1999) spatial illustration. The latter hypothesized, without formal derivation, that presidents who are more ideologically distant from majority party medians are less likely to issue EOs because these medians can play a significant role (using negative and positive agenda-setting by which proposals are kept off of or put onto the floor agenda) in statutorily overturning unilateral action. However, sustaining this hypothesis seems difficult, as other legislative pivots likely undermine such majority-leader attempts. Note also that the Deering/Maltzman analysis would not produce the other two hypotheses in the partisan-compliance model.

[29] However, data constraints – small sample size and the variables suggested in this hypothesis being highly correlated with divided government – make testing this hypothesis problematic, which is why we do not include it in Table 2.1.

The first hypothesis is analogous to those for the initial two models. The second integrates the potential importance of legislative parties and divided government, irrelevant for the earlier models, and can hold only when assuming that M_p directionally constrains presidential action. The condition for this hypothesis is typically found empirically. While this hypothesis has been proposed and tested elsewhere (Mayer 1999, Howell 2003), our derivation differs, and we make the theoretical assumptions and mechanism producing the effects of unified government more transparent and precise.[30] For instance, while previous studies suggest that congressional support drives unified government's effects, we deductively demonstrate how a *majority party*'s tacit approval for the President exercising his or her *discretion* results in these effects.

Conversely, our third hypothesis is novel, indicating that the interaction between unified government and the filibuster-tail's or override-tail's length positively increases $\Pr(Act)$, with the override-tail now defined as the distance between m_p and m_c. By detailing how the effects of factors related to the entire or partial EGI are conditioned by whether government is unified, we highlight the importance of developing individual models with consistent assumptions.[31]

An example of a presidential EO that would fit the partisan-compliance model (despite some contention involved) occurred in 1990, when George H. W. Bush issued EO 12711, allowing Chinese students to stay in the United States. This EO occurred at a time when there was much controversy about whether Chinese students should be permitted to remain in America in the aftermath of the suppression of pro-democracy movements in China, with the congressional Democratic majority being particularly in favor. Indeed, in late 1989, the Democratic Congress – led by liberal leaders such as Nancy Pelosi in the House and Edward Kennedy in the Senate – had passed a piece of legislation that did most of what the EO accomplished, but Bush, under heavy pressure from Chinese leaders, vetoed the legislation (the veto was not overridden). Interestingly, at first through more informal means and then via the EO, the President accomplished much the same goals but in a lower-key manner that was presumably somewhat more acceptable to government leaders in Beijing.[32]

PRESIDENTIAL POWER UNDER COMPETING MODELS

We have proposed a new theoretical framework where we can closely link theory to data in a manner that can allow us to assess unilateral action as

---

[30] This hypothesis is also more general than Howell's, regarding party effects. For one thing, he examines only when all pivots except the majority-party median are located identically under unified and divided governments, which is not the case in reality.

[31] Additionally, under this model Howell's two derived hypotheses – fragmentation and divided government – cannot hold simultaneously, no matter how we adjust our assumptions.

[32] Postscript: Pelosi would succeed in sponsoring the "Chinese Student Protection Act of 1992," which allowing Chinese nationals who had entered the US before the issuance of EO 12711 on April 11, 1990 to apply for permanent resident status.

a vehicle for presidential power and as a means of disentangling the enigma of presidential power. In doing so, we explicitly organized the insights of students of the institutional presidency with a research design focused on empirically discriminating between models. Thus, while our models all assume that Congress can constrain presidential unilateral action by passing legislation and that courts can prevent instances when they deem that legislatively or Constitutionally delegated discretion has been exceeded, each model has different implications for patterns of observed empirical data and the relationship between unilateral action and power. With the results presented earlier, we can now wrap up our discussion regarding how we will assess executive influence under the competing models that we have just specified.

Recall that in the unilateralism model, the President acts freely within the discretion limit, without any directional constraints. Any attempt by a legislative pivot to override a unilateral action through a statute will be stalled by another pivot. As Figure 2.6(a) shows, the President can move – but may lack incentives to shift – almost all status quos in any direction without the overt or tacit approval of any other political actors. Unilateral action is thus equivalent to presidential power to an extremely high extent, given our dual definitions.

By contrast, presidential power stemming from opportunities for unilateral action is substantially undercut in the chamber- and partisan-compliance models, as the President acts as if he or she cannot use discretion to shift a status quo without the overt or tacit approval of a critical actor in Congress, be it the chamber or the majority-party median. How much the President's expected utility rises from unilateral action is largely a function of the preference divergence between the President and this critical actor, as the latter constrains the President's directional use of discretion.

To measure the President's expected utility increase from unilateral action, for each model we compare the President's utility relative to a counterfactual where only a pivotal politics game, i.e., the second stage of our larger game, is played and no unilateral action can occur. In other words, imagine a world where the chief executive is void of the ability to act before the legislature moves, and compare it to a world where he or she can – how much better-off is the President under the latter conditions?

Proposition 4 (Appendix 1) demonstrates that the partisan-compliance model with unified government boosts the President's gain the most, followed by the unilateralism model, the chamber-compliance model, and the partisan-compliance model with divided government (where the chief executive benefits very little). Moreover, if we wish to combine the two variants of the partisan-compliance model, assuming that divided government's likelihood is not too low (reasonable, given that it occurs more than 50 percent of the time, post-World War II), we can establish under some fairly reasonable circumstances that the President's gain is the largest in the unilateralism model and the least in the partisan-compliance model.

Put differently, if we define presidential influence as the chief executive's utility gains stemming purely from unilateral action, the President becomes more influential from unilateral action in each of these models. However, the extent of the President's gain differs substantially depending on which of these models characterizes the world (and, for partisan-compliance, whether government is unified or divided).

While Proposition 4 confirms our intuition that the key difference in the discretion assumption in the three models has profound implications for presidential gains, the chief executive's increase in expected utility does not necessarily correspond to power, given either of our definitions. The President's gain from unilateral action is not agreed to by Congress or the courts in the unilateralism model, whereas it is agreed to in the chamber- and partisan-compliance models. Stated differently, the unilateralism model, which seemingly best corresponds to presidential influence and the insights of theoretical efforts such as Deering and Maltzman (1999), Krause and Cohen (2000), Mayer (2002) and elements of Howell (2003), implies the most presidential influence. Nonetheless, if the chamber- and partisan-compliance models, which highlight how overt or tactical approval may be required for presidents to act unilaterally, hold empirically, we must reassess the power associated with unilateral action.

CONCLUSIONS: WHAT PRESIDENTIAL INFLUENCE INVOLVES

While existing models of legislative and unilateral politics provide a promising foundation for establishing the theoretical framework to answer the fundamental question that motivates our analysis, they are not enough. To begin to understand the enigma of presidential power, we require directly comparable models that take into account different ways in which Congress and the courts might impact the presidential use of discretion. As such, we have built on these past insights, but in the process we have produced a new theoretical framework that will allow us to ascertain what presidential power looks like.

Specifically, our theoretical analysis – delineating three models that vary only in the assumption about discretion – makes clear what specific conditions must hold for presidents to employ unilateral action in an effective and powerful way. In doing so, we model the context where only formal statutory and judicial constraints matter, which is the principal way in which scholars have conceptualized the situation, and when extra-statutory constraints (as well as, in fairly rudimentary fashion, political parties) are also relevant, which others have increasingly realized may matter for unilateral action, and which are typically thought of us as important for how legislative-executive relations play out.

In a broad sense, these models force us to confront the fact that presidents' ability to successfully act unilaterally does not mean that the balance of power between political institutions is strongly biased toward the chief executive.

Rather, the presence or absence of such bias depends upon which of these models, with their contrasting discretionary constraints, most accurately corresponds to empirical reality.

Indeed, because the only element that differs across our competing models is our assumption about the direction of discretion, our theoretical analysis has the virtue of generating different hypotheses that can be directly compared. Depending on which of these hypotheses receives the most empirical support in our subsequent analysis, therefore, we will gain new insights into what role unilateral action in the form of EOs truly plays in the American political system. Our results should have important implications for understanding how constraining problems of collective action are: support for the unilateralism model would imply that Congress's collective action problems with respect to the use of extra-statutory means are neither substantially solved by the whole (consistent with the claims of Moe and Howell 1999a) or via parties; support for the chamber-compliance model would say that legislators as a whole can overcome these collective difficulties and effectively exercise extra-statutory means constraining presidential action; and support for the partisan-compliance model would indicate that parties, rather than the body of the whole, play this role.[33]

---

[33] We will, however, show in Chapter 5 that the relationship between the ability of parties to reduce presidential power by overcoming collective action problems is more complicated when different party roles are integrated into the legislative stage of our model.

3

Not All Unilateral Actions Are Created Equal: Measuring the Significance of Executive Orders

INTRODUCTION – THE IMPORTANCE OF SIGNIFICANCE

In January 2013, in light of a number of high-profile executive orders by President Barak Obama, Republicans and conservatives were in an uproar over the chief executive's use of unilateral actions. Rising to his defense, *Forbes* commentator Richard Salsman penned an essay titled, "When It Comes to Abuse of Presidential Power, Obama Is a Mere Piker."[1] Salsman's defense was a rather simple one – that by the number of EOs issued, Obama was rather circumspect in his activities:

> Republicans and conservatives have complained loudly lately that President Obama has been resorting to non-democratic and unconstitutional governance; imperiously ignoring the so-called "will of the people" by issuing a cascade of new executive orders. According to Senator Rand Paul (R-KY), Mr. Obama is acting "like a king" by issuing his recent executive orders on gun control. Conservative author and radio talk show host Mark Levin contends that Obama's executive orders are "un-American" and even "fascistic."
>
> If so, then certain Republican presidents – including Dwight Eisenhower, Gerald Ford and Ronald Reagan – must be classified as even more monarchical, un-American, and "fascistic"... *The average number [of executive orders issued post-1900] for all twenty presidents is 44 per annum... Mr. Obama has averaged 37.* [italics added]

However, as should be clear from our discussions in Chapter 1 overviewing unilateral action, not all unilateral actions generally, or EOs specifically, are created equal. While most popular commentators (including Mr. Salsman) and scholars recognize this at least implicitly, the tendency to count EOs has often crept into discussions of unilateral action and power. Not only have there been numerous discussions such as Salsman's over the years, but a good deal of the

---

[1] See www.forbes.com/sites/richardsalsman/2013/01/28/when-it-comes-to-abuse-of-presidential-power-obama-is-a-mere-piker/.

quantitative literature on unilateral action has done the same. Further, as we will detail shortly, even the work that has gone beyond just counting EOs has not provided what we would ideally like: a continuous measure of each action's significance, estimated with a solid statistical foundation. Such a measure will allow us to see the extent to which any empirical results we generate are sensitive to different levels of significance, ultimately providing us with more confidence in inferences drawn about the relationship between unilateral action and presidential power and the reconciliation of instances in which the chief executive appears to be powerful with those where he or she does not.

Happily, modern statistical techniques and the ability to collect data electronically make it possible to contemplate generating such a measure. As such, we will initially survey what steps previous analyses have taken and will then suggest a new hierarchical item-response theory (IRT) model, building upon previous statistical works and their applications in political science, notably to the statutory outputs of the United States Congress. IRT is a psychometric theory originally designed to measure characteristics such as a student's latent ability, but it has a variety of characteristics that make it quite appropriate for measuring the output significance of political institutions if enough so-called raters can be found (i.e., significance is a latent category being estimated). Our hierarchical IRT model is unique in that, besides incorporating the thresholds adopted by raters and their abilities to discriminate between EOs, we control for specific biases that these raters might bring to the table. Subsequently, we outline our data collection effort, which is considerable, and then estimate significance levels for our EOs. Before concluding, we show how significance levels vary by policy area.

SIGNIFICANT POLITICAL ACTIONS – INITIAL EFFORTS

As discussed above with respect to presidential choices, the nature of political outputs is such that actions that we compare and contrast typically vary greatly in their importance. "Importance" itself is, of course, a nebulous term. When we say that an output is important – be it a piece of legislation, a bureaucratic choice, a judicial decision or a unilateral action – we may be referring to the degree to which the action changes the status quo (as illustrated by our discussions in Chapter 2, where a policy can change the status quo on a spatial dimension), or the extent to which a resulting policy change effects societal welfare (is society better-off or worse-off as a whole as a result of this action?), or the manner in which a policy changes the distribution of benefits and costs (does one group lose at another's expense?), or the significances that elites or citizens ascribe to the issue in question (e.g., a social issue, such as stem cell research, may constitute a so-called wedge issue that arouses the passions of those who feel strongly about possible linkages with abortion). From our perspective as empirical scholars of institutional choice behavior, exactly *which* of these features is relevant is not key. What we focus on is measuring the relative extent to which politicians care about the changes being made by an action. In doing so, our fundamental interest is in finding an effective means of gauging this latent concept (the term used in this literature) of *significance*.

With respect to unilateral actions generally and EOs specifically (which have received most of the attention), scholars certainly understand that there is a wide range of significance, anchored by the extremely trivial (such as ordering a flag to half mast) to the quite profound (e.g., changing policies regarding segregation) (Howell 2005, Warber 2006).[2] Yet, lacking an easy alternative, many nonetheless have employed a count of executive orders. By treating all executive orders the same, they assume, whether implicitly or explicitly, that the acts being considered are of equal significance. To reiterate, this is not to say that those who do so believe this to be the case, only that this is the implication of their measurement choices. As such, any inferences drawn must be viewed with caution.

Others have tried to move beyond simple counts. Their approaches have taken two forms: either categorizing the actions according to their content or explicitly distinguishing significant EOs from insignificant EOs.

As for the first approach, for example, Warber (2006) categorized EOs into seven groups: symbolic, routine, policy, symbolic/routine, symbolic/policy, routine/policy and symbolic/routine/policy. Presumably, those actions that are considered *policy* would be viewed as more significant than those that are not, while those thought to be merely symbolic or routine would be considered as less significant. Obviously, this measure is discontinuous and, while likely correlated with significance (and it is, relative to the estimates that we generate), it does not make the finer-grain distinctions that we would prefer. Indeed, most EOs are graded as routine, with only a few designated as purely policy oriented (and, thus, significant). As such, Warber's typology is best conceptualized as the work of a single rater of EOs – albeit with a considerable amount of content analysis by the scholar doing the rating – or as a means of measuring specific characteristics of EOs.

Alternatively, following previous work on determining significant legislation (Mayhew 2005; originally 1991) and more in the spirit of our analysis in this chapter, Howell (2003, 2005) divided EOs into important and unimportant categories in several ways. In his initial work (Howell 2003), he coded an EO as significant for 1945 to 1983 if it was mentioned either in the appendix of the *Congressional Record* or in at least two federal court case opinions. For subsequent years (1986 to 1998) he adopted a more complicated procedure – running a regression of his initial measure using the number of EOs mentioned by the *Record* and judicial opinions on the corresponding number of EOs mentioned on the *New York Times* (*NYT*) front page, and then using the

---

[2] The same would certainly be true for others who have examined different sources of presidential unilateralism, such as executive proclamations (e.g., Rottinghaus and Maier 2007).

resulting coefficient to predict the expected numbers of significant EOs for 1984 to 1998. Two years later (Howell 2005), with the *Times* becoming available for electronic search, he then simply measured whether or not an EO appeared on the front page of the newspaper. Similarly, and again in the spirit of Mayhew's (2005) approach, Mayer (1999) and Mayer and Price (2002) measured significance over a subset of EOs (1,028 EOs in total, or 17.6 percent of the EOs issued between March 1936 and December 1999) from six sources (the press, congressional committee hearings on overriding an EO, mentions by students of law or of the presidency, the Presidents' public statements, federal litigation [if any] and whether an EO created a government organization),[3] considering any presence in one source as significant.[4]

While each of these approaches represents an important step forward, neither nears the ideal of a continuous, reliable measure of EO importance. Besides potentially serving as a useful single rating of EOs, Warber's analysis suggests that there are features of the content of EOs that we might want to take into account in our analysis – something we will do later when we disaggregate our analysis by policy type. Howell's effort, notably his *New York Times* measure (which we will principally discuss, as this is his preferred measure), produces a result that almost certainly correlates with an action's importance (e.g., the *New York Times* measure is correlated with our measure). Yet, not only does the dichotomous division mean that much other information is not incorporated, but relying on a single media source is problematic, as the standards employed for inclusion on the front page of any single newspaper, even a paper as prestigious as the *Times*, almost certainly reflect idiosyncratic factors other than executive order significance.[5] While Mayer, by himself and with Price, went beyond this by considering six sources, scoring a mention by any one of these sources as significant essentially means that there is essentially only one rater producing a single dichotomy (and, in this instance, for fewer than 18 percent of all EOs under study).[6]

Put differently, efforts using one or more sources demonstrate how we can produce a rating, if only a dichotomous one, that is certainly correlated with significance.[7] However, besides not providing a continuous significance

---

[3] We utilize a number of sources similar to those of Mayer and Price in our analysis, but we integrate them differently.

[4] We do not call these sources "raters" because they are utilized in a manner such that, as long as one source names an EO, it is irrelevant how many additional sources name it, in terms of the measured level of significance.

[5] For example, it has been suggested elsewhere that the *Times* might be biased toward reporting certain kinds of stories or issues (e.g., Groseclose and Milyo 2005, Gentzkow and Shapiro 2010), which may straightforwardly lead to a bias regarding what type of EOs are reported.

[6] After introducing our statistical model, we will expound upon the differences between our approach and that of Mayer (and Howell 2003, which essentially uses two or three sources for a single rater), including precisely distinguishing between a source and a rater.

[7] We will discuss a rater in the singular, even though the "rater" may be a product of multiple sources.

measure, doing so opens up a Pandora's box of problems associated with relying on a single rater for thresholds: we lack insight into the rater's objectiveness; we have no information about the threshold that the rater employs to distinguish significance from insignificance; we cannot judge whether this threshold is reasonable; and we cannot analyze the robustness of empirical analysis when thresholds of what constitutes significant actions are varied.

GOING BEYOND

It is possible to move beyond the kind of measures adopted in past research. Indeed, not only can we borrow from the measurement literature in statistics, we can also look elsewhere in recent analyses of American political institutions for inspiration.

Per the latter, those who have been actively involved in scholarly debates about legislative productivity, which has been a growth industry for well over two decades, have notably dealt with an analogous problem. Simply put, assessing a legislature's output dictates that scholars be able to establish a weight for each of the total actions by importance, for example each statute, produced during a specific period of time, such as a two-year US congressional term. This has meant, for instance, counting the number of bills that became law that exceeded a given significance threshold, or weighting all legislation by generating an individual measure of importance for each statute.

The foundational work in this literature is Mayhew (2005; to reiterate, originally 1991), who adopted the former tack of defining a list of important legislation. Specifically, he developed a measure of the amount of so-called landmark legislation produced in each post-World War II Congress by integrating systematically, although without employing an explicit statistical model, the views of policy experts and journalists as sources.[8] He relied upon both contemporary assessments of legislation (his so-called "Sweep One") and retrospective, historical, overviews (his so-called "Sweep Two"), and a statute was considered a landmark enactment if mentioned by either source.[9]

Inspired by this work, a proliferation of studies proposing alternative measures of significant bills ensued (e.g., Kelly 1993, Binder 1999, 2003, Howell et al. 2000, Clinton and Lapinski 2006, Grant and Kelly 2008). For our analysis, the most important work in this post-Mayhew genre is Clinton and Lapinski, which adopted an alternative approach: instead of counting the

---

[8] As noted, Mayhew's original work was published in 1991 (we cite the second edition here). Further, updated, data can be found at http://campuspress.yale.edu/davidmayhew/datasets-divided-we-govern/.

[9] We will also integrate contemporaneous and historical assessments of EOs in our analysis.

number of pieces of legislation reaching some threshold, à la Mayhew, they weighted all legislation by its importance. Building on Mayhew by applying a form of item-response theory (to reiterate, IRT) to handle statistically multiple raters (each of whom employs its own criteria in determining significance), it offered a better way of thinking about significance than past work, be it for legislation, EOs or other comparable outputs.[10] Thus, while the analyses of Mayer (1999), Mayer and Price (2002) and Howell (2003, 2005) all took inspiration from Mayhew (2005), Clinton and Lapinski's most directly motivates our efforts to tackle the measurement of presidential unilateral action. Our work on EOs builds on this analysis of significant legislation, with the notable improvement that we control rater biases while it does not.

As the discussion above should make clear, research on the significance of the President's unilateral actions, notably on executive orders, is very limited compared to legislative choices. Yet (to reiterate), like statutes, EOs range from the almost absurdly trivial – of little interest to all but a select few – to EOs that are important for those concerned about important policy outcomes. Contrast, for example, lame duck President Bush's issuance of EO 13485 in January of 2009, providing an order of succession within the Department of Transportation, with the newly inaugurated President Obama's issuance two months later, of EO 13505, dismantling barriers to conducting stem cell research. The former was certainly relevant only to a very few interested parties in the Department of Transportation, as it constituted little more than a matter of administrative bookkeeping; the latter engaged a wide range of interests, from scientists involved in research and concerned with impediments to progress to those with strong religious beliefs about the use of stem cells and its relationship to abortion. As such, while few political officials or related interest groups paid any observable heed to EO 13485, many were quite energized by EO 13505.

Nonetheless, as accounted above, in measuring EOs, there is far less work analyzing multiple sources akin to what Mayhew has done for legislation, no less formalizing the multiple rater approach analogous to Clinton and Lapinski for statutes. There are no obvious reasons for this, except perhaps that legislative activities have typically received more popular and scholarly attention. Such greater attention is likely a product both of EOs being, on average, less important than legislation, and of unilateral actions not winding through a publicly observable labyrinth in the manner that legislation must.

These distinctions between legislation and unilateral actions/EOs make the finding of appropriate raters more problematic and, as we will discuss further, generate concerns that highlight the need for improvements to the measurement

---

[10] See Johnson and Albert (1991) for a detailed discussion of the statistical model that Clinton and Lapinski applied in measuring legislation significance.

model as well. Indeed, while multiple raters are quite crucial for a more reliable measure of significance, as mentioned above, defining a group of raters is a major obstacle. Raters, to reiterate, discriminate among a set of actions by classifying some as significant and others as not. Some potential and actual raters may be more able than others to accomplish this task. Thus, we need raters of EOs who are qualified to distinguish between those that are significant and those that are not, and we need to account statistically for their differences in ability along the way. Yet, for example, with the exception of Cooper (2002), no general scholarly overview of landmark executive orders exists that is analogous to those for statutory enactments of Congress and can be straightforwardly identified as a rater.[11]

Still, the situation is far from hopeless. Beyond Cooper, there are other candidates that can serve as raters of executive orders. General and specialized newspapers, magazines and top legal journals all mention EOs to one extent or another – presumably, on average, those EOs that are more significant – and can therefore be employed as raters.[12] Happily, while using such sources might have seemed overwhelming in the past, the task, while still formidable, is feasible now without an army of coders. For example, technology makes it possible to search beyond a newspaper's front page à la Howell (2005; the *New York Times* in this case) so that, in essence, each paper can be thought of as two or more raters (e.g., front page and non-front page).[13] As we will detail subsequently in greater depth, we generate 19 raters altogether, providing us with the kind of data we need to produce a new and better measure of EO significance.[14] Specifically, our raters (listed in Table 3.1, and described later in more detail) range from daily newspapers, weekly magazines, court challenges, the congressional record and legal journals.[15]

As for the statistical model, as mentioned, we specify an extended IRT model that aggregates information from different raters in a systematic, comprehensive, and statistically defensible manner. It yields a measure that improves on previous efforts dealing with EOs and even upon what would be

---

[11] Warber's (2006) analysis might also be viewed as providing a rating. However, as will become clearer later, in implementing our statistical model we find it is more helpful to integrate his distinctions among EOs elsewhere in the analysis.

[12] These raters sometimes refer to past executive orders, but they principally focus on recent actions. In other words, they tend to draw attention to the contemporaneous rather than to the historical.

[13] Mention on a front page does not, either in theory or in fact, preclude discussion elsewhere in the paper. For example, prominent EOs may get first-page attention and then another treatment with more details in a separate article elsewhere in the newspaper.

[14] Note that, while some of the publications that we use for raters go back beyond the time that we include, we limit ourselves for obvious reasons to the time periods where we can perform electronic searches.

[15] One potential drawback of using electronic sources is that the mechanisms for searching may change over time, and this might lead to slightly different coding results at one point than at another.

TABLE 3.1 *Rater information*

Rater	Time period	EOs Rated	EOs Mentioned	Explanatory variables
New York Times – Front page	All dates	3515	320	1. Average number of articles appearing in its front pages
New York Times – Elsewhere	All dates	3515	949	None
Washington Post – Front page	All dates	3515	317	1. Government operation
Washington Post – Elsewhere	All dates	3515	776	1. Government operation
Wall Street Journal – Front page	All dates	3515	197	1. Macroeconomics 2. Labor, employment and immigration.
Wall Street Journal – Elsewhere	All dates	3515	428	1. Macroeconomics 2. Labor, employment and immigration.
National Journal	01/1/77 – 12/31/03	1377	137	1. Environmental protection
U.S. News & World Report	01/1/75 – 12/31/03	1500	50	1. Foreign policy
Newsweek	01/1/75 – 12/31/03	1500	51	1. Foreign policy
Congressional Quarterly Weekly Report	10/1/83 – 12/31/03	881	93	None
"American Presidency Project"	All dates	3515	730	None
Cooper	01/01/47 – 01/20/01	3336	126	None
Mentions by Courts and Congress	01/01/47 – 12/31/90	2933	424	None
Court challenge	01/01/47 – 12/31/94	3515	57	None
Chicago Law Review	All dates	3515	43	None
Columbia Law Review	All dates	3515	63	None
Harvard Law Review	All dates	3515	69	None
Stanford Law Review	All dates	3515	47	None
Yale Law Journal	All dates	3515	60	None

produced with a new application similar to what was previously employed for legislative productivity.

We will not detail the underlying mathematics here – leaving that to Appendix 2 – and will instead concentrate on discussing its many positive features for measuring EO significance. Specifically, we enumerate seven benefits from our approach. The first four are advantages that are associated with standard IRT, with the latter three being benefits stemming from our employment of a hierarchical structure and explanatory variables corresponding to raters.[16]

First, as indicated, we can employ multiple raters, as distinguished from utilizing an individual source or multiple sources to produce a single rating.[17] As mentioned, previous measures of identifying significant EOs rely on from as few as one (e.g., the *New York Times* front page) source to as many as six sources (i.e., an EO is identified as significant if one of the sources mentions it). By contrast, we include 19 raters, incorporating many more sources than in the past.

As long as the included raters mention an EO at least partially because of its significance, this expansion of the number of raters will generally increase the sample size for rating each EO, likely producing a more reliable measure of significance. To ensure this, while also ensuring that our measure incorporates more information than extant ones, we very selectively include data sources where we believe raters should be responding to EO significance.

Second, our method allows us to incorporate raters who are only covering a subset of the time being analyzed. For instance, if a political magazine or a newspaper was established in 1970 (or is electronically searchable only back to that time), we can still include it as a rater if we estimate EO significance, as we do, for a period that begins at an earlier time. By contrast, it would not make sense to include such information if we were simply counting whether one of many sources named a given EO, for example. Obviously, the virtue of having such flexibility is that it incorporates valuable information by making more raters eligible, without requiring arbitrary assumptions, than would be available if raters needed to assess the entire period under consideration. The result is a better measure than if raters were more severely restricted.

---

[16] All of these benefits but one (the sixth advantage) are associated with Clinton and Lapinski's approach as well.

[17] To follow-up on our earlier discussion, the distinction between a source and a rater is that a source need not help determine a final rating. For example, in Mayhew's or Mayer's method, a source may not help determine whether a law or an executive order (or whatever else is under consideration) is considered significant because, once one source makes a mention, it is irrelevant whether the others do (thus Mayer's analysis with six sources can be viewed as having only one rater, as can Howell's (2003) analysis that uses the appendix of the *Congressional Record* and federal court case mentions). By contrast, our method codes each rater's mention separately and raises the level of significance, to one degree or another, attributed to an output.

Third, we can deal with different thresholds employed by raters in mentioning an EO, as some raters may cite only a few acts and others may discuss many. Indeed, as seen in Table 3.1, some raters, such as newspapers, discussed hundreds of actions over our period of study, while others, such as weekly magazines, noted only scores during the same era. One strong possibility is that the latter raters adopt a higher significance threshold for mentioning an EO than the former because the number of stories that weeklies can cover in the aggregate is so much smaller. Regardless, the key point is that differences in raters' thresholds are handled well statistically.

Fourth, we can estimate different abilities of our raters in distinguishing between more- and less-significant actions. We take into account that some raters are better at mentioning which EOs are and are not significant and at ascertaining how significant an identified action is, relative to others.[18] For example, a rater tending to mention EOs only for idiosyncratic reasons or for systematic reasons that are not related to what other raters consider significance will be estimated to have a lower discriminative power. Similarly, if, in the real world, significance regarding EOs is distributed such that there are some EOs that are virtually insignificant, many have modest significance and a few have high significance, but a rater mentions similar numbers of EOs from each of these categories, this rater will also be considered to have a low power of discrimination.[19]

Fifth, turning to the improvements associated with our methodology over standard IRT applications, our approach helps distinguish even between the more than half of the EOs that are not mentioned by any rater, as well as among those that would otherwise be difficult to differentiate because they are mentioned by the same or similar sets of raters. Using standard models, the former, of course, would all be seen as having similar, low significance levels; the latter would be difficult to make any finer distinctions between, even if the significance level were not extremely low. To deal with such difficulties, we will incorporate additional information correlated with significance, such as whether an EO has policy content, creates a new organization, or represents routine administration. This data will help distinguish between the significance

---

[18] Note that one critical requirement for any good measure (in our case, of EO significance) is that the data employed to estimate or to measure it is correlated with or captures this underlying dimension for the object that we want to measure. As such, it is important that our rater's choices are correlated with the political significance of an EO. Later we will return to this concern when we present our estimation results.

[19] Per our earlier discussion of Howell's (2003) use of two sources (sometimes in conjunction with the *New York Times* front page) or Mayer's six sources constituting only one rater, their methods implicitly assume that all sources employ the same significance thresholds and have identical discrimination abilities (the same observation would apply to Mayhew's 2005 work on landmark legislation). Alternatively, our approach allows 19 different thresholds and discrimination abilities, corresponding to 19 raters.

of EOs that were not mentioned or were mentioned by the same set of raters and would otherwise be scored identically.

Sixth, we are able to account for rater biases. These biases are not ideological, per se, but rather are matters of emphasis or a function of other factors. In this vein, many of our newspaper and weekly political magazine raters appear to cover certain issues more than others. For instance, as a business paper the *Wall Street Journal* tends to cover more issues on macroeconomics and labor and employment, while – quite intuitively given its location – the *Washington Post* seems to focus on government operations. This could result in each covering EOs that address these corresponding issues. Moreover, a rater such as a newspaper could expand or shrink its pages over 50 or 60 years, impacting the number of articles at a given time and, thus, topics covered each day. This could lower or raise thresholds for mentioning an EO during some periods, relative to others. As we can deal with these potential rater biases, our analysis also goes beyond existing work such as Clinton and Lapinski and produces a measure of significance in which we can have more confidence.[20]

Finally, a huge advantage of our IRT method over extant measures for EOs is that the latter produce only a dichotomous measure of significance, despite the fact that significance is clearly a matter of degree. Given the IRT framework, an EO's significance and the threshold and discriminative power of each rater, all of which are continuous, are simultaneously estimated. Thus, we can examine hypotheses regarding unilateral action far more flexibly than in the past, assessing how statistical results depend on the threshold for EO significance.

DATA

Having described the strength of our methodological approach to measuring EO significance (again, see Appendix 2 for detailed technical information about our method), we now describe our data we will apply to our statistical model for estimating EO significance for 1947–2003.[21]

To recap, our model requires three types of information: (1) ratings from a set of raters; (2) explanatory variables for significance that we can use as additional leverage for distinguishing EO significance, particularly regarding unmentioned EOs; and (3) exogenous variables that we can incorporate to control for potential biases of raters. As such, for the 3513 EOs issued from

[20] As we discuss in Appendix 2, we deal with this bias by extending Johnson and Albert's (1991) hierarchical Item-Response Model by incorporating explanatory variables for some raters.

[21] Our data ends in 2003 because this is when the current data for the Policy Agenda Project (PAP) www.policyagendas.org/datasets/index.html, upon which we rely for a number of exogenous explanatory variables, currently ends. Also, at least half of our raters, including historical overviews, require a certain time period (say 10 years) for retrospective reviews of more recently issued EOs.

1947 through 2003, we define 19 raters, 11 exogenous variables for EO significance and 10 explanatory variables for rater bias. We discuss each of these measurement choices below.

Raters

Table 3.1 lists our raters, the years covered by each, the number of EOs during the covered period, and the number of EOs mentioned by each rater. As referenced, somewhat similar to Mayhew and Mayer and Price, we utilize a variety of sources, including historical overviews of EOs, top law reviews, national newspapers and politics-focused magazines.

For every rater and EO issued from 1947 to 2003, we code an EO as one if the rater in question mentions it, and as zero otherwise. As mentioned above, and as Table 3.1 documents, different periods are covered by each rater; times not covered are considered to be missing data.

In terms of historical overviews, we use four. As mentioned earlier, while there are few surveys of executive orders analogous to those that we find for legislation, Cooper (2002) is the one clear exception. He mentions 126 out of the 3512 EOs issued. However, we should acknowledge that even Cooper's effort was not specifically directed to name highly significant EOs; for example, it listed 18 actions of Bill Clinton designed to help implement Vice President Gore's National Performance Review, essentially an effort to improve the quality of government service, and the author included some examples to show what symbolic EOs look like. Although we could have eliminated EOs that we thought were not selected for reasons of significance, we chose to avoid doing so as a way to avoid the appearance that we were manipulating the information to our own advantage. Also, we employ data from the "The American Presidency Project,"[22] which includes a litany of presidential materials such as press conferences, signing statements, State of the Union addresses and the like. We searched the document archive for the phrase "executive order" to see when the president was referring to specific orders. As a third historical source, we used Howell's (2003) collection of EOs that were challenged in the courts, as it is likely that an EO taken up in the courts will tend to have major impacts on individuals or interest groups. Our final historical source is Howell's (2003; generously furnished by the author) detailing of which EOs got attention from Congress or the courts, based on the supposition that a more significant EO has a higher probability of having received such consideration. As discussed, Howell coded whether an EO was either mentioned in the appendix of the *Congressional Record* or in the federal court opinions of at least two different cases.

As for law reviews, we include the *Columbia Law Review, Harvard Law Review, Stanford Law Review, University of Chicago Law Review* and *Yale*

---

[22] The Project can be found at www.presidency.ucsb.edu.

Law Journal.[23] Naturally, these journals tend to have articles written by legal scholars that sometimes mention executive orders; these references can be relatively contemporaneous or, in other instances, can mention actions taken fairly long before. Presumably, more highly significant EOs are more likely to receive scholarly attention. For each of the legal journals, we employ the phrase "executive order" to search and see which EOs issued from 1947 to 2003 were mentioned in the publications from 1947 onward.[24] In general, these journals mention few EOs issued in the 60-year span being considered – only 56 EOs on average for each journal. As such, these journals will have much higher thresholds for significance than many other raters that we include. Not surprisingly, the types of EOs that might intuitively interest lawyers – such as those dealing with citizen rights (e.g., Truman's EO 10241, which established loyalty programs for the government workforce) or the boundaries of government authority over society (e.g., Reagan's Order 12333, which extended the powers of US intelligence agencies) – seem to attract more attention.

Similarly, we search the phrase "executive order" for four weekly magazines, including *Congressional Quarterly Weekly Report, National Journal, U.S. News & World Report* and *Newsweek*. These magazines cover political stories but, unlike newspapers, have to be very selective in choosing which issues should be included. Indeed, with respect to EOs they tended to focus on a few specific areas, such as South Africa at the time of apartheid (e.g., EO 12532, which put up trade restrictions in 1985) and intelligence issues (for instance, EO 12333, which we discussed with respect to our law reviews). Given their different foci and readerships, *Congressional Quarterly Weekly Report* and *National Journal* paid more attention to presidential and congressional policy-making, respectively, and covered more EOs than *U.S. News* or *Newsweek.*[25] Not surprisingly, the *Congressional Quarterly* was particularly concerned with EOs related to bills on the legislative agenda; as such, EOs dealing with issues such as homeland security, presidential records, regulatory cost–benefit analysis and dual-exports (where a good can have commercial and military uses) all got attention. The *National Journal* had some specific interests (such as access to presidential archives) that seemed somewhat unique and,

---

[23] All but *Chicago* (which we included because of the law school's intellectual prestige) are regularly ranked as the top legal journals (using the "Washington and Lee" rankings, which are the standard; see http://lawlib.wlu.edu/LJ/).

[24] These journals are available through www.heinonline.org. Searches were conducted in 2010 and included all issues of the journals that were available at that time (*Chicago* through Winter 2010, *Harvard* through November 2009, *Stanford* through March 2010 and *Yale* through October 2008).

[25] Both the *Congressional Quarterly* and the *National Journal* had search engines on their web sites; *U.S. News* and *Newsweek* were available via *LexisNexis* when the data were coded, circa 2010.

consistent with how the *Journal* is organized, tended to focus according to issue area, be it labor, environment or the like (e.g., EO 13203, issued by George W. Bush in early 2001, revoking labor-management partnerships that were designed to benefit organized labor). Also, just as, intuitively, the *Congressional Quarterly* talked about bills on the legislative agenda and the *National Journal* often discussed EOs in their formulation stages when agencies would be involved.

The rest of our raters, national newspapers covering daily political and economic news and sometimes including EOs, probably provide the most contemporaneous coverage of EOs. We picked three of the most prominent national newspapers: the *New York Times*, the *Wall Street Journal* and the *Washington Post*. Given the special attention often given to front-page stories, for each of these papers we distinguish between EOs mentioned on page one and those discussed elsewhere; i.e., we count each newspaper as being essentially two raters. Although each newspaper's content is generated from the same source regardless of page of publication, there are likely to be different discriminating abilities and thresholds between the front page and elsewhere, and for this reason two raters per paper should be defined. For these six total raters, we used the Proquest "historical newspapers" and its "national newspapers premier" databases up to and after 1989, respectively. We also employed more intensive search terms than just the phrase "executive order." Thus, unlike Howell (2003, 2005), which employed "executive order" to search the *Times* within one year of an EO's issuance, we included not only that phrase but also some key words or phrases for the specific EO for all of our newspaper raters, although our time span was from the issuing date to just one week after issuance. We made this tradeoff of more breadth in keywords over a shorter time period of search because we found that a large number of relevant newspaper articles mentioning an EO fail to contain the exact term "executive order."[26] This is reflected by the number of EOs mentioned in the *New York Times* being much larger in our search results (16.7 EOs annually, on average) than what Howell (2005) found (9.8 EOs annually, on average), even though we employ a much shorter time span for our search for each EO.

In coding the newspapers, several things are noteworthy. One is that in generating key phrases we tried to use words that were most likely to be adopted by reporters. For example, while sometimes the title of the EO itself could supply the phrase, in other instances it was marked by verbiage not common in journalism. Examples would be "Generalized System of Preferences" rather than "tariff" or "air carrier" rather than "airline." Of course, at other times the title of an EO was too vague or there was simply a note that it amended or eliminated a previous EO, meaning that one needed to

---

[26] For example, it was often common just to discuss the fact that the president had ordered that something be done without using the exact phrase "executive order."

either understand the substance of the EO and translate it into a key phrase or go back to a previous, referenced EO, whichever made the most sense in the specific instance.[27]

As seen in Table 3.1, the *New York Times* mentions beyond the front page are more numerous than any other raters, trailed by the *Washington Post*'s non-front-page coverage.[28] This is not surprising, given that the number of stories covered in a year is quite large. As such, the range of EOs discussed is quite a bit more comprehensive, overall, particularly in the *Times* and *Post*, which, unlike the *Journal*, purport to be all-encompassing. In terms of front pages, the *Times* and *Post* mentioned similar numbers of EOs. Not surprisingly, the *Post* tended to focus more on EOs involving civil service, while the *Journal* focused more on purely economic EOs. Also, many of the *Journal* front-page articles consist of just one paragraph, including a large number that deal with applications of the Taft-Hartley and Railway Labor Acts (the latter of which covers airline labor–management issues as well) designed to prevent or end labor unrest.

Explanatory Variables for Significance

As mentioned above, since many EOs were not referenced by any of our raters, furnishing more information, as long as it is relevant, will help us to distinguish between them in terms of their significance. Also, this additional information will add considerable precision to our estimates for those EOs mentioned by only a few raters.[29]

As such, we include a number of variables that should be correlated with significance. Specifically, as foreshadowed, we use Warber's (2006) assessments as to whether an EO is policy-oriented. Also, we include from the PAP (Policy Agenda Project) whether an EO: (1) covers a domestic issue; (2) deals with routine administrative matters; (3) is employed to create a new government organization; (4) is issued in the first 100 days of a President's term; (5) occurs after November 1 of the year in which the President's term is ending; (6) is issued

[27] For accuracy's sake, we coded 1947–1954 a second time, as we were worried that, with practice, we were getting better at finding EOs (and, therefore, that our early years might be under-counted). We did find some undercounting for the first several years only, which we rectified. We thus have confidence in the consistency of our method's application.

Also, we excluded letters to the editor, but their inclusion would change little. Finally, there are examples of EOs that do not get much attention in the period we are coding (the day of the EO and the next 7 days) but do get notice later (e.g., Reagan's efforts to get government workers to give to religious charities). However, the vast preponderance of attention (at least enough to get incorporated into our sample even if there was later coverage) was the eight-day period for which we coded.

[28] We did not include *New York Times* front-page mentions that directly referenced an article on another page.

[29] The only downside of including such information is that estimates will have slightly more variance. They will, however, be otherwise unaffected if the variables included are unimportant.

by a Republican President; (7) is made during a period of divided government;[30] (8) is promulgated during a presidential transition; (9) is issued during a presidential election year; or (10) is put forth during a congressional election year.

Explanatory Variables for Controlling Rater Biases

Per our previous discussion, and as also shown in Table 3.1, we include explanatory variables for some raters to control potential biases. For the front page of the *New York Times*, the average number of articles appearing on page one is added to control for its varying threshold over time (see Howell 2003, 2005). While Howell included this measure as a variable (along with congressional fragmentation and divided government) directly in his statistical estimation of how many significant EOs are predicted to be issued in a given period, it is better to incorporate the average number of articles into the rating of an individual EO's significance, as it captures the direct impact of the variation in the number of such articles. When the average number is higher (or lower), an EO is more (or less) likely to be included as a cover story.

In addition, we have good reason to believe that some of our raters tend to cover certain issues more than others. For the *Wall Street Journal*, it appears that three concerns – macroeconomics, labor and employment, and immigration – tend to receive more attention, everything else being equal.[31] The *Washington Post*, given its location in the nation's capital, seems to focus more on issues related to government operation, the *National Journal* comes across as particularly interested in environmental issues and the *U.S. News & World Report* and *Newsweek* appear to pay special attention to foreign policy.

ESTIMATES OF EO SIGNIFICANCE

Figure 3.1 displays the estimates of EO significance generated by our model.[32] Scores range from a low of −0.994 to a high of 3.491, with a mean of 0 and a variance of 0.677. Clearly, and not surprisingly, a substantial percentage of EOs are attributed little significance. Also not surprisingly, low-significance EOs tend to be mentioned by none of our raters. Such unmentioned EOs usually have significance scores in the range of −1 to 0, with other explanatory

---

[30] Our estimates are little changed if we exclude divided government.

[31] Such beliefs are largely a function of spending hours poring over these sources during the coding process.

[32] With a one-dimensional IRT estimation, 93 percent of observations are correctly classified, demonstrating that the data are essentially unidimensional. In other words, our results indicate that the latent trait of significance has only one dimension, ranging from low to high.

FIGURE 3.1 Estimates of executive order significance

variables helping distinguishing between them (more information about this is given below). This contributes to a spike between −1 and 0. EOs mentioned by at least one rater generally have scores above zero, but how much a rater's mention contributes to this value depends on how well any rater making a mention actually discriminates EO significance (which is also detailed below).

The five EOs with the highest significance scores are EO 10925 (Kennedy's establishment of a committee on equal opportunity at a time of considerable racial tensions in America), EO 10340 (Truman's seizure of the American steel industry), EO 12356 (Reagan's tightening of national security information disclosure, reversing a trend toward easing such disclosure), EO 12333 (Reagan's rule for CIA discretion for spying and the banning of political assassinations) and EO 11615 (Nixon's wage and price controls).

All of these are certainly intuitively significant, since all were dealing with widely debated policies that were central to controversies at their time of issuance. Kennedy's establishment of a committee on equal opportunity was an initial foray of the new administration to deal with the hot-button issue of race; given the president's role as head of the executive branch, he could push to make the federal government and its contractors more progressive in terms of civil rights. Truman's efforts with respect to the steel industry have already been mentioned. That the chief executive would try, in essence, to take over a large industry in the name of providing for the military was, naturally, a galvanizing consideration. When the case went to the Supreme Court, of course, it meant that even greater attention was given to this issue. EO 12333, which we mentioned earlier, and EO 12356 both involved considerations about how much discretion the president should have in an area where political accountability is inherently difficult, given the need for secrecy. Reagan's actions in particular came in the midst of great controversy about the administration's actions in Central America. Finally, Nixon's EO on wage and price controls, instituted at a time of spiraling inflation in America, was an example of a President employing his authority in a way that impacted every citizen as well as many organized groups, such as unions and business associations.

Having looked at significance estimates, we will now examine how our method does by sequentially presenting the results for the performance of each rater, our explanatory variables for significance and the variables included to control for raters' biases, and by different thresholds as well. Subsequently, we will show how significance levels vary across policy areas,

Each Rater's Performance

Table 3.2 shows, as estimated by the IRT's discrimination parameter, how well each rater distinguishes significant from insignificant EOs. The higher the parameter's absolute value, the better the rater's ability is to discriminate on the underlying, latent dimension of significance. We find considerable, generally unsurprising differences in how our raters are able to distinguish between significant and non-significant concerns.

Daily newspapers and weekly magazines with a political emphasis have the greatest discrimination power. The front pages of the *New York Times* and the *Washington Post* do the best, with the *Wall Street Journal*'s front page, the paper's stories not on the cover page (labeled "Other") and the *U.S. News* following. After these raters, the *Congressional Quarterly Weekly Report* and *Newsweek* do roughly as well as the first two newspapers' other pages.

Among the remaining raters, the five law journals perform relatively better. Of course, these types of raters are not obligated to review all EOs systematically, even those that are quite important, so the fact that they do not do as well as those mentioned above might not be surprising. Other raters follow, with the worst being, a bit surprisingly, Howell's measure of whether an EO was mentioned in the appendix of the *Congressional Record* or in at least two federal court cases. However, even this rater still adds to our significance estimates, as the 95 percent confidence interval of the discrimination parameter is far from zero. Interestingly, Cooper's analysis, which was not explicitly designed as an effort to systematically list significant EOs (as our noting of his listing of a multiplicity of Clinton EOs designed to implement the National

TABLE 3.2 *Raters' discrimination parameter estimates*

Raters	Discrimination parameter (β_j)	Standard deviation
Amer. Presidency Project	0.906	0.046
Congressional Quarterly	1.242	0.132
National Journal	0.797	0.073
U.S. News	1.311	0.148
Newsweek	1.191	0.142
History of EOs (Cooper)	0.758	0.067
Courts & Congress (Howell)	0.667	0.046
New York Times (front)	1.656	0.100
New York Times (other)	1.132	0.051
Washington Post (front)	1.618	0.109
Washington Post (other)	1.125	0.051
Wall Street Journal (front)	1.466	0.113
Wall Street Journal (other)	1.351	0.078
Court challenge	0.976	0.101
Harvard Law Review	1.076	0.105
Yale Law Journal	0.933	0.106
Stanford Law Review	0.973	0.110
Columbia Law Review	0.950	0.112
Chicago Law Review	1.003	0.100

Note: Estimates demonstrate the ability to discriminate EO significance. For example, these findings indicate that the front pages of the *New York Times* and the *Washington Post* appear to have the greatest discrimination power; this is likely at least partially because these raters span our entire period, while many others do not.

Performance Review suggests), did rather poorly. This is not to suggest any problem with Cooper's work as a study of presidential unilateralism, but it does indicate that his effort to discuss unilateralism did not focus squarely on the latent attribute of significance that we are trying to measure.

Exogenous Variables for Significance

Our results, provided in Table 3.3, strongly demonstrate that the inclusion of a hierarchical structure for significance is beneficial. Also, given the intuitive effects that relevant variables have on EO significance, we produce evidence that the underlying dimension we estimate is, indeed, interpretable as EO significance.

Several variables, discussed in descending order of importance (but all statistically significant), are correlated with significance. An EO issued to

TABLE 3.3 *Exogenous variables for significance*

Variables	Coefficients	Std. errors
Constant	−0.152	0.111
Policy oriented	0.359	0.101
Beginning of term	0.464	0.085
End of term	−0.026	0.731
Republican Pres.	0.075	0.049
Divided govt.	−0.192	0.050
Pres. transition	0.024	0.737
Routine admin.	−0.224	0.096
Domestic issue	0.041	0.054
New organization	0.555	0.047
President election yr.	−0.055	0.059
Congress election yr.	0.040	0.047
τ^2	0.838	0.022
N	3512	

Note: Results demonstrate benefits of a hierarchical structure for significance. As shown, many of the exogenous variables are quite important for establishing significance, with the dummy variables for whether the EO is policy relevant, is at the beginning of a presidential term and creates a new government organization all particularly relevant; this is especially pronounced for significance scores lower than one. See Figure 3.2 for estimates with and without the hierarchical structure.

create new organizations has the strongest effect, as such actions usually have major policy impacts or are related to presidential control over agencies to steer policy changes. The variable with the second highest magnitude is the beginning of a term, i.e., the first 100 days of a new presidency, as – consistent with our Chapter 1 review of past findings – the chief executive tends to respond to new electoral mandates or public demands or simply to dissatisfaction with the inherited status quo through a series of unilateral actions. We also find that EOs with policy content tend to be more significant. Finally, acts are generally less significant when an EO addresses routine administration or is issued during an era of divided government.

Furthermore, Figure 3.2 contrasts our model's estimates with those from an IRT model without a hierarchical structure, illustrating that incorporation of these exogenous variables substantially distinguishes the significance of less-frequently mentioned EOs (these EOs are usually scored in the lower part of the distribution). As we see, effects are especially pronounced for significance scores lower than one. Indeed, in the IRT model without a hierarchical structure, EOs mentioned by no rater typically are scored near −1. With the information from our additional exogenous variables, these EOs

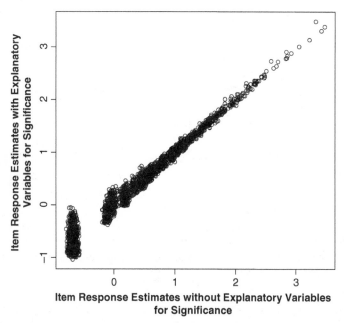

FIGURE 3.2 Comparing significance estimates with and without explanatory variables for significance

are distributed between −1 and 0. Similarly, those EOs mentioned by only one rater tend to obtain significance scores near 0 without information from these exogenous variables, but are distributed between −0.4 and 0.3 once we incorporate this information. Our hierarchical structure improves our estimation, even for EOs mentioned by multiple raters, although such ratings are less impacted because we possess a great deal of other information to distinguish them.

Explanatory Variables Used to Control for Rater Biases

Likewise, the introduction of explanatory variables for raters proves to be fruitful (Table 3.4). As expected, the *Wall Street Journal* tends to have lower thresholds for macroeconomics and labor and employment on its front page. The effects are quite strong. Also as expected, the average number of articles on the front page of the *New York Times* significantly conditions its threshold for reporting an EO – this effect is quite substantial, as demonstrated by the fact that the variable ranges from 6.9 to 13.1. Surprisingly, for an EO related to foreign affairs to receive a mention in the *U.S. News & World Report* actually requires a still higher threshold. *Newsweek* does tend to be more likely to cover EOs that deal with foreign affairs, the *National Journal* has a higher propensity

TABLE 3.4 *Explanatory variables for raters*

Variables	Coefficients	Std. errors
National Journal – Environment	0.471	0.240
US News – Foreign affairs	−0.897	0.288
Newsweek – Foreign affairs	0.544	0.205
New York Times – Num. front-page articles	0.154	0.019
Wash. Post (front) – Govt. operations	0.299	0.110
Wash. Post (other) – Govt. operations	0.210	0.073
Wall St. Journal (front) – Macroeconomics	0.586	0.243
Wall St. Journal (front) – Labor and empl.	0.639	0.131
Wall St. Journal (other) – Macroeconomics	1.327	0.202
Wall St. Journal (other) – Labor and empl.	1.093	0.103

Note: These estimates show that the introduction of explanatory variables for raters is fruitful. See Figure 3.3 for estimates with and without controls for rater biases.

to cover EOs related to environmental policy and the *Washington Post* does deal more with EOs concerned with government operations, although the estimated effect is rather modest.

Given the litany of findings for our control variables for rater attributes, it is not surprising that incorporation of rater attributes affects our estimates of significance. Figure 3.3 compares the estimate of our hierarchical IRT with and without the rater attribute variables. The mean difference between the two scores is roughly 0.25, with a maximal difference of 0.58. Also (and not surprisingly), relative to the very uneven effect on significance of adding a hierarchical structure, the effect of adding control variables impacts all EOs more evenly. Regardless, our estimates are more precise than they would be without integration of rater attributes and we can have greater confidence in the validity of our measure than we would otherwise have.

Significant EOs with Various Thresholds

As we have discussed, our approach not only includes much richer information for retrospective and contemporary raters than past analyses, it also integrates data in a far more systematic and reasonable way. And, because our EO significance measure is continuous, we can select varying thresholds for determining which EOs are counted as significant and study how the relations we are concerned about are conditioned by these choices.

Figure 3.4 displays the number of significant EOs per Congress for a variety of different thresholds, starting with all EOs (−1) and increasing the threshold

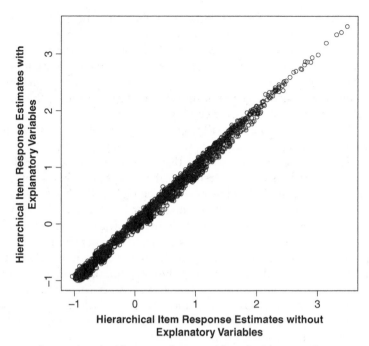

FIGURE 3.3 Comparing significance estimates with and without explanatory variables for raters

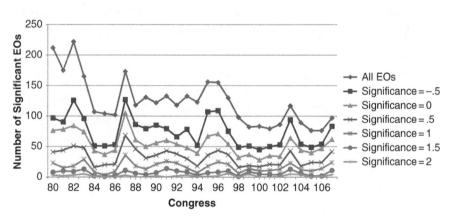

FIGURE 3.4 Significant EOs per Congress.
Note: Each curve corresponds to a threshold for determining a significant executive order.

progressively by 0.5.[33] Several interesting patterns are evident. First, the fluctuation over Congresses is fairly continuous and lacking in dramatic changes when we gradually increase the thresholds.[34] This suggests that, in conducting our empirical examinations, comparison of competing models and the like by utilizing such incremental increases of the significance threshold will not be problematic, as we will not be missing dramatic changes in the number of EOs if alternative thresholds were employed.

Second, while the count of EOs per Congress seems to have trended downward over time, this effect essentially goes away with a sample restricted to more significant actions. We witness this trend when we examine all EOs or when we hold the significance threshold to be −0.5, but it abates considerably when we employ 0, and it disappears with even higher thresholds. This implies that any claims that EOs diminish in importance are overstated. Furthermore, Figure 3.4 serves as a cautionary note that any empirical results and inferences regarding what explains the number of significant EOs per Congress could be a function of the threshold that we adopt in defining significant EOs (and, indeed, we will find some evidence for this). Finally, not only does holding the significance threshold at 2 give us a very flat curve, but, as there are only 63 EOs (2.5 per Congress) whose significance scores are sufficiently high, it could be problematic to conduct empirical analysis for EOs with a higher threshold, as there is little variance to be explained.

Third, regardless of the threshold, we consistently observe several peaks for the number of significant EOs per Congress. Such peaks occurred during the first terms of the Kennedy, Carter and Clinton administrations, at which point there was also unified government (with the president's party controlling a supermajority in the House and Senate during the first two). We also observe a peak during Truman's final two years, but only when a low significance threshold is employed, implying the issuance of a substantial number of less significant EOs.

Note that our measures of significant EOs with various thresholds are correlated with, but are not identical to, Howell's *New York Times* measure (2005). For any threshold below 1.9, the correlation coefficient between our measure and Howell's is between 0.6 and 0.74, with the strongest correlation at a 0 threshold. However, the correlation between the two measures slowly decreases as thresholds increasingly exceed 1.9. The sum of squares of the differences between the number of significant EOs per Congress in our and in Howell's measure is minimized at a 1.25 threshold.

---

[33] We estimate EO significance for all EOs issued from 1947 to 2003, but because the 108th Congress lasts from 2003 to 2004, we omit it from this Figure and from our empirical analyses when we focus on the number of significant EOs per Congress.

[34] While Figure 3.4 increases the threshold by 0.5, even if we utilized a smaller rate of change (e.g., by 0.25 or 0.1), the pattern remains continuous.

TABLE 3.5 *Number of executive orders by policy area: 1947–2002*

Topics code	Policy areas of Policy Agenda Project (PAP)	Number of executive orders
1	Macroeconomics	73
2	Civil Rights, Minority Issues and Civil Liberties	149
3	Health	54
4	Agriculture	35
5	Labor, Employment and Immigration	317
6	Education	41
7	Environment	62
8	Energy	82
10	Transportation	87
12	Law, Crime and Family Issues	68
13	Social Welfare	30
14	Community Development and Housing Issues	53
15	Banking, Finance and Domestic Commerce	91
16	Defense	682
17	Space, Science, Technology and Communications	75
18	Foreign Trade	155
19	International Affairs and Foreign Aid	391
20	Government Operations	810
21	Public Lands and Water Management	216

Note: Code numbers 9 and 11 are purposely omitted.

Significant EOs across Policies

Finally, we turn to whether the number of significant EOs per Congress substantially differs across policy areas. To do so, we employ the PAP's codings for 19 major policy topics, focusing on the 7 for which a considerable number of EOs were issued between 1947 and 2002: (1) Civil Rights, Minority Issues and Civil Liberties; (2) Labor, Employment and Immigration; (3) Defense; (4) Foreign Trade; (5) International Affairs and Foreign Aid; (6) Government Operations; and (7) Public Lands and Water Management.[35] Table 3.5 details the number of EOs in each policy area; we look first at those with the most EOs. We examine patterns for both the total number of EOs per Congress for each policy and the numbers deemed

---

[35] The other 12 policy areas have fewer than 100 EOs in total. We excluded them from detailed analysis.

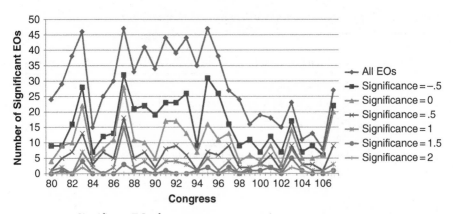

FIGURE 3.5 Significant EOs for government operations.
Note: Each curve corresponds to a threshold for determining a significant executive order.

significant. In general, each policy tends to follow its own patterns, some of them unique. While certain policy areas follow very different patterns for more and less significant EOs per Congress, others follow similar patterns. And some policies' patterns are closer than others to the patterns for all EOs, as shown in Figure 3.4.

Government operations is the largest EO policy category, comprising about 23 percent of EOs issued, and the number of significant EOs per Congress follows a similar pattern to that for all the EOs, with some small differences (Figure 3.5). Presidents Johnson and Nixon issued many insignificant EOs for routine government operations. Once we exclude EOs not mentioned by our raters (i.e., those with significance scores below zero), patterns look even more similar to those for all EOs. However, there are two additional peaks that were not previously evident: Presidents Eisenhower and Nixon issued a number of significant EOs for government operations during their first two and four years, respectively.

For significance thresholds higher than 1, a number of Congresses saw no government operations EOs. When a 1.5 threshold is employed, many more Congresses have no EOs. A threshold greater than 2 leaves only a handful of actions. These include EO 10450, issued by President Eisenhower in the first months of his administration to set up a new means of rooting-out disloyal federal employees during the time of McCarthyism; EO 10479, promulgated a few months later and designed as a means to support equal employment opportunity (e.g., as a function of race, creed or national origin), complete with creation of a Government Contract Committee to ensure compliance; EO 12291, announced early in the Reagan administration to formalize review of new major regulations as part of the new President's efforts to rein in the bureaucracy; two early Clinton edicts – EO 12834, an EO signed on

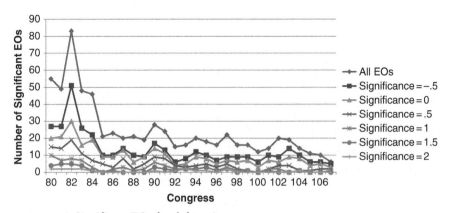

FIGURE 3.6 Significant EOs for defense issues.
Note: Each curve corresponds to a threshold for determining a significant executive order.

inauguration day requiring senior political appointees to restrict themselves by signing an ethics pledge, and EO 12866, another landmark regulatory review EO, signed in September 1993 – and a 1995 Clinton action, EO 12954, a pro-union change requiring that executive agencies withhold contracts from employers that replace striking employees; and, finally, EO 13233, issued by George W. Bush during his first year in office to limit the public's access to the records of former Presidents.

EOs for defense issues make up the second-largest policy group (Figure 3.6), comprising about 19.6 percent of our total. Note that the PAP's defense issues category includes weapon procurement, veteran's affairs and military preparations. The number of significant EOs for this policy area looks slightly different than for government operations or all EOs. Many insignificant EOs regarding defense were issued in President Truman's last two years, seemingly related to the aftermath of World War II. For defense issues EOs with significance scores higher than 0 the peaks become less obvious and they tend to appear during the Truman years and Johnson's last two years (the height of American involvement in Vietnam).

The third-largest policy area for EOs is international affairs and foreign aid. Interestingly, as seen in Figure 3.7, the temporal pattern for EOs per Congress for this policy area is different from those we have discussed so far. Presidents Truman and Johnson issued numerous such EOs during their third and fourth years, respectively. President Reagan did the same during his first two years[36]

---

[36] One tricky consideration is that Reagan issued a series of EOs (EOs 12276–12285) more or less in the wake of a crisis with Iran in which American hostages were being released. As they are closely related and were issued on the same day, it is unclear whether they should be regarded as 1 or 10 [quite significant] EOs.

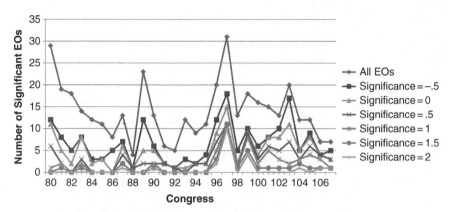

FIGURE 3.7 Significant EOs for international affairs and foreign aid.
Note: Each curve corresponds to a threshold for determining a significant executive order.

and his fifth and sixth years, while Clinton promulgated a substantial number of significant EOs during his first two, fifth and sixth years as well. In general, the peaks for EOs for this policy area did not occur for the same presidencies as those for other matters. Moreover, regardless of the significance threshold adopted, and in contrast to the earlier policies that we discussed, the patterns for this policy look similar.

Labor, employment and immigration is the fourth-largest policy area for EOs, and has patterns that are still different from what we have observed thus far (Figure 3.8). Most notably, there are two dramatic peaks – during President Truman's last four years and Kennedy's first two – with numbers per Congress otherwise rather flat with only mild fluctuations.

The other three policy areas, (1) public lands and water management, (2) international trade and (3) civil rights, minority issues and civil liberties, each have 4 to 7 percent of all EOs. We show these patterns in Figures 3.9, 3.10 and 3.11. Briefly, the pattern for public lands and water management is somewhat similar to that just shown for labor, employment and immigration; the pattern for civil rights, minority issues and civil liberties is roughly analogous to that for government operations; and the pattern for international trade is dramatically different from any previously seen, with President Truman having issued very few EOs and Presidents Ford, Reagan (the third through sixth years) and Clinton (the first two years) having issued more significant and insignificant EOs than others.

In summary, EOs for different policy areas tend to exhibit different patterns from one another. Also, for some areas, there is a clear distinction when we look exclusively at significant EOs. Finally, the patterns for certain policies roughly correspond to the pattern for our entire sample, while those for others deviate markedly from that norm.

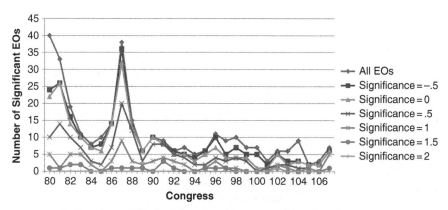

FIGURE 3.8 Significant EOs for labor, employment and immigration.
Note: Each curve corresponds to a threshold for determining a significant executive order.

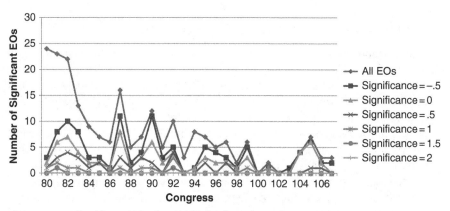

FIGURE 3.9 Significant EOs for public lands and water management.
Note: Each curve corresponds to a threshold for determining a significant executive order.

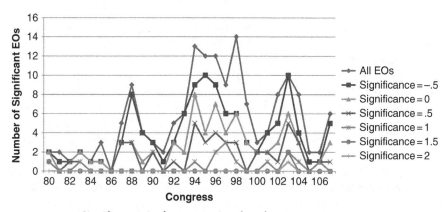

FIGURE 3.10 Significant EOs for international trade.
Note: Each curve corresponds to a threshold for determining a significant executive order.

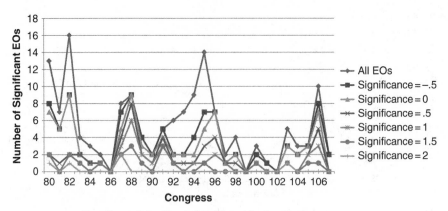

FIGURE 3.11 Significant EOs for civil rights and minority issues.
Note: Each curve corresponds to a threshold for determining a significant executive order.

CONCLUSIONS: LAYING THE FOUNDATIONS

Unilateral actions in general, and executive orders specifically, as we have already repeated several times, are not all created equal. As such, a tally of actions will not suffice to bring us to our goal of achieving a better understanding of how actions of the chief executive impact presidential power and the separation-of-powers system in the United States.

Recognition that the actions we are examining are heterogeneous in a variety of ways, including with respect to the latent trait of significance, is not a new epiphany. However, as we have laid out in detail, previous research has not provided measurements that make it possible to distinguish the examination of unilateral actions according to their exact level of significance, measured continuously from very to unimportant to extremely important, of the choices being made. Our analysis in this chapter provides the foundation for accomplishing this task and generating insights into the enigma of presidential power.

We have invested much effort into delving deep into the minutiae of measurement, with the goals of delineating patterns of unilateral action and producing the dependent variable that we need if we are to be able to assess presidential power under unilateralism. To do so, we extended the IRT methodology – employed elsewhere in political science but not by past scholars of unilateral action – by accounting for rater biases. This is an important improvement over existing approaches, where raters assessing the object of interest may have discernible biases. We then developed a series of raters, using more contemporary and retrospective information about presidential EOs than were used in earlier analyses, and applied our specified model in order to estimate a continuous measure of EO significance. The overall distribution of EOs provides many insights, including the realization that the seeming decline of activity over time largely dissipates once we examine more highly significant actions.

Further, in examining both the total number of EOs per Congress for each policy area and those EOs identified as significant, we find that some policies follow their own patterns while others follow patterns very similar to those of the entire EO universe. Additionally, some of these patterns are impacted by our choice of threshold level and some are not. Regardless, our results suggest that breaking our analysis out further by policy type, which we will do in the chapters that follow, is highly advisable.

Our new, flexible measure is a necessary condition for taking the theories that we specified in the previous chapter and applying them to the data to provide an answer to the enigma of power. This is where we now turn our attention.

4

The Race for Power: Empirically Examining
Competing Models

INTRODUCTION

We began our analysis in Chapter 1 by recognizing that power and unilateral action need not be equivalent and that their relationship is rather a matter for analytic inquiry. One could imagine a world where a president, despite issuing unilateral actions, would find his or her actions considerably constrained beyond the limits associated with statutory or judicial overrides.

In Chapter 2 we specified models that would capture alternative ways in which presidential discretion, particularly in terms of its ideological direction, would be constrained. In the unilateralism model there would be no directional constraints, in the chamber-compliance model the chamber median would constrain and in the partisan-compliance model the majority party median would constrain.

We also noted that different EOs could be seen as roughly corresponding to these models: a series of regulatory EOs dealing with cost–benefit analysis seemed consistent with the unilateralism model, an EO involving US relations with Central America appeared to fit the chamber-compliance story and an immigration EO allowing Chinese students to remain in the US corresponded to the partisan-compliance model.

Now, with our competing theories and our measure of EO significance in hand, we are well positioned to examine our central question regarding the extent to which unilateral action is the equivalent of presidential influence and power. As each competing model is associated with a different level of presidential influence and power and is characterized by theoretically derived hypotheses (which differ by model, except for how the president should act in the early part of his or her first term), we can test these hypotheses and draw inferences about presidential power in the context of presidential unilateral action.[1] To

---

[1] We are not the first to examine competing models in order to tease out and differentiate between their respective inferences. Other such efforts include: Krehbiel's (1991) testing of alternative

reiterate, past research has either ignored the issue of presidential power in this realm or has largely assumed it to be trivial by positing that the exercise of unilateral action is tantamount to the usage of power. By contrast, we bring considerations of power to the forefront and drop any assumption of equivalency between unilateral action and power. Moreover, given the EO significance measure presented in Chapter 3, we can examine whether the relationship between unilateral action and presidential power depends on how we define significant EOs.

Furthermore, motivated by our recognition that different EOs appear to match our theoretical models, we break down the universe of Orders by policy type. While we can find examples of different unilateral acts matching different theories, we also expect that there may be systematic differences in the way Orders are perceived for different policy types, for a variety of reasons. Some policies may be more politically sensitive than others from the perspective of members of Congress, some may be more amenable to the use of extra-statutory mechanisms (such as those that would require budgetary outlays) and the associated costs of legislative interference for some policies may be greater than for others.

Thus, we now empirically examine the hypotheses generated by the unilateralism, chamber-compliance and partisan-compliance models. We initially focus on the number of significant EOs, by Congress, from the 80th to the 107th Congress, with varying EO significance thresholds. Then we analyze these competing predictions across policy areas to explore in what ways the relationship between unilateral action and presidential power depends on policy context. We conclude by assessing what our results tell us about the enigma of power that motivates us.

COMPETING MODELS WITH ALL EXECUTIVE ORDERS

Our primary analysis involves a statistical examination of our EO data, for each Congress, with independent variables directly derived from the competing models. Once this has been presented, we will extend our analysis by including other independent variables previously regarded as germane.

---

models associated with distributive and informational theories of legislative organization in his pioneering work on the use of closed rules regarding amendments in the US House; Chiou and Rothenberg's (2003, 2006, 2009) investigations of the roles of parties in legislative productivity; Primo, Binder and Maltzman's (2008) application of multiple pivotal politics models for examining judicial appointments; Cameron, Groseclose and McCarty's analyses of veto bargaining where models generate different predictions about vetoes and veto threats (see Cameron and McCarty 2004 for a survey); and Canes-Wrone's (2005) investigation into when presidents issue public appeals.

Dependent Variable

Our principal dependent variable for this section is the number of significant EOs, as measured in Chapter 3, promulgated in each Congress from the 80th to the 107th Congress.[2] Significance itself depends on the threshold we adopt from the measure generated by our extended IRT model.

We focus on the individual Congress as a unit of analysis even though alternatives have been explored in the empirical literature. While Howell (2003) analyzed a comparable dependent variable in terms of time (i.e., by Congress), many previous empirical studies of EOs, such as Deering and Maltzman (1999), Howell (2005) and Mayer (2002), focused on yearly, quarterly or monthly data. Although partitioning the data more narrowly would have the virtue of providing a larger sample size, doing so can be rather arbitrary, as it is unclear why and how we should choose a certain time period out of an infinitely large set of possible alternatives. Rather, our theoretical models seem to suggest that a focus on the data for each Congress is the most natural and defensible. For instance, in these models the president decides whether to issue an EO by anticipating congressional and judicial reactions, with the former including the discretion constraint and the option of passing a law to override an EO. As congressional constraints vary almost exclusively by Congress, where the preferences of key players are likely to shift principally by member turnover, analyzing data by Congress seems the most obvious and intuitive way to conduct our comparative model testing.[3]

In terms of employing contrasting significance thresholds (as displayed in Figure 3.1), in theory we have many possible ways to define significant EOs. Recall that the values of our EO significance estimates generated by our extended IRT model range from -0.994 to 3.491. By definition, this continuous measure provides infinitely many possible significance thresholds on the basis of which to determine which EOs will be seen as significant. For a given significance threshold, EOs whose significance scores are higher than that threshold level are seen as significant while, conversely, those whose scores are lower are seen as insignificant. After deciding on a threshold, we can calculate the number of significant EOs per Congress.

In our analysis we will incrementally increase significance thresholds. As Figure 3.4 in the previous chapter illustrates, changes in the number of

[2] To reiterate, we do not expand our data to recent Congresses, partly because we rely on the Policy Agenda Project for many of our variables, some of which were no longer coded for the years after 2003 and partly because some of our raters for measuring EO significance are historical overviews, and it will require some years to review more recent EOs.

[3] Although Deering and Maltzman (1999) mentioned similar reasons in their discussion of units of analysis, they nonetheless utilized yearly data.

significant EOs per Congress are, by and large, continuous, with incremental increases of significance thresholds. Because of this, we can examine how our empirical results are a function of the threshold employed with step (rather than with marginally continuous) increases from the lowest to 2 by 0.25 changes (as mentioned in the previous chapter, only 63 Orders exceed this level from 1947 to 2003). To save space, we present our results with incremental changes of 0.5, noting any abnormal patterns from the results with smaller increases along the way.

Consequently, we shift from looking at the universe of EOs to more realistic measures of significance and finally to a maximum threshold of 2 for highly significant EOs. This allows us to explore whether, and how, our results qualitatively hinge on how we define a significant EO.

Independent Variables

For independent variables, we first focus on those variables derived from our competing models, partly because we are mainly interested in testing these models and partly because we are concerned about our rather small sample size, given that the number of EOs issued is being measured for each Congress rather than for shorter periods. Later, as mentioned, we will report our results with some additional independent variables that have been previously regarded as important in the literature and also vary within the span of a Congress. For now, though, we describe the set of independent variables that our models explicitly suggest.

Specifically, per Table 2.1, we include for all three models a dummy variable for first-term, scored as 1 in the first two years of an administration if a new president's party is different from his predecessor's during his initial term and scored as 0 otherwise (Table 4.1 provides descriptive statistics for this and all other independent variables). For the unilateralism and the chamber median models, we incorporate the lengths of the filibuster- and the override-tails of the EGI. Recall that, in particular, whether the override-tail has a positive or a null impact on the dependent variable is critical for distinguishing whether the unilateralism or the chamber-compliance model performs better empirically. To reiterate, the equilibrium gridlock interval is the set of *status quos* that cannot be changed statutorily in equilibrium, the override-tail is the interval between the median and the override pivot closer to the president, and the filibuster-tail is the interval between the median and the filibuster pivot further away from the president. The unilateralism model suggests that the filibuster-tail and override-tail parts of the EGI each will have distinct, positive effects on unilateral action (the former having a smaller effect than the latter). By contrast, the chamber-compliance model posits that only the filibuster-tail of the EGI will have a positive effect, while the partisan-compliance model suggests that unified government has a positive effect. Finally, as also indicated in Table 2.1, for the partisan-compliance

TABLE 4.1 *Summary statistics for independent variables*

Variable	Mean	Standard deviation	Min.	Max.
First-term	0.250	0.441	0	1
Divided government	0.643	0.488	0	1
Filibuster-tail EGI	0.135	0.053	0.050	0.288
Override-tail EGI	0.219	0.069	0.094	0.404

Notes: N = 28.

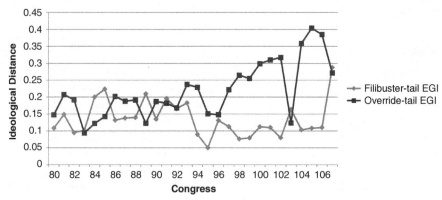

FIGURE 4.1 Filibuster- and override-tails of the EGI

model the key variable is divided government, which we measure as a dummy variable.[4]

To ensure comparability among chambers and across Congresses, we measure preferences using Poole's (1998) common space scores in calculating EGIs and determining the ideal points of the filibuster and override pivots and the chamber medians.[5] Figure 4.1 displays the value of the filibuster- and the

---

[4] In addition to this variable, this model has two other variables: interaction terms between unified government and the filibuster- and the override-tails of the EGI. Each of these variables is substantially correlated with divided government (at an absolute value greater than .89). Moreover, given our model sample size and given that there are only ten Congresses characterized by unified governments, we have a limited ability to examine this interaction.

   Also and as foreshadowed in Chapter 2, one potential concern arising from testing between the competing theories is that, given the reasons stated above, our focusing only on divided governments for the partisan-compliance model, compared with the EGI tails of the other two models, may make it easier for the former to be judged the best fit. In Chapter 5 we propose a new empirical strategy to examine competing models that eliminates any worry of such a bias.

[5] As mentioned in Chapter 2, as a means of capturing bicameralism we measure the ideal points of the override pivots and chamber medians according to our theoretical definitions. We determine the ideal point of the pivots from common space scores estimated from 75th through 110th

override-tail EGIs over time. While each tail seems to go up and down, the filibuster-tail is the more stable of the two. Moreover, while the former tends to decrease until the 107th Congress, the latter tends to increase, with the exception of Clinton's first term. Interestingly, these two variables are only moderately negative correlated at –0.285.

Empirical Results

Given that our dependent variable is a count of significant EOs, negative binomial regression is an appropriate estimation technique. Tables 4.2 and 4.3 provide our results for each of our three models for discrete changes in significance thresholds (results are very much continuous).[6]

One pronounced pattern is that the first-term variable is almost always significant and correctly signed. From this vantage point, all three models receive support. However, support for the universalism model is undercut by the override-tail of the EGI's coefficient being sometimes significant but always wrongly signed, and support for the chamber-compliance is undermined, given that the same is true of the filibuster-tail of the EGI, the key variable for assessing this (and the unilateralism) model.[7] As such, neither model receives much support.

By contrast, as Table 4.3 shows, the partisan-compliance model receives very strong confirmation.[8] Except for thresholds exceeding 1.65, divided government always has the predicted negative effect on significant EOs, with

---

Congresses from Poole's Voteview website (www.voteview.com). Alternatively, in addition to common space scores, we examine our models using common space DW-NOMINATE scores to measure preferences (also available at www.voteview.com). However, because the results of the two are similar (these two scores being strongly correlated), we only present the results using common space scores.

[6] Given that each model has its own set of independent variables, some highly correlated, and because of our modest sample size, we do not test the three models within the same regression model.

[7] In principle, we should test the chamber-compliance model without including the irrelevant variables, such as the EGI override-tail. However, because the results are not qualitatively different regardless of whether or not we include this variable, we do not present the corresponding results.

[8] Although multicollinearity prevents testing the interaction of unified government and EGI length, we jointly test divided government and this interaction and find that our core results are unchanged. When we include the interaction terms, holding the means of the two EGI tails constant, divided government's effect is negative and statistically significant up to a threshold of 1.5. The joint test on divided government and the two interaction terms between unified government and the filibuster- and override-tails of the EGI leads us to reject the null hypothesis that these three variables simultaneously equal zero (the sign of the first interaction is always correct, while that of the second is not) except for thresholds over 1.25. Due to serious multicollinearity, the sign of the interaction term between unified government and the filibuster-tail of the EGI is seemingly wrong, but it becomes consistent with our theoretical expectation once we drop the extremely correlated variables.

TABLE 4.2 *Determinants of number of significant executive orders: Universalism and chamber-compliance models*

	Expected sign		T = -1 (All EOs)	T = -0.5	T = 0	T = 0.5	T = 1.0	T = 1.5	T = 2.0
	Unilateralism	Chamber-compliance							
First-term	+	+	0.041	0.237**	0.260**	0.370***	0.551***	0.665***	0.907**
			(0.096)	(0.108)	(0.114)	(0.140)	(0.155)	(0.172)	(0.399)
Filibuster-tail EGI	+		-1.416	-0.720	-0.416	0.214	-0.317	0.364	-2.293
			(0.810)	(0.907)	(0.973)	(1.210)	(1.345)	(1.466)	(3.389)
Override-tail EGI	+		-2.791	-2.079	-1.726	-1.935	-1.287	-1.640	-0.391
			(0.544)	(0.611)	(0.643)	(0.808)	(0.914)	(1.126)	(2.402)
Constant			5.585***	4.782***	4.345***	3.751***	2.953***	1.988***	0.738
			(0.183)	(0.204)	(0.217)	(0.269)	(0.300)	(0.347)	(0.756)
Alpha			0.036***	0.043***	0.045***	0.067***	0.064***	0.024	0.311*
Log-likelihood			-129.85	-119.27	-112.14	-103.21	-88.57	-69.43	-49.57

Notes: $N = 28$. Negative binomial regression coefficients with standard errors in parentheses. T represents the threshold used to ascertain Executive Order significance: higher T values represent a more restrictive threshold. Two-tailed tests are conducted for the constant term and one-tailed tests for the rest of the parameters. *** p-value $< .01$ ** $.01 < p$-value $< .05$ * $.05 < p$-value $< .1$

TABLE 4.3 *Determinants of number of significant executive orders: Partisan-compliance model*

	Expected sign	T = −1 (All EOs)	T = −0.5	T = 0	T = 0.5	T = 1	T = 1.5	T = 2
First-term	+	0.066	0.211***	0.233***	0.357***	0.529***	0.685***	0.858**
		(0.108)	(0.079)	(0.092)	(0.110)	(0.138)	(0.171)	(0.383)
Divided Government	−	−0.345***	−0.455***	−0.398***	−0.476***	−0.327***	−0.276*	−0.061
		(0.097)	(0.072)	(0.084)	(0.101)	(0.130)	(0.169)	(0.375)
Constant		5.006***	4.518***	4.165***	3.652***	2.837***	1.852***	0.399
		(0.091)	(0.063)	(0.073)	(0.087)	(0.115)	(0.150)	(0.344)
Alpha		0.050***	0.019***	0.026***	0.034***	0.047***	0.029**	0.319*
								(0.290)
Log-likelihood		−134.00	−111.71	−107.06	−97.70	−86.71	−69.22	−49.80

Notes: $N = 28$. Negative binomial regression coefficients with standard errors in parentheses. T represents the threshold used to ascertain Executive Order significance; higher T values represent a more restrictive threshold. Two-tailed tests are conducted for the constant term and one-tailed tests for the rest of the parameters. *** p-value < .01 ** .01 < p-value < .05 * .05 < p-value < .1

statistical significance.[9] Holding all other variables constant, divided government decreases the expected number of EOs by around 30 percent, except for thresholds that exceed 1.5. Beyond this threshold, the effect gradually diminishes. Note that, as discussed with respect to the so-called evasion hypothesis, while some previous studies also find significant evidence that divided government dampens EO production, our analysis is distinguished in that we find this relationship to exist, virtually regardless of our EO significance criteria, except in the case of an extremely high threshold.

Note that even if we include presidential popularity and the so-called misery index (the two independent variables sometimes included in explaining the use of EOs[10]) the results shown in Tables 4.2 and 4.3 are qualitatively unchanged (these findings are available from the authors).[11] Moreover, we discover that presidential popularity is not always statistically significant and is negatively signed if it is (meaning that more popular presidents do not take advantage of their popularity by issuing more EOs), while the misery index tends to have a negative sign but is often statistically insignificant.

Overall, the partisan-compliance model receives much stronger empirical support than the chamber-compliance and unilateralism models.[12] Admittedly, the partisan model tends to do worse with very high significance thresholds, suggesting either that there is just not enough variance in the dependent variable or that the model is of limited value in explaining extremely significant EOs.

Obviously, these results have considerable ramifications for our analysis of power. Recall that, in discussing the implications stemming from each of the three competing models in Chapter 2 we noted that, while the president gains more policy influence through unilateral action under each of the models, the president achieves the most under the unilateralism model, trailed by the chamber-compliance and the partisan-compliance models. More importantly, with the Dahlian definition of power, where power is defined as freedom to pursue something in spite of opposition from others, the president is quite powerful and can alter status quos without approval (and even in light of opposition) from Congress under the unilateralism model, but is constrained

[9] To foreshadow our results in Chapter 5, findings for divided government will not necessarily prove robust when we build in other party effects in the legislative stage.

[10] Gallup Organization polls are employed quarterly to measure popularity; the misery index simply adds the inflation and unemployment rates, on the supposition that higher scores correspond to greater misery.

[11] In the literature, and as mentioned in Chapter 1, other variables such as congressional fragmentation or majority strength are sometimes utilized, but, because they are captured in our model by our preference measures, adding them to our empirical models would be problematic.

[12] Employing the Bayesian information criterion (BIC; Raftery 1995, and, for application, see Clarke 2001; Primo, Binder and Maltzman 2008), which is a means of distinguishing between models based on how they fit the data, also clearly reveals that the partisan-compliance model outperforms the other two alternatives.

and requires approval from Congress, be it the chamber median or the majority party median, under the other two models.

Our results, leading to the inference that presidential unilateral action is neither consistent with the unilateralism model nor the chamber-compliance model, and corresponds much more to the partisan-compliance model, imply that the strength of the relationship between unilateral action and presidential power may be considerably less than had been thought. Instead of exercising power that is only constrained by statutory overrides and judicial limits on discretion, the president must anticipate extra-statutory costs. The chief executive has to account for congressional preferences (and, perhaps, for judicial efforts to enforce such legislative will) in deciding whether and how to issue an EO, even when there is high legislative gridlock. This is striking, given that presidential unilateral action has so often been depicted as resulting in unilateral power. Our findings clearly reject this presumption and, instead, imply that so-called presidential lawmaking involves bargaining and reaching agreement with other actors.

Additionally, in the context of previous literature, it behooves us to note that our results are in the spirit of consistent findings that reject the evasion theory, that the chief executive will act more given a unified government. This is true regardless of the significance level, indicating that this result is not conditioned by which threshold is employed. Here we have established one reason for this lack of evidence, which is that extra-statutory mechanisms may undermine the president when he would otherwise have reason to behave as the evasion theory predicts.

PRESIDENTIAL CALCULATIONS ACROSS POLICY AREAS

The findings above, nonetheless, pose a puzzle, given the deep impression that the president buttresses his power as a result of executive action. For instance, is the example of cost-benefit Orders – by which chief executives, especially Reagan, acted in obvious contradiction to legislative preferences in order to push regulatory initiatives – very rare in reality? Given the implications for institutional design and presidential power, the effort to assess whether there are definable conditions under which the president employs unilateral authority to guide policy changes, even with congressional opposition, is essential.

To address this issue, it is critical that we again emphasize that for our models, in contemplating unilateral action, whether the president needs to take into account how Congress may possibly respond with statutory and extra-statutory means is key. Variance in presidential expectations about possible congressional willingness and ability to respond through these two avenues can substantially impact the chief executive's likelihood of taking action, which in turn implies various degree of presidential power.

One seemingly fundamental source for differing congressional responses, and hence presidential expectations, involves the various policy areas. A key component driving our findings is that Congress can, and will in fact want to, wield extra-statutory means to impose nontrivial costs – be they a function of calendar control, impacts on budgets, stalling appointments, or what have you – on a president whom they see to be taking unwanted unilateral action.

For some policy areas, however, this might not always be desirable or effective. In particular, Congress might have weaker electoral incentives to incur costs for punishing the president in some policy areas, such as those involving national rather than local interests (Howell and Jackman 2013). Also, in a related vein, congressional statutory abilities may vary across policy areas. It has long been acknowledged that different policy areas are characterized by distinctive political environments when considered by Congress. For example, Lowi (1964) and Wilson (1974) categorized types of policy areas according to the characteristics of their costs and benefits. Alternatively, Ripley and Franklin (1984) arrayed six policy areas based on interest group mobilization and the relationship between the executive and legislative branches.

More recently, detailed empirical work by Lapinski (2008) demonstrated that lawmaking might differ according to policy substance. He classified laws into four main policy areas – sovereignty, organization and scope, international relations and domestic policy – finding that legislative accomplishments and factors that induce greater legislative productivity differ substantially. For instance, while political polarization appears not to impact legislative productivity where it concerns international affairs issues and sovereignty, it does influence congressional output regarding organization and scope and domestic policy. Similarly, the majority party's strength, measured by the difference in size between the House majority and minority parties, positively impacts significant domestic legislation but negatively influences organization and scope legislation. Also (intuitively), war affects only international affairs legislation. In general, this analysis provides a strong case in support of the idea that the pooling of policies can lead to a misguided understanding of relevant dynamics, due to differences in congressional abilities and incentives across policies.

More broadly, and as discussed in our introduction to this chapter, if the policy area strongly conditions congressional actions and responses, it could very well influence the calculations behind a president's unilateral actions in a corresponding manner. By extension, this distinction between policy types has a crucial ramification for our above findings, generated from pooling all EOs. Alternative models might better correspond to EO production in some policy areas than in others. For instance, will the same model correspond to civil rights EOs such as EO 11246 – Lyndon Johnson's 1965 Order establishing non-discriminatory employment practices for federal contractors – and to public lands Orders such as EO 11644 – a 1972 Nixon EO governing how increasingly popular off-road vehicles could be ridden on federal lands? Civil rights might involve stronger electoral considerations, while public lands management, particularly when no budgetary outlay is required, could allow the president somewhat more latitude. In general, if empirical support for these competing models differs across substantive areas, it would indicate that presidents have varying degrees of freedom to act unilaterally, even in light of congressional opposition, depending on policy type.

To examine whether policy characteristics and political environment might structure congressional responses and affect presidential calculations with regard to EO production, we need to distinguish between policies. We begin with the PAP's coding for major policy topics, which separates all 3471 EOs issued between 1947 and 2002 into 19 major policies (as detailed in Table 3.5). As discussed in Chapter 3, not all policies contain enough EOs to make statistical examination possible. The 12 policy topics individually averaging fewer than four EOs per Congress (with many instances of no EOs issued in a given Congress) are omitted for now, while we again investigate the 7 policy areas with more than 100 EOs, which were detailed in Chapter 3 – (1) Civil Rights, Minority Issues and Civil Liberties, (2) Labor, Employment and Immigration, (3) Defense, (4) Foreign Trade, (5) International Affairs and Foreign Aid, (6) Government Operations and (7) Public Lands and Water Management.

Analogous to our analysis of all EOs, we incorporate each EO's salience or importance for each of the policy types. Because a given action can vary from being symbolic or routine to having critical policy impacts, we continue to consider whether findings and inferences are conditioned by how we define which EOs are measured by our dependent variables, i.e., what significance threshold we adopt. So we once more conduct analyses including only those EOs with significance scores higher than a given threshold. Hence, the dependent variable is the number of significant EOs for a major policy area within a Congress, with the significance threshold ranging from the lowest to one that is reasonably high.[13] Figures 3.5 to 3.11 plot the dependent variables for each of the seven major policies.

To uncover whether the president factors in different considerations when deciding upon EOs for contrasting policy types, we study the different policy areas in parallel fashion. In all instances, we examine our three competing models by investigating how well the independent variables from each of the competing models explain the variance of the same dependent variable.[14]

[13] Analysis of the number of significant EOs in a Congress also requires that roughly 100 EOs be issued for the covered time period, because otherwise the dependent variable's score for most Congresses is 0 once we start to increase the threshold level for significance.

[14] Our empirical results are robust if we additionally include presidential approval and the misery index, which, to reiterate, control for the possibilities that presidential popularity helps chief executives to act unilaterally or to circumvent Congress or that favorable economic conditions can undermine or boost presidential bargaining power with Congress.

Again, a dummy variable for first-term is incorporated in all models. The lengths of the EGI filibuster- and override-tails, measured with common space scores, are included for the unilateralism model, only the EGI filibuster-tail is utilized for the chamber-compliance model and divided government is added for the partisan-compliance model. This allows us to determine which model, if any, fits unilateral actions for each policy area, paving the way for examination of whether and how the relationship between EOs and presidential power is conditioned by policy area.

Analogous to the work presented in Chapter 3, we present our empirical results for the seven policy areas in an order that roughly corresponds to the number of EOs (of course, with more EOs we are able more easily to examine how our results are conditioned by EO significance level). Table 4.4 displays negative binomial regression results for testing the three competing models with EOs that address government operations, which constitute about one-quarter of the entire EO universe. Consistent with our analysis of all EOs, while we estimate our analysis for a whole distribution of threshold significance scores, the results are rather continuous and, hence, we present them at intervals of 0.5 on the significance scale from -1 up to 1.[15]

The unilateralism model does a much poorer job of explaining domestic EOs than do the chamber-compliance and partisan-compliance models. In Table 4.4(a), while first-term's coefficient is always statistically significant (which makes sense, given the casual observation that government operations are quickly dealt with by the president in his role as titular head of the bureaucracy), the override-tail EGI hypothesis, that distinguishing between the unilateralism and the chamber-compliance models, is never supported (i.e., statistically significant coefficients signs contradict theoretical expectations). The filibuster-tail EGI hypothesis does not receive strong empirical support, with marginal support only when the significance threshold is held to be moderate. By contrast, the partisan-compliance model does much better in explaining the number of significant EOs for this policy area. Recall that the main variables in testing the partisan-compliance model include first-term and divided government. Table 4.4(b) shows divided government's coefficient to be almost always statistically significant and correctly signed, while first-term's coefficient is statistically significant.[16] Divided government decreases the expected number of EOs by around 40 percent for significance thresholds lower than 1.5. These

---

[15] There are 82 government-operations EOs from 1947 through 2002 with significance scores higher than 1. Because we wanted to be able to compare our results for this policy area with other policies, where the number of EOs beyond this significance threshold is even smaller, we decided to not go beyond this threshold level. (Later, we will increase the maximum threshold up to 2, when we combine several policies into one category.)

[16] As mentioned, the model suggests interaction terms between unified government and the EGI override-tail and the EGI filibuster-tail. When these terms are included, the divided government coefficient is insignificant but joint tests show strong evidence of multicollinearity.

TABLE 4.4 *Determinants of number of significant executive orders for government operations*

(a) Testing Unilateralism and Chamber-Compliance Models

	Expected sign	T = –1	T = –0.5	T = 0	T = 0.5	T = 1.0
First-term	+	0.181†	0.444***	0.757***	0.788**	1.263***
		(0.135)	(0.156)	(0.142)	(0.179)	(0.271)
Filibuster-tail EGI	+	–0.090	0.953	1.813†	2.259†	0.116
		(1.136)	(1.304)	(1.180)	(1.506)	(2.274)
Override-tail EGI	+	–3.707***	–2.913***	–1.709*	–2.623**	–1.407
		(0.844)	(0.974)	(0.935)	(1.235)	(1.838)
Constant		4.094***	3.108***	2.191***	1.672***	0.845†
		(0.270)	(0.308)	(0.281)	(0.360)	(0.549)
Log-likelihood		–98.733	–86.212	–72.994	–62.259	–50.846

(b) Testing Partisan-compliance Model

	Expected sign	T = –1	T = –0.5	T = 0	T = 0.5	T = 1.0
First-term	+	0.258*	0.477***	0.806***	0.842***	1.211***
		(0.152)	(0.151)	(0.144)	(0.178)	(0.246)
Divided Govt.	_	–0.390***	–0.448***	–0.233†	–0.365**	–0.430*
		(0.138)	(0.141)	(0.142)	(0.176)	(0.250)
Constant		3.522***	2.885***	2.210***	1.644***	0.828***
		(0.121)	(0.123)	(0.129)	(0.159)	(0.232)
Log-likelihood		–103.148	–86.564	–74.657	–63.765	–49.853

Notes: N = 28. Negative binomial regression coefficients with standard errors in parentheses. T indicates the significance threshold for determining a significant EO. Likelihood ratio tests for each regression that alpha equals zero all strongly suggest the existence of overdispersion, especially for lower significance thresholds. Two-tailed tests are conducted for all parameters. *** p-value < .01 ** .01 < p-value < .05 * .05 < p-value < .1 † .1 < p-value < .2

results suggest that the president faces constraints from Congress (at least from congressional majority parties) when organizing government operations. While admittedly speculative, one possibility is that government operations require budgetary outlays, and this provides Congress with a higher extra-statutory influence relative to other policy arenas.

Similar empirical results are found for defense-related EOs, but with two important differences (Table 4.5). One is that the first-term hypothesis now receives no support. While a new president whose party differs from his

TABLE 4.5 *Determinants of number of significant executive orders for defense*
(a) *Testing Unilateralism and Chamber-Compliance Models*

	Expected sign	T = −1	T = −0.5	T = 0	T = 0.5	T = 1.0
First-term	+	−0.368[†]	−0.246	−0.253	−0.100	−0.177
		(0.200)	(0.229)	(0.226)	(0.299)	(0.377)
Filibuster-tail EGI	+	−4.217**	−4.077**	−3.092[†]	−3.026	−5.909*
		(1.784)	(2.018)	(2.023)	(2.725)	(3.550)
Override-tail EGI	+	−5.708***	−4.942***	−5.028***	−7.652***	−8.016***
		(1.146)	(1.315)	(1.349)	(1.992)	(2.532)
Constant		5.015***	4.210***	3.792***	3.637***	3.402***
		(0.401)	(0.451)	(0.464)	(0.628)	(0.804)
Log-likelihood		−100.792	−87.598	−79.374	−68.265	−53.765

(b) *Testing Partisan-Compliance Model*

	Expected sign	T = −1	T = −0.5	T = 0	T = 0.5	T = 1.0
First-term	+	−0.245	−0.203	−0.178	0.046	0.039
		(0.236)	(0.237)	(0.241)	(0.321)	(0.402)
Divided Govt.	−	0.519**	−0.621***	−0.546**	−0.728**	−0.635*
		(0.210)	(0.210)	(0.213)	(0.287)	(0.358)
Constant		3.556***	2.993***	2.639***	2.063***	1.321***
		(0.185)	(0.182)	(0.184)	(0.244)	(0.304)
Log-likelihood		−171.130	−90.074	−82.433	−72.004	−57.539

Notes: N = 28. Negative binomial regression coefficients with standard errors in parentheses. T indicates the significance threshold for determining a significant EO. Likelihood ratio tests for each regression that alpha equals zero all strongly suggest the existence of overdispersion. Two-tailed tests are conducted for all parameters. *** p-value < .01 ** .01 < p-value <,05 * .05 < p-value < .1 [†] .1 < p-value < .2

predecessor's may prefer to use EOs to restructure his administration or to tighten his controls over an agency in his first two years in order to implement his new electoral mandates, he may not necessarily have incentives to issue more defense EOs during this period.[17] The second difference between

[17] According to the PAP coding, 37 percent of defense EOs are devoted to manpower, military personnel and dependents (Army, Navy, Air Force and Marines), trailed by 9.2 percent for military intelligence and CIA, 7.9 percent for general defense issues (such as the operation of Department of Defense), 7.6 percent for national guard and reserve affairs, 6 percent for arms

government operations EOs and defense EOs is that the chamber-compliance model receives as little support as the unilateralism model for the latter. The coefficient for the filibuster-tail of the EGI is always wrongly signed and is not statistically larger than that of the override-tail of the EGI. The partisan-compliance model receives even more support relative to the other two competing models.

Tables 4.6 to 4.8 examine EOs for (1) Labor, Employment and Immigration, (2) Public Lands and Water Management and (3) Civil Rights, Minority Issues and Civil Liberties. Empirical patterns for each policy area are almost identical to those for defense, with the partisan-compliance model receiving strong empirical support and the other two models getting little. Moreover, the first-term hypothesis is not borne out, so that, as with defense, there appears to be less discontinuity in policy with new administrations in these areas than in some others. The latter result is quite different from that found by previous studies such as Howell (2003, 2005) and from our own analysis for the universe of EOs, all of which highlights the importance of paying attention to individual policy areas.

Among the seven policy areas we examine, results for international affairs and foreign aid and for foreign trade stand in contrast to the patterns uncovered above, as well as for our pooled results. In particular, as seen in Table 4.9, the unilateralism model actually outperforms the other two models in explaining the 391 EOs issued for international affairs and foreign aid. Regardless of significance threshold, the divided-government coefficient is either statistically insignificant or, if significant, incorrectly signed. For higher significance thresholds, on the other hand, the override-tail EGI coefficient is correctly signed and statistically significant. Also, the first-term hypothesis gains strong empirical support. Finally, none of the chamber-compliance model's hypotheses receive empirical support. Overall, our results suggest that, at least for moderate or quite high significance thresholds, the president possesses more leverage to act unilaterally in international affairs and foreign aid and is particularly active in these areas during his first two years.

Interestingly, there is little empirical evidence for any of the competing models when applied to foreign trade EOs (Table 4.10). The only exception is that the divided-government hypothesis holds when we establish a very moderate significance threshold (around 0), providing some support for the partisan-compliance model. There is no evidence for the first-term hypothesis, regardless of the model specification or significance thresholds.

In broad strokes, then, we find great disparities between policy areas in terms of relative empirical evidence for the competing models. The partisan-compliance model receives stronger support than the other two models,

control, 5.5 percent for direct war-related issues and less than 5 percent for the other 12 subtopics.

TABLE 4.6 *Determinants of number of significant executive orders for labor, employment and immigration*

(a) Testing Unilateralism and Chamber-Compliance Models

	Expected sign	T = −1	T = −0.5	T = 0	T = 0.5	T = 1.0
First-term	+	−0.009	0.049	0.049	0.175	0.541†
		(0.292)	(0.296)	(0.329)	(0.355)	(0.352)
Filibuster-tail EGI	+	−2.223	−1.501	0.484	0.368	2.349
		(2.697)	(2.746)	(3.056)	(3.279)	(3.034)
Override-tail EGI	+	−4.961***	−5.824***	−6.132***	−6.589***	−5.257**
		(1.801)	(1.923)	(2.125)	(2.496)	(2.523)
Constant		3.756***	3.591***	3.398***	2.872***	1.341*
		(0.589)	(0.614)	(0.672)	(0.736)	(0.696)
Log-likelihood		−89.674	−83.462	−82.296	−70.898	−50.337

(b) Testing Partisan-Compliance Model

	Expected sign	T = −1	T = −0.5	T = 0	T = 0.5	T = 1.0
First-term	+	−0.058	−0.009	0.015	0.229	0.640*
		(0.299)	(0.295)	(0.324)	(0.326)	(0.353)
Divided govt.	−	−0.558**	−0.732***	−0.788***	−0.849***	−0.587*
		(0.268)	(0.264)	(0.290)	(0.294)	(0.336)
Constant		2.764***	2.614***	2.520***	2.020***	0.910***
		(0.236)	(0.230)	(0.252)	(0.248)	(0.288)
Log-likelihood		−91.037	−84.105	−82.718	−70.738	−51.583

Notes: N = 28. Negative binomial regression coefficients with standard errors in parentheses. T indicates the significance threshold for determining a significant EO. Likelihood ratio tests for each regression that alpha equals zero all strongly suggest the existence of overdispersion. Two-tailed tests are conducted for all parameters. *** *p*-value < .01 ** .01 < *p*-value < .05 * .05 < *p*-value < .1 † .1 < *p*-value < .2

except in the areas of international affairs and foreign aid, where the unilateralism model holds up best when we have moderately or very high significance thresholds for defining significant EOs, and of foreign trade, where no model does particularly well. Additionally, the first-term hypothesis gains much in the way of empirical confirmation only for government operation and international affairs and foreign aid, a result that is very different from that found in previous studies.

TABLE 4.7 *Determinants of number of significant executive orders for public lands and water management*

(a) Testing Unilateralism and Chamber-Compliance Models

	Expected sign	T = −1	T = −0.5	T = 0	T = 0.5	T = 1.0
First-term	+	−0.286	0.157	−0.018	−0.168	−1.082
		(0.330)	(0.361)	(0.399)	(0.438)	(0.850)
Filibuster-tail EGI	+	−3.137	−3.052	−4.317	−2.855	−4.359
		(2.993)	(3.277)	(3.787)	(3.965)	(6.948)
Override-tail EGI	+	−5.723***	−2.876†	−1.462	−6.90**	−8.989*
		(1.899)	(2.053)	(2.185)	(3.018)	(5.279)
Constant		3.700***	2.307***	1.847**	0.041**	1.839
		(0.646)	(0.725)	(0.834)	(0.969)	(1.735)
Log-likelihood		−81.610	−65.797	−57.222	−39.795	−23.183

(b) Testing Partisan-Compliance Model

	Expected sign	T = −1	T = −0.5	T = 0	T = 0.5	T = 1.0
First-term	+	−0.276	0.027	−0.199	−0.108	−0.873
		(0.348)	(0.296)	(0.350)	(0.394)	(0.799)
Divided govt.	_	−0.703**	−0.980***	−0.827***	−1.018***	−0.909†
		(0.308)	(0.267)	(0.306)	(0.362)	(0.582)
Constant		2.508***	1.846***	1.463***	0.784***	−0.089
		(0.268)	(0.218)	(0.251)	(0.269)	(0.431)
Log-likelihood		−83.096	−61.540	−54.734	−39.188	−23.839

Notes: N = 28. Negative binomial regression coefficients with standard errors in parentheses. T indicates the significance threshold for determining a significant EO. Likelihood ratio tests for each regression that alpha equals zero all suggest the non-existence of overdispersion. Two-tailed tests are conducted for all parameters. *** p-value < .01 ** .01 < p-value < .05 * .05 < p-value < .1 † .1 < p-value < .2

However, as mentioned, the existing literature suggests that there are other sensible ways of grouping data by policy area. As such, we now combine multiple major policy topics defined by the PAP in a manner consistent with earlier research.

In particular, we employ Lapinski's (2008) four policy categories: (1) sovereignty, (2) organization and scope, (3) international relations and (4) domestic affairs. While the first two policy categories roughly correspond to the PAP's coding of "civil rights, minority issues and civil liberties" and

TABLE 4.8 *Determinants of number of significant executive orders for civil rights, minority issues and civil liberties*

(a) Testing Unilateralism and Chamber-Compliance Models

	Expected sign	T = −1	T = −0.5	T = 0	T = 0.5	T = 1.0
First-term	+	−0.049	0.063	−0.214	0.190	0.1475
		(0.348)	(0.366)	(0.412)	(0.430)	(0.477)
Filibuster-tail EGI	+	−5.061*	−3.283	−5.222†	−1.852	−0.590
		(3.010)	(3.232)	(3.915)	(3.978)	(4.376)
Override-tail EGI	+	−3.033†	−1.907	−3.029†	−1.830	−1.543
		(1.923)	(1.999)	(2.220)	(2.479)	(2.771)
Constant		2.983***	2.088***	2.489***	1.144†	0.563
		(0.657)	(0.693)	(0.825)	(0.888)	(0.984)
Log-likelihood		−73.476	−64.072	−60.836	−48.625	−41.491

(b) Testing Partisan-Compliance Model

	Expected Sign	T = −1	T = −0.5	T = 0	T = 0.5	T = 1.0
First-term	+	−0.132	−0.095	−0.349	0.067	0.021
		(0.346)	(0.317)	(0.346)	(0.386)	(0.437)
Divided govt.	−	−0.664**	−0.830***	−1.014***	−0.862**	−0.820**
		(0.308)	(0.279)	(0.296)	(0.350)	(0.393)
Constant		2.083***	1.740***	1.731***	1.004***	0.634**
		(0.269)	(0.231)	(0.237)	(0.282)	(0.313)
Log-likelihood		−73.388	−61.102	−57.533	−46.158	−39.627

Notes: N = 28. Negative binomial regression coefficients with standard errors in parentheses. T indicates the significance threshold for determining a significant EO. Likelihood ratio tests for regressions with lower significance thresholds that alpha equals zero all strongly suggest the existence of overdispersion. Two-tailed tests are conducted for all parameters. *** *p*-value < .01 ** .01 < *p*-value < .05 * .05 < *p*-value < .1 † .1 < *p*-value < .2

"government operations," respectively, the latter two require the incorporation of multiple PAP policy topics.[18] "International relations" essentially

---

[18] Implementing earlier policy categorizations such as those in Wilson (1974) and Ripley and Franklin (1984) is not feasible, as mapping which EOs would then go into which different categories is extremely problematic. By contrast, while Lapinski's typology does not exactly fit with amalgamation of the PAP categories (e.g., he does not consider immigration issues, for which there are very few EOs, to be a domestic policy as does the PAP), there is a strong match.

TABLE 4.9 *Determinants of number of significant executive orders for international affairs and foreign aid*

(a) Testing Unilateralism and Chamber-Compliance Models

	Expected sign	T = −1	T = −0.5	T = 0	T = 0.5	T = 1.0
First-term	+	−0.007	0.360†	0.509*	0.845**	0.981*
		(0.193)	(0.270)	(0.309)	(0.362)	(0.527)
Filibuster-tail EGI	+	−2.897*	−2.955	−4.792*	−6.547*	−11.805**
		(1.733)	(2.463)	(2.902)	(3.355)	(5.544)
Override-tail EGI	+	−1.886*	−0.610	0.353	2.860†	5.463*
		(1.104)	(1.509)	(1.682)	(1.941)	(2.900)
Constant		3.428***	2.343***	2.025***	1.129†	0.589
		(0.398)	(0.553)	(0.630)	(0.704)	(1.104)
Log-likelihood		−87.911	−76.185	−70.293	−59.906	−48.729

(b) Testing Partisan-Compliance Model

	Expected sign	T = −1	T = −0.5	T = 0	T = 0.5	T = 1.0
First-term	+	0.016	0.291	0.395	0.547†	0.405
		(0.200)	(0.266)	(0.316)	(0.380)	(0.563)
Divided govt.	−	−0.164	−0.195	0.001	0.278	0.503*
		(0.180)	(0.245)	(0.294)	(0.362)	(0.358)
Constant		2.735***	1.957***	1.509***	0.844**	0.249
		(0.159)	(0.217)	(0.264)	(0.331)	(0.479)
Log-likelihood		−89.562	−76.577	−71.838	−63.059	−53.116

Notes: N = 28. Negative binomial regression coefficients with standard errors in parentheses. T indicates the significance threshold for determining a significant EO. Likelihood ratio tests for each regression that alpha equals zero all strongly suggest the existence of overdispersion. Two-tailed tests are conducted for all parameters. *** p-value < .01 ** .01 < p-value < .05 * .05 < p-value < .1 † .1 < p-value < .2

encapsulates three PAP policy areas that we have analyzed: defense, international affairs and foreign aid, and foreign trade. "Domestic affairs" include all remaining EOs, including the other two policy areas that we have investigated (i.e., labor, employment, and immigration, and public lands and water management) and those EOs that we previously put to the side and were not able to assess (i.e., policy areas with fewer than 100 EOs total). Since we analyzed Lapinski's first two policy types above, we will focus on his last two here.

TABLE 4.10 *Determinants of number of significant executive orders for foreign trade*

(a) Testing Unilateralism and Chamber-Compliance Models

	Expected sign	T = −1	T = −0.5	T = 0	T = 0.5	T = 1.0
First-term	+	0.326 (0.318)	0.381 (0.321)	0.251 (0.337)	0.576[†] (0.420)	0.950[†] (0.689)
Filibuster-tail EGI	+	−4.511* (2.567)	−3.230 (2.639)	−5.519* (2.985)	−8.774** (4.138)	−9.909[†] (7.676)
Override-tail EGI	+	−0.008 (1.876)	−1.342 (1.932)	−1.586 (2.007)	−0.654 (2.503)	0.304 (4.197)
Constant		2.209*** (0.615)	1.981*** (0.626)	1.946*** (0.680)	1.555* (0.883)	0.168 (1.560)
Log-likelihood		−73.225	−64.927	−54.411	−44.363	−24.438

(b) Testing Partisan-Compliance Model

	Expected sign	T = −1	T = −0.5	T = 0	T = 0.5	T = 1.0
First-term	+	0.213 (0.330)	0.299 (0.315)	0.222 (0.346)	0.359 (0.403)	0.875[†] (0.608)
Divided govt.	−	−0.069 (0.302)	−0.347 (0.291)	−0.108*** (0.320)	−0.441 (0.378)	0.232 (0.623)
Constant		1.696*** (0.271)	1.496*** (0.256)	0.964*** (0.287)	0.622* (0.330)	−1.136* (0.598)
Log-likelihood		−74.72	−65.080	−56.152	−46.317	−25.649

Notes: N = 28. Negative binomial regression coefficients with standard errors in parentheses. T indicates the significance threshold for determining a significant EO. Likelihood ratio tests for regressions with low significance thresholds that alpha equals zero all strongly suggest the existence of overdispersion. Two-tailed tests are conducted for all parameters. *** p-value < .01 ** .01 < p-value < .05 * .05 < p-value < .1 [†] .1 < p-value < .2

Altogether, 1228 EOs fall into Lapinski's categorization of international relations, of which 56 percent are defense, 32 percent are international affairs and foreign aid and 12 percent are foreign trade.[19] Recall that these three policy areas produced different results earlier, with defense and international affairs

[19] As we will discuss in Chapter 6, some of these EOs largely include domestic content.

and foreign aid EOs being more consistent with the partisan-compliance and unilateralism models, respectively, and foreign trade EOs being essentially inconsistent with any of the competing models. Given this heterogeneity of findings and given that defense constitutes the lion's share of the amalgamated category, it is not shocking that the partisan-compliance model does best under some circumstances (when the significance threshold is set to a low or moderate level) and no model does particularly well otherwise (when the threshold is higher than .7; see Table 4.11). In other words, in light of our combining of EOs with very different underlying patterns into a single category, with the president seemingly possessing very different calculations about how he should unilaterally act, we produce somewhat muddled findings.[20]

As for Lapinski's categorization of domestic affairs, there are 1,284 EOs, of which 25 percent are about labor, employment and immigration, 17 percent pertain to public lands and water management and the remaining deal with 13 major policies which have not been analyzed above, each constituting less than 7 percent of all domestic EOs (banking, finance and domestic commerce; energy; transportation; space, science, technology and communications; macroeconomics; law, crime and family issues; environment; health; community development and housing issues; education; agriculture; and social welfare).[21] Interestingly, Table 4.12 demonstrates that, for this amalgamated policy category, a determination of which model receives the most support depends on how we define significant EOs. When we fix the threshold lower than .5, the partisan-compliance model does best. When we employ higher significance thresholds, the chamber-compliance model receives the most support, as all of its hypotheses hold and the other two models' hypotheses do not. Jointly, from these results we can infer that, regardless of significance threshold, the president has to account for congressional constraints that are beyond statutory means in contemplating unilateral action for Lapinski's policy category of domestic policy, with majority parties playing an active role in directionally constraining the use of discretion in issuing an EO when the significance threshold is lower.

DISCUSSION AND CONCLUSIONS

It is now common among political scientists and legal scholars to assert that the tools of institutional influence, of which the executive order is a primary means,

---

[20] As our empirical distinctions are not as clear-cut as we would, ideally, prefer, and as our manner of differentiating among policies might be criticized as somewhat arbitrary, we will return to this issue from the perspective of the two-presidencies conjecture, i.e., that there is a strong chief executive for areas of foreign affairs and a more quiescent chief executive for areas of domestic affairs, in Chapter 6.

[21] For clarity, we distinguish this category as domestic affairs, as defined by Lapinski, and we will redefine domestic policy later in a broader manner when we turn to the two-presidencies conjecture.

TABLE 4.11 *Determinants of number of significant executive orders for Lapinski's category of international relations*

(a) *Testing Unilateralism and Chamber-Compliance Models*

	Expected sign	T = −1	T = −0.5	T = 0	T = 0.5	T = 1.0	T = 1.5	T = 2.0
First-term	+	−0.154	0.052	0.048	0.270†	0.349***	0.607*	0.927*
		(0.132)	(0.150)	(0.154)	(0.183)	(0.286)	(0.351)	(0.492)
Filibuster-tail EGI	+	−3.781***	−3.615***	−3.746***	−4.665***	−8.139***	−9.056**	−7.053†
		(1.159)	(1.314)	(1.386)	(1.695)	(2.867)	(3.643)	(4.984)
Override-tail EGI	+	−3.674***	−2.951***	−2.747***	−2.473**	−1.180	−1.908	−0.738
		(0.758)	(0.860)	(0.893)	(1.091)	(1.639)	(2.208)	(3.255)
Constant		5.092***	4.272***	3.923***	3.385***	2.844***	2.370***	1.105
		(0.265)	(0.297)	(0.313)	(0.376)	(0.599)	(0.773)	(1.098)
Log-likelihood		−108.364	−95.578	−87.541	−77.159	−67.853	−54.074	−43.395

(b) *Testing Partisan-Compliance Model*

	Expected sign	T = −1	T = −0.5	T = 0	T = 0.5	T = 1.0	T = 1.5	T = 2.0
First-term	+	−0.101*	0.037	0.053	0.239	0.274	0.587*	0.914*
		(0.162)	(0.154)	(0.168)	(0.189)	(0.300)	(0.355)	(0.484)
Divided govt.	−	−0.353**	−0.449***	−0.328**	−0.382**	−0.139	−0.188	0.212
		(0.145)	(0.138)	(0.151)	(0.173)	(0.276)	(0.337)	(0.485)
Constant		4.019***	3.439***	3.042***	2.482***	1.654***	0.930***	−0.099
		(0.128)	(0.121)	(0.133)	(0.151)	(0.242)	(0.296)	(0.437)
Log-likelihood		−115.487	−97.396	−91.009	−79.683	−71.751	−57.306	−44.323

Notes: N = 28. Negative binomial regression coefficients with standard errors in parentheses. T indicates the significance threshold for determining a significant EO. Likelihood ratio tests for each regression that alpha equals zero all strongly suggest the existence of overdispersion. Two-tailed tests are conducted for all parameters. *** p-value < .01 ** .01 < p-value < .05 * .05 < p-value < .1 † .1 < p-value < .2

TABLE 4.12 *Determinants of number of significant executive orders for Lapinski's category of domestic affairs*

(a) *Testing Unilateralism and Chamber-Compliance Models*

	Expected sign	T = -1	T = -0.5	T = 0	T = 0.5	T = 1.0	T = 1.5	T = 2.0
First-term	+	0.136	0.307**	0.256^	0.337*	0.544†	0.612**	1.545**
		(0.129)	(0.135)	(0.156)	(0.187)	(0.211)	(0.300)	(0.742)
Filibuster-tail EGI	+	-0.238	0.360	0.722	2.082†	2.791†	6.672**	2.016
		(1.092)	(1.137)	(1.322)	(1.595)	(1.740)	(2.462)	(4.767)
Override-tail EGI	+	-1.635**	-1.184†	-1.037	-1.505†	-1.629	-1.116	5.327
		(0.720)	(0.776)	(0.882)	(1.097)	(1.295)	(1.969)	(4.165)
Constant		4.169***	3.555***	3.218***	2.656***	1.801***	0.027	-3.024**
		(0.244)	(0.258)	(0.297)	(0.357)	(0.399)	(0.583)	(1.241)
Log-likelihood		-110.548	-101.457	-97.789	-89.999	-74.051	-53.238	-19.478

(b) *Testing Partisan-Compliance Model*

	Expected sign	T = -1	T = -0.5	T = 0	T = 0.5	T = 1.0	T = 1.5	T = 2.0
First-term	+	0.144	0.274**	0.221	0.365**	0.644***	0.862**	1.595**
		(0.126)	(0.111)	(0.132)	(0.165)	(0.217)	(0.342)	(0.619)
Divided govt.	–	-0.256**	-0.391***	-0.401***	-0.475***	-0.245	0.033	1.357*
		(0.115)	(0.102)	(0.120)	(0.151)	(0.207)	(0.339)	(0.799)
Constant		3.943***	3.592***	3.342***	2.895***	1.969***	0.671**	-2.554***
		(0.101)	(0.088)	(0.105)	(0.130)	(0.181)	(0.303)	(0.852)
Log-likelihood		-110.601	-96.703	-94.025	-87.635	-75.460	-56.605	-18.695

Notes: N = 28. Negative binomial regression coefficients with standard errors in parentheses. T indicates the significance threshold for determining a significant EO. Likelihood ratio tests for each regression that alpha equals zero all strongly suggest the existence of overdispersion. Two-tailed tests are conducted for all parameters. *** p-value < .01 ** .01 < p-value < .05 * .05 < p-value < .1 † .1 < p-value < .2

117

provide the chief executive with great power that has heretofore been underappreciated. While we agree with the general premises that the chief executive's institutional position is a key to understanding his impact and that presidential influence should be conceptualized as stemming from the strategic context in which he operates, the more specific conclusion that "action is tantamount to power" does not stand up when we actually turn to analyzing the data.

In Chapter 2 we saw that different assumptions about the ideological direction in which discretion is employed by the president can impact the patterns of his unilateral action (far more than can assumptions about the size of this discretion) that we can expect to witness in subtle and previously unrecognized ways. When we analyze our data – including in total, by significance levels and by different categorizations of policy areas – if there is one overarching inference to be drawn it is that we should be careful in our claims about power. Overall, the president behaves in a manner much more consistent with bargaining, particularly with majority party leaders, in the context of relevant extra-statutory constraints. In particular, our analysis underscores that partisan constraints may limit the ideological direction in which the president can take policy when exercising his discretion.

Thus, when it comes to unilateral action, the amount of power – at least power as defined by the ability to move the status quo without some form of approval from the other key political players – that goes with unilateralism should not be overstated, as the president's directional use of discretion is limited.[22] Rather, the underlying process that generates executive orders is more akin to separation-of-powers bargaining than to a president acting, and daring others to respond, with Congress unable to mobilize due to its own collective action problems or policy gridlock and the courts generally compliant, and the president winning the vast majority of the time. While the press may, for understandable reasons, focus on instances of seeming presidential power where the chief executive dares a legislature to act or the courts to overrule (even if this is "off-the-equilibrium" path behavior), the larger picture is generally inconsistent with this viewpoint.

Yet it is often the case that other political actors, notably legislative parties or their surrogates in the courts, must be willing to go along even when statutory overrides are not feasible. Perhaps this should not surprise us, given both that there is acknowledgement in the mainstream Congress literature that legislators have abilities to impact outcomes, that go beyond their passing a statute, to move a status quo directly by exercising the extra-statutory means described in Chapter 1. Moreover, parties can help overcome collective action problems, strengthening the effectiveness of Congress in responding to presidential

---

[22] Recall that this Dahlian view of power is only one of our two definitions of power; the other involves moving policy toward the president's ideal point even if other political leaders also prefer a change.

unilateral actions. While Moe and Howell (1999a, b) argue that collective action problems hamper the Congress and provide the president with a considerable advantage, we find in the context of our analysis that the ability of subsets of members (i.e., members of a majority party) to act collectively and impact the unilateral action is especially effective in undercutting the chief executive's power and influence. All in all, these processes contribute to the stability of separations of power and prevent the seeming excesses of an imperial presidency.

Our findings are not equivalent to saying that the president is never powerful. There may be specific occasions in which the chief executive acts in a relatively unconstrained manner, worrying only about whether the legislature will act statutorily and the courts will rule his actions out of bounds. We certainly witness this in examining EOs for specific policies. For example, we find that while the president often has to solicit tacit support from Congress in most major policy areas, he retains greater leverage to act unilaterally on more significant issues related to international affairs and foreign aid. And, in the name of full disclosure, we also find a few instances, such as with respect to international relations issues using Lapinski's typology and a modestly high or quite high significance threshold, in which the executive's actions seem not explicable at all, in that none of our models fits well.

Even in other policy areas where the patterns of action are generally consistent with bargaining, we can occasionally point to cases that suggest that the president at least attempts to act unilaterally against congressional will. For example, in November of 2014 President Obama issued a series of highly controversial actions to protect up to 5 million undocumented persons from deportation despite strong congressional opposition; this seems to contrast with our statistical findings, which are consistent with the notion that the president will shy away from actions that will inflame a hostile Congress.[23]

Yet, while these examples are certainly important for understanding how the president promulgates unilateral actions, they constitute only a small portion of the universe of unilateral actions and may be impacted by factors that are sufficiently idiosyncratic that we have not integrated them into our general analysis of actions. For example, immigration may be affected by the fact that Hispanics make up a large national voting bloc (particularly in presidential elections) that is sympathetic toward a lenient policy regarding those already in the United States, albeit illegally. Reflecting this possibility, President Obama was quite hesitant early in his administration to loosen immigration policy in a way that would postpone deportation, but he did so initially in the summer of 2012, with his reelection looming that November, issuing a unilateral action to

---

[23] As we mentioned earlier, these were not technically EOs but illustrate the point well.

postpone deportation for young undocumented persons; presumably, his action would substantially help consolidate support from Latino voters (he won Hispanic votes by such a large majority that some saw it as decisive for his ultimate victory). Conversely, worried about the consequences of further loosening of the immigration law, given the attitudes of non-Hispanic Americans in the lower-turnout midterm elections, the president postponed additional, more dramatic action until after the voting.[24] Unsurprisingly, when Obama did move immediately after the 2014 election, Republican majority leaders in Congress were quite upset, and acted in what we have characterized as extra-statutory ways, most notably by holding the Department of Homeland Security budget hostage during a three-month showdown before acquiescing. In addition, Republicans attempted to add amendments to the defense budget. Finally, underscoring the extreme nature of Obama's use of discretion, the courts invalidated his 2014 immigration changes, ruling that they went beyond his delegated authority (specifically, the president's position lost in the appellate court, and a deadlocked Supreme Court allowed that decision to stand). All in all, Obama's actions opposing the congressional majority precipitated legislative costs and an eventual loss in the courts; for the president and his party, these choices may still have had electoral benefits by appealing to a large and growing electoral bloc, but they also demonstrate the corresponding costs.

Finally, it behooves us to acknowledge two things. First, and as we will see again in the next chapter, while our inferences are often invariant with regard to the significance of the EOs being considered, this is not always the case. Beyond our increased confidence in our results, based on our ability to employ a continuous measure of significance, we also find instances such as that for domestic policy (using the Lapinski typology) where our determination on whether to infer that the key legislative player is the chamber or the partisan median depends on what set of Orders we are considering. Second, and to foreshadow our study of the two presidencies in Chapter 6, our results for policy types are not as definitive as we might like, and some thinkers might take exception to our distinctions between policy types.

Before turning to the latter concern, however, we see our analysis as having one considerable, but remediable, limitation: the modest manner in which we have treated political parties in the legislative stage of our models. Parties can execute a variety of roles in the legislative process. This multiplicity of roles has received great emphasis in recent years in the literature on Congress, including

---

[24] Interestingly, during his presidency, Obama resisted pressure from gay rights groups to produce executive orders that would have likely conflicted with the Republican Congress. Ultimately, in 2015 the United States Supreme Court did what many in the gay rights community were urging the president to do by unilateral action.

analysis that specifically highlights the importance of parties in producing legislative outputs (e.g., Chiou and Rothenberg 2003). Nonetheless, we have restricted our attention to how various party roles can structure presidential calculations with regard to unilateral action, and thus impact presidential power. Our next chapter addresses these issues by peeling back the onion a good deal further as a means of exploring the multifaceted features of political parties.

5

Bringing the Parties In: Legislative Partisan Influence and Presidential Power

INTRODUCTION: BRINGING LEGISLATIVE PARTIES
TO THE PRESIDENCY

To this juncture, in our effort to shed light on the enigma of presidential power, we have focused on integrating our theoretical and empirical analyses by looking principally at the interplay between the chief executive, legislators and judges. We have specified a theoretical framework with competing models that corresponds to different levels of presidential power, measured executive order significance empirically in a reliable and valid way and examined which of our competing models corresponds best to the empirical data.

In one sense, by concentrating our attention on the back-and-forth between the President, members of Congress, and the courts, we have mimicked past practices in institutional presidential research. While this makes sense as an initial step, one obvious critique of our approach is that we direct insufficient attention toward the concerns of others who study institutions more broadly. As such, we may be ignoring critical factors that can impact the ability of Congress to respond to unilateral action and, in turn, whether, how and when the President takes unilateral action to change policy. This has the potential to dramatically impact how we understand presidential power arising from unilateral action. Specifically, another key actor pinpointed in the broader literature, especially with respect to the legislature, is the political party.[1] In our initial theoretical and empirical analysis, while we incorporated a role for political parties as part of our effort to understand the nature and importance of presidential discretion, we followed convention in the study of

---

[1] Admittedly, in Chapter 2 we consider partisan influence over discretion and provide a somewhat arbitrary role for the majority party in the legislative process; however, as we will see, we omitted a great deal more about what roles parties might play.

unilateral action by not integrating parties into what we called the legislative stage of the process. As discussed, this facilitated a clear analysis with general assumptions, allowing us to gain insight into the relevance of assumptions regarding the direction of discretion for how unilateral action impacts presidential power.

However, just as the analysis of the modern presidency has been dramatically reshaped by institutional scholars, views regarding political parties, and in particular their potential roles in the legislature, have experienced a revolution of sorts (e.g., Monroe, Roberts and Rohde 2008; for a review, see Smith 2007 and the collection in Maisel and Berry 2010). As David Rohde (2010, p. 323) put it several years back, "What a difference twenty-five years makes."

Thus, our next step, in broad strokes, is to move beyond our initial analysis and examine whether partisan roles in the legislature can have independent effects that condition unilateral action generally and presidential power specifically. The importance of understanding such legislative partisan roles is underscored by the fact that parties are increasingly considered as potentially key congressional actors. While there was a period where scholars conceptualized parties as having little or no legislative role in terms of preferences – and some, such as Krehbiel (e.g., 1993 for an early discussion), continue to press this viewpoint (but, see, for example, Krehbiel, Meirowitz and Romer 2005 for a more balanced perspective) – this is no longer the case.

This is not to assert that universal agreement exists, even among those touting the importance of partisan organizations, about the precise mechanisms through which parties influence the legislature. Indeed, this is a subject of much debate and consternation. Perspectives range from negative agenda-setting, by which majority parties possess the ability to keep items off the agenda (e.g., Cox and McCubbins 2005), to positive agenda-setting, by which majority parties can conditionally or unconditionally determine which choices are placed to a vote (Rohde 1991, Cox and McCubbins 2005), to influencing member choice behavior (e.g., on roll calls) through, albeit imperfect, party discipline (e.g., Snyder and Groseclose 2000, Cox and Poole 2002, Evans and Grandy 2009), by which members vote (or act in other manners) differently than they otherwise would as a function of partisan pressures and enticements.

Yet, despite parties' reemergence as central to the study of institutional politics, presidency research has not integrated these multiple partisan roles into the analysis of executive actions or influence. At most, the focus has been on exploring party effects in reduced form, by which varied impacts are aggregated – and even these studies have tended to ignore unilateral action. As such, we lack assessments of whether and in what contexts different, specific party effects exist. Presidential scholars have suggested the potential importance of divided government (e.g., Lewis 2008), partisan support of presidents in the legislative arena (e.g., Bond and Fleisher 1990), majority party status for distributive spending (Berry, Burden and Howell 2010), and co-partisanship (where the President and a legislator are from the same party) for disaster expenditures (e.g., Kriner and Reeves 2012). The detailed analysis of varied party roles that has been stressed for more than two decades has been substantially lacking for presidential studies in general and for unilateral action in particular. Indeed, as Howell (2005, p. 437) pointed out in his overview of the unilateralism literature a number of years ago, "[I]ssues that have received enormous amounts of attention within the legislative politics literature remain essentially unexamined in the emerging unilateral politics literature."[2] Thus, our analysis here differs from previous research by focusing on how specific partisan roles might impact executive decisions overall and unilateral actions in particular.

One possible reason for the past omission of legislative partisan roles from analyses of choices such as executive actions may stem from a presumption, which we believe deserves questioning, that these various party roles in the legislative stage matter little for such decisions. Admittedly, unambiguous, empirical documentation of the exercise of these types of party powers, not to mention detailing the exact mechanisms employed, based on discussions of individual executive orders, is problematic. Nonetheless, we have already said in earlier chapters that not only does a President often seem to cooperate with congressional leadership in his or her unilateral actions, but in practice this sort of consultation is not principally with legislative medians or pivots, but with party leaders (e.g., Boyle 2007). Such leaders appear to have impacts ranging from restraining what presidents include in EOs, on the one hand, to making positive changes more to legislators' likings, on the other.

For example, one time when combat between parties in the legislature and the chief executive particularly came to the fore was in the period immediately after the House and Senate swung dramatically to the Republican Party, to the consternation of President Bill Clinton, in 1994 (e.g., Turner 1996). One area of conflict where partisan roles did seem to come into play, for instance, involved protecting unions involved with federal contractors. Notably, when Clinton issued EO 12954 in early 1995, which banned the government from doing business with companies that hired permanent strike replacement workers, congressional Republicans sprang into action. The House voted to deny funding for enforcement of the EO in committee and Republican Kansas Senator Kassenbaum attached the same provision to a Defense Appropriations bill, which, however, stalled on the Senate floor as Republicans coordinated to

---

[2] Reinforcing Howell's point and our earlier comments, the relationship between parties and presidents has not gone completely unexplored. However, features about parties that have gotten a great deal of attention from students of legislatures, the integration of which, we are suggesting, is needed for a clear understanding of the institutionalized presidency and presidential power, have not received comparable treatment. For another example of where attention has previously been directed, others have focused principally on the dynamic between the chief executive and parties in terms of the degree to which the former relies on the latter in pursuing objectives such as electoral success and effective communication with the electorate (for a review, see, e.g., Milkis and Rhodes 2010).

maintain unity. Senate Republicans tried to win over a few conservative Democrats in the process, but were unable to break a Democratic filibuster. Subsequent partisan attempts to undermine the EO continued, with the courts eventually siding with the Republican interpretation. Clearly, this was a case where partisan agenda control and party discipline seemed to come into play (although the actual application of pressure by leaders on party members is always difficult to pinpoint) to at least inflict costs on the President when he acted against the majority interests.

In this spirit, those at the helm of political parties may conceivably play several relevant roles in producing such outcomes. For example, they could influence legislators' voting behaviors through persuasion, inducement or coercion. This, in turn, could help determine the extent of legislative gridlock, for example impacting the likelihood that unilateral actions would be overridden or that other parts of the presidential agenda would be realized. Along similar lines, as we implied earlier, party leaders could be central for agenda control. Party leaders are usually viewed as being in the thick of efforts to manage the legislative calendar as a means of thwarting executive initiatives – either by keeping items off the agenda or by adding them on.

If, through such functions, parties are key forces in determining legislative behavior that may, in turn, shape the strategic choices of presidents, a failure to account for their influence could result in incorrect inferences and serious misstatements about the amount of influence that presidents can and do wield. As described in Chapter 2, the game sequence suggested by previous unilateral action studies is that the President moves initially by deciding whether and how to take unilateral action, which is followed by possible reversal by Congress through passage of legislation and then by the courts' enforcement of discretion limits. If parties are a fundamental element in the legislative stage, they condition the ability of Congress to respond to unilateral action that will, in turn, shape the strategic choices of presidents. Put simply, the roles that parties may play can impact presidential influence or power.

In related fashion, examination of various party functions with regard to unilateral action will help us assess the actual extent of collective action problems that, some have claimed, undermine congressional efforts to thwart presidential moves, per our discussion in Chapter 1. As we elaborated in that discussion, the likelihood that collective action problems will deter legislative action is fundamental for understanding the unilateral executive actions that are of interest to us for assessing presidential power. Yet there is widespread disagreement over the severity of such obstacles. Recall that, in their groundbreaking work, Moe and Howell (1999a, b) asserted that Congress greatly suffers from such problems. Interestingly, party scholars such as Cox and McCubbins (2007), who argued that parties emerge to resolve collective action problems by forming a procedural cartel, and Rohde (1991), who maintained that party leaders discipline their rank and files and exercise positive agenda-setting, might be seen as offering contrasting views even though they focus on the collective action of subsets of legislators rather than on chambers as wholes. In Chapter 2, we incorporated parties principally in the unilateral action stage of our model, emphasizing their potential to impact the directional use of discretion. In this instance, parties and their leaders are presumed to help overcome collective action problems through the use of extra-statutory means in the unilateral action stage. Now, by incorporating possible party roles in the legislative stage, including the lack of a partisan impact, we will be able to gauge to what extent parties can further help overcome collective action problems in this stage, and whether (and how) doing so counteracts or encourages presidential unilateral actions and subsequent assessments of power.

To sum up, not only might a failure to consider partisan roles at the legislative stage lead to problems in theoretically and empirically ascertaining the part that presidents play; it could result in serious misstatements about the amount of influence presidents can and do wield. In light of such possible flexing of party muscles, it is important to consider parties as member-influencers and agenda-setters – even at the cost of parsimony and a need to include some restrictive theoretical assumptions – given our interest in comparing models as a way to shed light on the enigma of presidential power.

This, in turn, has two principal ramifications for our analysis of the degree to which inter-branch relationships impact presidential power. First, we need to take partisan roles as seriously as those of legislators, bureaucrats, judges or voters. As the findings in our earlier chapters indicate, these functions impacting the executive may actually extend beyond the legislature, per se, to the actual implementation of presidential discretion to move policy. Second, while these roles are not typically pinned down, because party influence mechanisms are myriad and can occur in different policy-making process stages, an encompassing theoretical framework allowing for these various possibilities and derivation of corresponding hypotheses is essential. Although, combined with the nuances of presidential strategic action, such an approach is necessarily somewhat cumbersome, it promises to be illuminating.

Hence, building on our work in Chapter 2 (which, to reiterate, only integrates the matter of whether parties can constrain the directional uses of discretion by the chief executive), we stipulate a more encompassing theoretical framework. It is encompassing in that it incorporates many competing models without initially fully specifying a game sequence or players and, while still including alternative discretion assumptions, effectively accounts for the alternative roles that parties might play: no role, negative agenda-setting, positive agenda-setting and imperfect party discipline. We then conduct a corresponding empirical analysis, employing the measure of EO significance that we developed in Chapter 3, in tandem with a novel approach that makes comparing models possible and straightforward, to ascertain both whether parties take on important functions in the unilateral action process and to refine our inferences about presidential power.

BROADENING OUR THEORETICAL FRAMEWORK TO INCLUDE POLITICAL PARTIES[3]

While sharing the features of our general setup in Chapter 2, our more encompassing theoretical framework here is able to capture 18 competing models.[4] Each varies the roles of parties in the presidential unilateral action and the legislative stages. In turn, such different functions have implications for how the president can employ discretion and for how the relevance of these possible roles shapes both agenda power and the extent of congressional fragmentation that impact presidential incentives. This permits us to derive and then compare the set of status quos where the president will undertake unilateral action in equilibrium in each of the competing models.[5]

For those not wishing to slog through the technical apparatus (they can pick up with the summary in the final two paragraphs of this section), we will show that partisan roles can impact legislative gridlock. This (following Chapter 2's logic and discussion of the gridlock incentive) can structure presidential opportunities for taking unilateral action because the President has more leeway to move a policy when gridlock is expanded. Additionally, the President's motivation to use discretion to move the status quo as close to the override pivot as possible to prevent the chamber median from adjusting it further away (what we labeled the preemption incentive in Chapter 2) can be impacted if parties can exercise positive agenda-setting, as such an ability can shift the agenda-setter's relative position to the chief executive and the override pivot. Positive agenda-setting's effect is conditioned by the directional constraint assumption, as discussed with respect to the discretion incentive in Chapter 2, so its effect hinges crucially on whether government is unified or divided.

For those who worked through Chapter 2 and desire to continue further, our game's general sequence should be familiar, albeit with some discrepancies (Figure 5.1):[6] (1) *Nature* randomly selects a level of discretion (t) and a status

---

[3] In presenting our framework, we include some deliberate redundancy with Chapter 2 so that the reader need not flip back and forth between chapters.

[4] Consistent with Chapter 2, our model is also more realistic than past efforts in that we assume a bicameral rather than a unicameral legislature.

[5] As in Chapter 2, we focus on generating predictions directly from our models. Here, predictions are based on models that assume alternative sets of party roles as well as the different directional constraints on presidential discretion used earlier, which we then compare with respect to how they fit the data. As we discussed in Chapter 4, this approach is similar in spirit to work such as Chiou and Rothenberg's (2003) analysis of law-making and Primo, Binder and Maltzman's (2008) study of federal judicial appointments – where formal theories are explicated. It is also, we might add, comparable to research that is exclusively empirical but where assumptions are nonetheless made, if less explicitly, comparing different statistical models or even testing a single model (e.g., Shipan 2004).

[6] For example, Figures 2.4 and 5.1 are analogous, except that the latter reflects the more encompassing approach by leaving unspecified, for the time being, who can set the agenda or veto

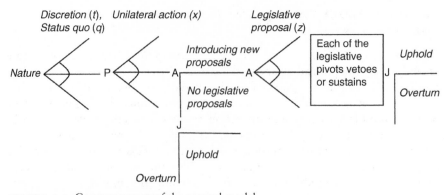

FIGURE 5.1 Game sequence of the general model.
Note: P, A and J denote the President, the agenda-setter in Congress and the court, respectively.

quo (*q*) from their respective distributions and reveals them to all the players; (2) the President (*P*) decides whether to take no unilateral action (at which point the game ends) or to choose an action, $x \in R$, to move the status quo; (3) the agenda-setter in Congress chooses whether to introduce a proposal (if not, the court will decide whether to uphold or to overturn the presidential action and the game ends); (4) the agenda-setter chooses a proposal, $z \in R$; (5) each legislative pivot decides whether to veto; and (6) the court (*J*) chooses whether to uphold or overturn the presidential action. Step (2) of the sequence represents the game's unilateral action stage, steps (3), (4) and (5) constitute its legislative stage and step (6) its judicial stage. In other words, after a status quo and discretion are drawn, the game has three sequential stages (the second of which actually involving a number of actions): presidential unilateral, legislative and judicial. In contrast to Chapter 2 and as mentioned with respect to Figure 5.1, we are bringing far more models under a single umbrella. As a result, our overarching theoretical framework does not, for the time being, specify the exact agenda-setter or explicitly define the group of actors making up the legislative pivot set, as each varies by model. The six different party roles (or combinations of roles) in the legislative stage and the three possible discretional constraints in the unilateral action stage produce the 18 combinations and corresponding models.

As indicated above, these party roles are drawn from the literature on legislative institutions, which is rife with competing claims about how parties operate in the legislative stage. Previous scholars have asserted that parties play no substantive role (i.e., only preferences matter; see, e.g., Krehbiel 1993), that they exercise negative or positive agenda-setting (keeping issues off or putting

legislative proposals. If we treat the filibuster pivot and either the President or the override pivot – whichever is less extreme – as comprising the set of actors who can veto proposals, Figure 2.4 is essentially a special case of Figure 5.1.

them on the agenda of the whole; see, e.g., Cox and McCubbins 2005, Rohde 1991) or that they impact the actions of their members through (imperfect) party discipline (e.g., by changing a member's vote; see, e.g., Snyder and Groseclose 2000, Cox and Poole 2002, Evans and Grandy 2009). Per the last partisan role, like Volden and Bergman (2006) and Chiou and Rothenberg (2009) we assume that a rise in imperfect party discipline will shift a party member closer to his or her party median, with the degree of change hinging on the effectiveness of party pressure.[7] As such, a legislator's *induced* preference will replace his or her *primitive* preference (for our purposes, the latter is a representative's preference net of party influence) in determining legislative policy outcomes.[8]

Given these different possibilities, and as Table 5.1 lays out, there are six different combinations of party roles in the legislative stage: (1) no role, so that only preferences matter; (2) negative agenda-setting only; (3) imperfect party discipline only; (4) positive agenda-setting only; (5) negative agenda-setting and imperfect party discipline jointly; and (6) positive agenda-setting and imperfect discipline jointly.[9] As Table 5.1 indicates, each combination implies an agenda-setter and a set of legislative pivots.

Specifically, the chamber median in one chamber, given either his or her original or party-induced preference, will be the agenda-setter in models without positive agenda-setting.[10] With positive agenda-setting, either the

---

[7] Originally proposed by Volden and Bergman (2006), the approach implies that the ideal points of members from each party will move toward their party medians in a one-dimensional policy space. Increasing party discipline will gradually bifurcate the legislature, and perfect discipline will result in all members converging at their party medians.

[8] In balancing comprehensiveness and parsimony, we omit one potential party role – the President serving as his or her party's leader to control the legislative agenda or to discipline the party's members (e.g., Patterson and Caldeira 1988, Sundquist 1989, Rohde 1991, Miller 1993). We make this choice because assuming that the President (rather than party medians) is the party leader changes results very little (see Chiou and Rothenberg 2003 for empirical and theoretical evidence), but adds another set of models, dramatically increasing the number of models requiring analysis and greatly complicating presentation of theoretical and empirical results.

[9] In a model with unicameralism, positive agenda-setting subsumes negative agenda-setting, as the member given positive agenda power will not propose legislation undermining his or her interests, and he or she therefore possesses negative agenda power. However, with bicameralism, there are two chamber/party medians. While one chamber/party median possessing positive agenda power can also exercise negative agenda power, it is unclear, given positive agenda-setting, what role the other chamber/party median plays. To be concise, when incorporating positive agenda-setting in our model, we assume that the latter has negative agenda power; however, our theoretical and empirical results for when the President will act unilaterally are almost identical without this assumption.

[10] Since each chamber has a median, we assume that one median is the agenda-setter and the other is a legislative pivot. As which median is more justifiably the agenda-setter is unclear, we essentially assume that each is equally likely to be and we average out our results at the end. An analogous assumption is made for the model where the majority party has positive agenda power.

TABLE 5.1 *Set of pivots in the legislative stage under alternative party roles*

Party role	Set of pivots
Preference-based	i) Filibuster and override pivots ii) Non-agenda-setting chamber's median
Negative agenda-setting	i) Filibuster and override pivots ii) Non-agenda-setting chamber's median iii) Majority party medians
Imperfect party discipline	i) Party-induced filibuster and override pivots ii) Party-induced median of other chamber
Negative agenda-setting and imperfect party discipline	i) Party-induced filibuster and override pivots ii) Party-induced median of the other chamber iii) Majority party medians
Positive agenda-setting	i) Filibuster and override pivots ii) Chamber medians iii) Non-agenda-setting chamber's majority party median
Positive agenda-setting and imperfect party discipline	i) Party-induced filibuster and override pivots ii) Party-induced median of the two chambers iii) Non-agenda-setting chamber's majority party median

Note: While there is only one filibuster pivot, each chamber has an override pivot, a median and a majority party median.

House or the Senate majority party median serves the agenda-setter role. In the same vein, and as Table 5.1 specifies, the set of legislative pivots depends on how one perceives the institutional structure underlying the policy-making process. Following Krehbiel (1998) and Chiou and Rothenberg (2009), we incorporate a filibuster pivot and House and Senate override pivots. Imperfect party discipline will induce these pivots' preferences. Thus, the set of legislative pivots when only preferences matter includes the filibuster and override pivots and the chamber median not serving as the agenda-setter.[11] With negative

[11] Without loss of generality, we assume a Republican President. Since the President is, empirically, at least as extreme as the override pivots or majority medians, we make this assumption so that the override pivots rather than the President are relevant in determining the gridlock interval. By the same token, we assume that the President is more conservative than the majority party medians and the filibuster pivot. Relaxation of these assumptions alters our results very little.

agenda control, the two majority party medians are additional pivots. The induced pivots comprise the set when there is imperfect party discipline.

In terms of possible directional constraints on presidential discretion's use, which we have already shown are intimately intertwined with how presidential discretion selected by *Nature* actually functions, we include the same three assumptions laid out and justified in Chapter 2: (1) the President's action is always within the boundary of delegated discretion (i.e., the President can move policy in a manner that makes Congress worse-off, as long as it is within the range of t); (2) the President can move the status quo only in the direction consistent with the interests of the chamber median; or (3) the interests of the majority party median rather than the chamber median serves as a de facto directional constraint on discretion.

As noted, and in contrast to Chapter 2, our theoretical framework here is encompassing in that it requires no specific game sequence (as the sequence is unspecified until we stipulate party roles) and allows for many possibilities at the legislative stage. For example, Howell's models or any additional models further generated from his theoretical framework can be derived from ours, but not vice versa. As such, in integrating the impact of party roles on presidential power, our competing models go well beyond prior work (remaining details of our formal setup and our theoretical results summarized in proposition form are available in Appendix 3). Moreover, our theoretical framework can be flexibly applied or extended to investigate other issues.[12]

Before presenting our theoretical results for how party roles shape presidential incentives, it is helpful to emphasize that presidential incentives for unilateral action can be decomposed into three types: gridlock, preemption and discretion, as we briefly discussed in Chapter 2 and mentioned above. Considering in detail how each corresponding incentive is directly triggered by legislative gridlock, the President's attempt to preempt, and the discretion given to the President, respectively, provide insights into the total effects of incorporating party roles into the legislative stage of our framework.

Figure 5.2, where no party roles in the legislative stage and no directional constraints on discretion are assumed, illustrates each incentive type. As indicated, the President possesses incentives to act unilaterally in equilibrium for status quos between $f - t/2$ and $2v - m_c + t$ (where f, v, m_c and t denote the filibuster and override pivots, the chamber median, and a given level of discretion).[13] Following Chapter 2, the gridlock incentive exists when a status quo is within the EGI – to reiterate, the set of status quos unaltered in the legislative stage in equilibrium – so that the President can move it closer to

[12] For example, we could adapt our framework to include myriad models where the court is a strategic actor with preferences that differ from those of other players, or we could focus on particular policies by including relevant committee medians as pivots.

[13] Despite assuming bicameralism in our models, we assume unicameralism in our figures in order to make them more easily understandable.

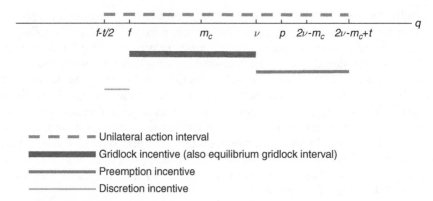

FIGURE 5.2 Unilateral action interval (assuming no party role or constraint on discretion direction).

Note: f, v, p, m_c, m_p, q and t denote the ideal points of the filibuster and override pivots, the President, the medians of the chamber and the majority party, the status quo and the level of discretion, respectively. The three types of incentives are the presidential incentives for unilateral action, which are indicated by the unilateral action interval, the set of status quos where P will take unilateral action in equilibrium.

his or her own ideal point without running the risk that Congress will pass a bill overriding this unilateral action.

The preemption incentive appears when the status quo falls between the override pivot and $2v - m_c + t$, where $2v - m$ is the chamber median's reflection point, allowing the President to use discretion to move the status quo as close to the override pivot as possible to prevent the chamber median from adjusting it further away. In contrast to the gridlock incentive, the magnitude of the preemption motive depends only on the gridlock interval's right tail, i.e., the interval between the median and the override pivot, in addition to discretion levels.

Finally, the discretion incentive, as indicated by the very thin line in Figure 5.2, involves the presidential incentive to bring a status quo close to, and to the left of, the filibuster pivot inside the EGI in order to take advantage of sufficiently large discretion, given congressional gridlock (i.e., it operates in conjunction with gridlock). If the President does not act, the chamber median still can move a status quo closer to the median's ideal point, a change that will also benefit the President. However, with sufficiently large discretion, the President can do better by moving the status quo within the gridlock incentive zone. Therefore, while the President can undermine Congress's attempt to move a status quo further away, given preemptive incentives, he or she acts due to discretion incentives because the chamber median cannot move enough.

Hence, a (possibly empty) set of status quos constituting an interval exists such that the President prefers to act unilaterally for each type of incentive.

The gridlock incentive segment is located between the preemptive incentive and the discretion incentive. When a status quo is located outside the EGI but near the President, the President has the preemption incentive to act unilaterally to constrain or forestall congressional action. With a status quo outside the EGI where the President and Congress locate on the same side of this status quo, the President shares congressional preferences and acts because legislative gridlock stops Congress from moving sufficiently.

It is particularly important to point out that, while each incentive is directly or indirectly triggered by elements of gridlock, only the gridlock incentive is a function of EGI *size*. Consistent with Chapter 2, the EGI cannot be directly employed as a predictor of unilateral action. Alternatively, to facilitate our analysis here, we define the unilateral action interval (UAI) as the set of status quos where the President prefers to act unilaterally in equilibrium. The UAI represents the union of all status quos associated with each of the three incentives for the chief executive to act and underpins the differences between our competing models.[14]

In turn, there are three noteworthy features when these different incentives are compared and contrasted. First, corresponding to Figure 5.2, the gridlock incentive is the most dominant of the three, since the vast majority of status quos locate within the EGI.

Second, while the discretion incentive is fully shaped by the delegated level of discretion, the gridlock incentive requires only a positive discretion level (which tends to hold in reality); i.e., the discretion level size does not affect this incentive.[15] Party roles and directional constraints on discretion, as will be shown, do not impact the discretion incentive much. Overall, the amount of discretion given to the President is minimally important for explaining presidential incentives for unilateral action in the models. Rather, what determines EGI size (e.g., preferences, party roles) and directional constraints on discretion largely shape presidential incentives.[16]

Third, divided government plays a critical role for how some of the President's incentives play out when we assume that either positive agenda-setting or majority parties act as a constraint on the direction of discretion. In the latter situation, presidential gridlock incentives for unilateral action are seriously undercut only under divided government, as shown in Chapter 2, since the preferences of the President and of the majority party median are generally very similar under unified government but they typically differ dramatically under divided government. In contrast, if the President does not face such a partisan directional constraint or is constrained by the chamber median, positive agenda-setting actually causes

---

[14] To foreshadow our data analysis, we will incorporate an additional step beyond measuring the UAI when empirically comparing the competing models.

[15] The preemption incentive is determined partially by the EGI (i.e., the EGI's right tail) and partially by the discretion level.

[16] This is why we get very similar results even if we assume that discretion is a function of the status quo or that the status quos are not concentrated within the EGI.

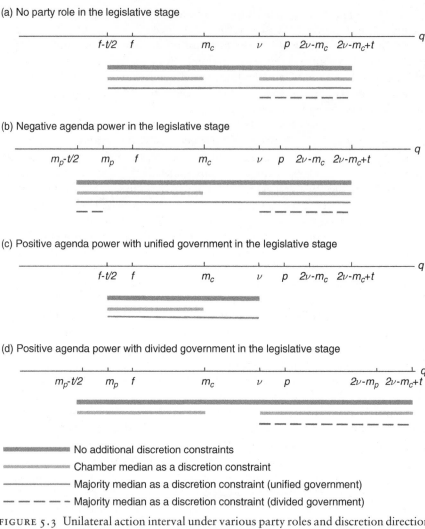

(a) No party role in the legislative stage

(b) Negative agenda power in the legislative stage

(c) Positive agenda power with unified government in the legislative stage

(d) Positive agenda power with divided government in the legislative stage

━━━━━ No additional discretion constraints

┅┅┅┅┅ Chamber median as a discretion constraint

──────── Majority median as a discretion constraint (unified government)

─ ─ ─ ─ ─ Majority median as a discretion constraint (divided government)

FIGURE 5.3 Unilateral action interval under various party roles and discretion direction assumptions.
Note: f, v, p, m_c, m_p, q and t denote the ideal points of the filibuster and override pivots, the President, the medians of the chamber and the majority party, the status quo and the level of discretion, respectively. Bold lines indicate the unilateral action interval, the set of status quos where the President will take unilateral action in equilibrium under various discretion assumptions.

substantially more gridlock under divided government, triggering greater gridlock or preemption incentives for unilateral action.

Figures 5.3(a) through 5.3(d), which correspond to each type of party role and demonstrate the UAI under possible directional constraints, illustrate and characterize the effects of various party roles on these three incentives for the

President to act, given discretion assumptions.[17] We can see that, when assuming no directional constraint (as indicated by the boldest lines in the Figures), party roles impact presidential incentives to varying degrees. Comparing Figures 5.3(a) and (b), the negative agenda power tends to reinforce presidential incentives for unilateral action (i.e., by expanding the UAI) through an extended gridlock interval.[18] This suggests that negative agenda-setting tends to augment presidential influence; i.e., stronger parties mean more presidential power. Even more pronounced is the effect of positive agenda power on the UAI, which is positive under divided government but is negative under unified government, because the President has much greater incentive to preempt when the opposition party rather than his or her own party exercises positive agenda control. As demonstrated by contrasting Figures 5.3(c) and (d), where the UAI is indicated by the boldest lines, the preemption motive evaporates under unified government but strengthens dramatically under divided government, with the gridlock motive slightly increasing under both types of government regimes. Positive agenda-setting at the legislative stage does not impact presidential influence under unified government, since the President will obtain similar policy outcomes regardless of whether or not he or she can act unilaterally. However, positive agenda-setting, given divided government, provides the President with opportunities to undercut majority parties' agenda power and increase his or her influence. One interesting difference between negative and positive agenda control is that the former affects the gridlock incentive, while the latter shapes that for preemption.

Also, Figure 5.3 illustrates that whether the chamber or the majority party median constrains directional use of discretion has great, but distinct, effects on presidential incentives for unilateral action, as measured by UAI length. When the chamber median is the force that limits, the gridlock motive shrinks under various party roles, as this discretion assumption rules out presidential attempts to move status quos between the chamber median and the override pivot. The effects of various party roles under this discretion constraint assumption are identical to those that pertain under no directional constraint.

---

[17] For comparison and illustration, we fix the preferences of relevant players and assume that the presidential party's median coincides with the override pivot.

[18] Several additional features not illustrated in Figure 5.3 should be pointed out. First, as we assume for illustrative purposes that the preferences of the President's party median and override pivot are identical, and then show the effect of negative agenda-setting under divided government, we omit several alternative possibilities. Notably, with unified government the effect of negative agenda-setting is conditioned by the relationship between the party median's and the override veto's preferences. If the party median's preference is at least as moderate as the override pivot's, negative agenda-setting does not augment presidential incentives for unilateral action. Alternatively, negative agenda-setting will reinforce these incentives if the party's median preference is more extreme than that of the pivot. Second, Figure 5.3 does not demonstrate the effects of imperfect party discipline. Quite similar to the effect of negative agenda power under various discretion assumptions, such discipline generally simultaneously expands both EGI boundaries, augmenting the gridlock and the preemption motives.

By contrast, Figure 5.3 indicates that the impact of the majority party median directionally constraining discretion is far more nuanced, as it depends on party roles and on government type. With either no partisan role or each of various party roles in the legislative stage, this directional discretion constraint has no effect on presidential incentives under unified government. Conversely, with divided government there exists a strong negative impact, as the President's choices to move the status quo are greatly limited. Under this discretion constraint, negative agenda power generally triggers more presidential unilateral action because of augmented gridlock incentives. However, the effect of positive agenda power depends on whether government is unified. Given unified government, the preemption motive disappears analogous to when there is no directional discretion constraint, while, by contrast, under divided government the preemption motive is dramatically extended and the gridlock motive completely disappears. Note that the effect of positive agenda power under this directional discretion assumption is the opposite of its impact under the other two discretion assumptions.

In conjunction with Figure 5.3 and our discussion of different incentives for presidential action, we can roughly summarize the effects of party roles under various directional constraint assumptions. Without directional constraints, both negative agenda power and imperfect party discipline increase the UAI, while positive agenda-setting shrinks it under unified government but substantially enlarges it under divided government. Adding the chamber median as a directional constraint universally reduces the UAI, whatever party role is assumed; the effects of each party role under this directional constraint assumption are similar to those with no directional constraint. In contrast, if the majority median acts as a directional constraint, the UAI under unified government is impacted little, whereas it is reduced dramatically with divided government. Under this directional constraint assumption, while the effects of negative agenda power and imperfect party discipline remain the same as those under the first two directional constraint assumptions, the impact of positive agenda power is the opposite of what it would be if it were assumed that there is no directional constraint or that the chamber median serves as a directional constraint.

These theoretical results highlight the importance of incorporating party roles into presidential unilateral action decisions at the legislative stage, as such party roles affect the gridlock interval and the length of its right tail, which impact the President's gridlock and preemption incentives, respectively. Consequently, the UAI length varies across competing models. Moreover, the interplay between party roles and assumptions regarding the direction of discretion has a significant impact on our expectations for presidential action, with government regime types conditioning the effects. These complications make investigation of this relationship a crucial step for our empirical analysis, which, as we will see, requires considerable effort in measurement.

INVESTIGATING THE MODELS EMPIRICALLY

Having laid out our general theoretical framework, we now investigate whether any of the competing models gains empirical support and, if so, which model or models best correspond to the data, given our theoretical results. This demands a research design that allows us to capture and compare the theoretical results from each model empirically, without biasing findings in favor of any given model. As before, we require a dependent variable that measures the number of significant EOs with varying significance thresholds. But now, we also need an independent variable capturing differences in presidential incentives for issuing EOs that correspond to each theoretical model. This is essential for evaluating and comparing these competing models, relative to one another and in an absolute sense, to see if any model is good in terms of both theoretical predictions being borne out and fitting the empirical data well.

Following Chapter 4, our dependent variable for assessing our competing models is a count variable of the number of significant EOs issued by presidents in each Congress using a given significance threshold. Analogous to our analysis in that chapter, for each significance threshold we distinguish the empirical support for our competing theoretical models. Unlike Chapter 4, here we do not examine subsets of EOs by policy type, since breaking out actions by individual policy is far too cumbersome, and we will examine the most distinct policy difference, that between foreign and domestic EOs, in our forthcoming analysis of the two presidencies.[19]

Regarding independent variables, we again focus on those directly stemming from our theoretical framework, although much differently now that we are investigating 18 models, and we once more check for our results' robustness by including control variables common in previous studies. Given our theoretical discussion in the current chapter, it is clear that our key independent variable must capture the total difference in presidential incentives to act unilaterally, as defined by each competing model. Yet, this is more easily said than done. Essentially, as we will explain shortly, the empirical strategy in Chapter 4 will not work for evaluating the competing models here.

While our theoretical results that, for a given status quo, presidents have incentives to take unilateral action in some models but not in others would make measuring presidential incentives for unilateral action, as illustrated in Figure 5.3, relatively straightforward if we possessed reliable information about each status quo, we unfortunately lack such status quo data. Alternatively, analogous to previous efforts testing pivotal politics models of legislative productivity using the EGI, we could utilize each model's UAI length, which, to reiterate, summarizes the set of status quos where the President prefers to act unilaterally. However, the requisite assumption that status quos are uniformly

---

[19] Obviously, estimating 18 models for multiple policy types and EO significance levels would produce thousands of estimates that would be impossible to summarize in an accessible fashion.

distributed (i.e., that they are equally distributed at each point on the ideological spectrum) could be criticized on the grounds that it is contrary to the more accepted, and intuitive, wisdom that status quos are concentrated within the gridlock interval or in the center of the ideological distribution.

Given our lack of data about status quo placement and our reluctance to assume that status quos are uniformly distributed, we develop a predictor for unilateral action, which we call the expected incentive for unilateral action (Appendix 3 provides a formal definition). This measure corresponds to the UAI for each theoretical model under the reasonable assumption that status quo distributions are centrally concentrated.

This approach to measurement, of course, differs markedly from what we employed in Chapter 4, where we used different independent variables suggested by each model. There are four related reasons why we adopt this alternative tack here.

First, it is impossible to distinguish empirically between models that make the same discretion assumption but stipulate a different assumption about parties. For instance, for the partisan-compliance model, the main predictor is divided government, regardless of our assumption about party roles in the legislature. Thus, to gauge how parties in the legislature condition presidential incentives we must apply our alternative approach of integrating the expected incentive for unilateral action.

Second, while this chapter's empirical approach is somewhat less intuitive than that in Chapter 4 and requires a more restrictive assumption about the distribution of status quos (that they are normally distributed), its advantage is that the main predictor for each competing model is derived identically, except for assumptions about legislative partisan roles and the discretion constraint. In other words, at the cost of some intuitiveness and a need for specificity regarding the status quo distribution, we benefit from seemingly fairer comparisons.

Third, our new means of analysis makes it much easier to compare large numbers of models than does that employed in Chapter 4. As we will see, as long as the coefficients are in the theoretically predicted directions, we can just compare model fit with a single statistic.

Finally, our employment of two different approaches, each with its pros and cons, provides a robustness check of sorts. The analysis in Chapter 4 is not restrictive about status quo assumptions, while our analysis here is encompassing and allows cleaner model comparisons. Thus, for example, if we continue to uncover evidence that the partisan-compliance model performs best – obviously, in this chapter, there are six variants of it – we can be more confident of our inferences, given that they come from two very different empirical approaches.

With this in mind, we measure the expected incentive for unilateral action for each model for each Congress in three steps: (1) we again employ Poole's (1998) common space scores to place the ideal points of the relevant pivots (as enumerated in Table 5.1) for each Congress in the same ideological space, as illustrated in Figure 5.2; (2) we solve, for each status quo, whether the President will unilaterally act in equilibrium; and (3) we average the overall incentives to act unilaterally by placing greater weight on status quos that are closer to the chamber median in the previous Congress, assuming a uniform distribution of discretion.

The first two steps determine the UAI with uneven weights, which are employed, given that we assume that more status quos locate in the center or within the gridlock interval. The third step then generates the variable by integrating the UAI over distributions of discretion and status quos. Although, as discussed in our theoretical analysis, the extent of discretion given for each status quo impacts presidential incentives rather little, we allow for a distribution of discretion to capture the minor effect that does exist. Based on our theoretical framework, higher values of the resulting variable predict more unilateral action for each of our 18 models.

To illustrate this complicated procedure, consider a hypothetical example. Suppose that we obtain common space scores for a given Congress for the ideal points in Figure 5.2.[20] In this situation, there are two sets of conditions under which the President will move unilaterally. First, the President will act unilaterally with respect to status quos that are located between the filibuster pivot and the reflection point (i.e., $2v - m_c$), regardless of the discretion level. The probability that status quos locate on this interval is the major element for the expected incentives measure and corresponds to the gridlock and part of the preemption incentives discussed in the previous section. Second, the President may act unilaterally as a result of the expected probability that status quos outside this interval are sufficiently close to its boundaries that the distance is smaller than the relevant discretion. This likelihood is a secondary component (in terms of its magnitude) for the expected incentives measure, and corresponds to the rest of the preemption incentive and the entire discretion incentive.

Assuming normal and uniform distributions for status quos and discretion, respectively, we will also conduct sensitivity analyses when we estimate our models. Specifically, since the EGI length for each model ranges from 0.3 to about 0.7 and the chamber medians are close to 0, we assume that discretion is uniformly drawn between zero and γ, which can range from 0.1 to 0.5.[21] We follow past research by assuming a normally distributed status quo,[22] and capture the inheritance of status quos from the past Congress by assuming that

---

[20] We illustrate our approach assuming unicameralism but assume bicameralism in calculating the expected incentive for unilateral action.

[21] While the discretion level should not be crucial in assessing our competing models, for consistency with our theoretical assumptions we assume that it is drawn from a uniform distribution, with various upper bounds examined while conducting sensitivity analysis. As expected, changing the assumption about discretion's upper bound does not change our empirical results.

[22] This assumption is roughly consistent with Howell (2003) and with Poole and Rosenthal (1997).

the mean of the distribution is around the midpoint of the two chamber medians in the previous Congress. For sensitivity, we will check with standard deviations ranging from 0.2 to 0.5 (the former being a natural boundary because any standard deviation less than 0.2 implies that status quos are almost always located within the EGIs). To display our empirical results more concisely, we present findings using the quite reasonable assumptions that the status quo distribution's standard deviation is 0.4 and that the discretion distribution's upper bound is 0.3.[23]

Regardless of partisan roles in the 18 models, those assuming no additional constraints on discretion, on average, have much larger means for expected incentives than do others (see Table 5.2).[24] In turn, models where the chamber median is assumed to constrain presidential discretion have slightly higher expected incentives than those where the party median is assumed to constrain discretion. This pattern is consistent with our assertion that the President will tend to take advantage of unilateral action when his or her discretion is not further constrained.

Finally, along the lines of our specifications in Chapter 4, as our theoretical framework indicates that the more issues or the larger the agenda considered in a Congress, the more significant EOs are to be expected, we include a dummy variable for first-term that captures the first two years of a new administration when the ruling party changes.

As in the previous chapter, we estimate negative binomial models, this time for our 18 models. To determine which model receives more support, we first check whether the expected incentive variable has the theoretically expected positive sign with statistical significance (using a 95 percent significance level, given a one-tailed test) and then compare the BIC (Bayesian Information Criterion) of each model (Raftery 1995; for political science applications, see

---

[23] We calculate the induced preferences of relevant players by taking a linear combination of their party leaders' and their own primitive preferences, with the weight being the level of party pressure, which is estimated in Snyder and Groseclose (2000). As the Snyder/Groseclose estimates are only up to the 105th Congress, we employ the same estimate for the next Congresses, partly because party pressure seems rather stable between the 104th and 107th Congresses and partly because the numerical values of the dependent variable have to be identical across the models we seek to compare.

[24] Since this independent variable is generated partly from common space scores (which we also use in Chapter 4) and partly from our theoretical models, we admittedly omit controlling for the standard errors arising from estimating these scores, as does all previous work employing common space scores. Solving this problem would require information for both the standard error of each pivot's common space score and the correlation between relevant pivots determining the UAI, the latter of which is unavailable. In principle, we could alternatively control for these errors by using a Bayesian procedure to jointly estimate common space scores of all legislators voting from 1947 through 2002, producing standard errors for each legislator and the UAI and estimating the posterior mean of the coefficient of the expected incentive. In reality, this is computationally formidable at present, given the sheer numbers of legislators and votes involved.

TABLE 5.2 *Expected incentive for unilateral action for competing scenarios*

Scenario		Obs.	Mean	Std. dev.	Min.	Max.
No additional constraints on discretion	Preference	28	0.6213004	0.073441	0.4840943	0.8044157
	Negative agenda-setting	28	0.6767778	0.0837712	0.5202063	0.8572445
	Imperfect party discipline	28	0.6332084	0.093662	0.5041489	0.9092045
	Negative agenda-setting and imperfect party discipline	28	0.6668417	0.0988317	0.5118089	0.9198217
	Positive agenda-setting	28	0.6653042	0.1723815	0.3369217	0.9268267
	Positive agenda-setting and imperfect party discipline	28	0.6447517	0.1671723	0.3721006	0.9383636
Discretion constrained by chamber median	Preference	28	0.4178783	0.0485607	0.3306843	0.5286368
	Negative agenda-setting	28	0.4599089	0.0511911	0.3681644	0.5565296
	Imperfect party discipline	28	0.4094702	0.0746292	0.2326688	0.5574602
	Negative agenda-setting and imperfect party discipline	28	0.4363654	0.0765441	0.2593113	0.5555325
	Positive agenda-setting	28	0.4218609	0.1587048	0.1820642	0.6921486
	Positive agenda-setting and imperfect party discipline	28	0.3846696	0.1280933	0.181470	0.6238374
Discretion constrained by party median	Preference	28	0.3402446	0.1641133	0.1188154	0.6058175
	Negative agenda-setting	28	0.3855268	0.1650752	0.2004372	0.668612
	Imperfect party discipline	28	0.3419837	0.1577746	0.1197617	0.598914
	Negative agenda-setting and imperfect party discipline	28	0.3719526	0.1572001	0.1509248	0.6839797
	Positive agenda-setting	28	0.3659164	0.0931876	0.1720075	0.4967428
	Positive agenda-setting and imperfect party discipline	28	0.3442042	0.0957146	0.1714386	0.5213954

Clarke 2001, Primo, Binder and Maltzman et al. 2008).[25] As mentioned in Chapter 4, the BIC is a means of selecting which of a finite set of models is better, with smaller BIC values preferred. According to Raftery (1995; see his Table 6), differences in BICs greater than 10 are very strong, differences between 6 and 10 are strong, those between 2 and 6 are positive and those less than 2 are weak.[26]

RESULTS

We are principally interested in what roles, if any, parties play in conditioning legislative influence on presidential unilateral action. However, to reiterate, in understanding any such relationship or impact, we want to know how it may shift as a function of EO significance, and so we report our results using a variety of significance thresholds.

Table 5.3 displays – as accessibly as possible, given our sheer volume of results – the negative binomial parameter estimates, the log-likelihood functions and the BIC scores for our 18 models for the entire sample of EOs, while Table 5.4 demonstrates corresponding results for the significance threshold of 2 (see Appendix 4 for additional information and regression results for representative threshold levels ranging from very low to quite high). Table 5.5, in turn, compares the competing models with various significance thresholds in summary form. To reiterate, in making comparisons we focus both on whether the variables, particularly the expected incentive measure, work as theorized and the smallness of a model's BIC score.[27]

For example, consider Table 5.3, which presents results with the lowest significance threshold of −1 (i.e., encompassing all EOs issued from 1947 to 2002). Findings for the models without directional discretion constraints are unimpressive because the coefficients for expected incentives, which are our main focus among all the coefficients, are wrongly signed (although they would be significant with two-tailed tests). For models where the President's discretion is subject to chamber constraints, the main coefficient is sometimes correctly signed with statistical insignificance and sometimes wrongly signed (if statistically significant with two-tailed tests). Furthermore, the BIC scores of the models under these two discretion direction assumptions (i.e., the first 12 models in

---

[25] We take advantage of our theoretical results to guide our empirical investigation by requiring that the sign of the coefficient be consistent with our theoretical expectation. Even if we adopt a barefoot empiricist perspective and do not consider such expectations in ascertaining which model(s) best fit the data, our empirical conclusions largely hold.

[26] Specifically, the BIC is −2*log-likelihood + (number of parameters)*ln(number of observations) (see equation 23 in Raftery 1995). An alternative to the BIC is the Akaike Information Criterion (AIC), but whether we adopt the BIC or AIC is immaterial because the only difference between the two in assessing model fit is how they account for the number of independent variables, and all of our estimates are based on the same number of independent variables.

[27] First-term is virtually always correctly signed and significant.

TABLE 5.3 *Alternative models and the production of significant executive orders (negative binomial estimates with significance threshold equaling −1)*

Model		Constant	First-term	Expected incentives for unilateralism	2* log-likelihood	BIC
No additional constraints on discretion	Preference	6.27***(0.43)	0.06(0.11)	−2.38(0.68)	−267.9	281.2
	Negative agenda-setting	6.38***(0.37)	0.05(0.10)	−2.35(0.53)	−263.6	276.9
	Imperfect party discipline	5.80***(0.35)	0.07(0.11)	−1.60(0.53)	−270.8	284.1
	Negative agenda-setting and imperfect party discipline	5.82***(0.35)	0.08(0.11)	−1.56(0.50)	270.4	283.7
	Positive agenda-setting	5.46***(0.21)	0.04(0.11)	−1.01(0.29)	−268.3	281.6
	Positive agenda-setting and imperfect party discipline	5.36***(0.21)	0.07(0.11)	−0.90(0.30)	−270.7	284.0
Discretion constrained by chamber median	Preference	4.68***(0.50)	0.16(0.13)	0.24(1.19)	−278.4	291.7
	Negative agenda-setting	5.70***(0.48)	0.15(0.12)	−2.02(1.04)	−274.9	288.2
	Imperfect party discipline	4.37***(0.32)	0.12(0.13)	1.01(0.80)	−277.1	290.4
	Negative agenda-setting and imperfect party discipline	4.53***(0.33)	0.13(0.13)	0.57(0.77)	−278.0	291.3
	Positive agenda-setting	5.01***(0.16)	0.12(0.12)	−0.55(0.35)	−275.9	289.2
	Positive agenda-setting and imperfect party discipline	4.91***(0.18)	0.15(0.13)	−0.35(0.43)	−277.8	291.1
Discretion constrained by party median	Preference	4.44***(0.11)	0.12(0.11)	0.97***(0.30)	−269.1	282.4
	Negative agenda-setting	4.36***(0.12)	0.12(0.10)	1.06***(0.28)	−266.6	279.9
	Imperfect party discipline	4.41***(0.11)	0.12(0.11)	1.06***(0.30)	−268.0	281.3
	Negative agenda-setting and imperfect party discipline	4.36***(0.12)	0.11(0.10)	1.13***(0.30)	−266.1	279.4
	Positive agenda-setting	4.11***(0.20)	0.21**(0.11)	1.75***(0.51)	−268.8	282.1
	Positive agenda-setting and imperfect party discipline	4.19***(0.18)	0.15*(0.11)	1.66***(0.50)	−269.3	282.6

Note: $N = 28$. One-tailed tests are used for first-term and expected incentives for unilateralism and standard errors are in parentheses. *** $p < .01$, ** $.01 < p < .05$, * $.05 < p < .10$

TABLE 5.4 *Alternative models and the production of significant executive orders (negative binomial estimates with significance threshold equaling 2)*

	Model	Constant	First-term	Expected incentives for unilateral action	2* log-likelihood	BIC
No additional constraints on discretion	Preference	0.60 (1.55)	0.86** (0.39)	-0.39 (2.44)	-99.6	112.9
	Negative agenda-setting	-0.40 (1.47)	0.93*** (0.38)	1.10 (2.09)	-99.3	112.6
	Imperfect party discipline	-0.75 (1.21)	0.98*** (0.37)	1.69 (1.81)	-98.7	112.0
	Negative agenda-setting and imperfect party discipline	-1.01 (1.23)	0.99*** (0.37)	1.99 (1.76)	-98.4	111.7
	Positive agenda-setting	0.47 (0.80)	0.85** (0.40)	-0.16 (1.10)	-99.6	112.9
	Positive agenda-setting and imperfect party discipline	0.10 (0.79)	0.91*** (0.39)	0.38 (1.12)	-99.5	112.8
Discretion constrained by chamber median	Preference	0.64 (1.52)	0.88*** (0.37)	-0.68 (3.65)	-99.6	112.9
	Negative agenda-setting	-0.53 (1.61)	0.88*** (0.37)	1.91 (3.43)	-99.4	112.7
	Imperfect party discipline	-1.25 (1.14)	0.68** (0.38)	3.97* (2.74)	-97.5	110.8
	Negative agenda-setting and imperfect party discipline	-1.68* (1.18)	0.64** (0.36)	4.68** (2.64)	-96.6	109.9
	Positive agenda-setting	0.62 (0.55)	0.83** (0.38)	-0.61 (1.17)	-99.4	112.7
	Positive agenda-setting and imperfect party discipline	0.48 (0.59)	0.87*** (0.37)	-0.33 (1.42)	-99.6	112.9
Discretion constrained by party median	Preference	0.36 (0.42)	0.88*** (0.37)	-0.01 (1.09)	-99.6	112.9
	Negative agenda-setting	0.23 (0.47)	0.86** (0.37)	0.33 (1.09)	-99.5	112.8
	Imperfect party discipline	0.17 (0.44)	0.85** (0.37)	0.56 (1.13)	-99.4	112.7
	Negative agenda-setting and imperfect party discipline	0.07 (0.47)	0.84** (0.37)	0.79 (1.13)	-99.1	112.4
	Positive agenda-setting	0.53 (0.70)	0.86** (0.37)	-0.48 (1.80)	-99.6	112.9
	Positive agenda-setting and imperfect party discipline	0.12 (0.65)	0.87*** (0.37)	0.68 (1.77)	-99.5	112.8

Note: $N = 28$. One-tailed tests are used for first-term and expected incentives for unilateralism and standard errors are in parentheses. *** $p < .01$, ** $.01 < p < .05$, * $.05 < p < .10$

TABLE 5.5 *Alternative models, significant executive orders, and model fit (negative binomial estimates with increasing significance thresholds [T])*

Competing models/threshold		-1	-0.75	-0.5	-0.25	0	0.25	0.5	0.75	1	1.25	1.5	1.75	2
No additional constraints on discretion	Preference													
	Negative agenda-setting													
	Imperfect party discipline													
	Negative agenda-setting and imperfect party discipline													
	Positive agenda-setting													
	Positive agenda-setting and imperfect party discipline													
Discretion constrained by chamber median	Preference													
	Negative agenda-setting													
	Imperfect party discipline													
	Negative agenda-setting and imperfect party discipline												■	
	Positive agenda-setting													
	Positive agenda-setting and imperfect party discipline													
Discretion constrained by party median	Preference		■	■	■	■	■	■	■					
	Negative agenda-setting	■	■	■	■	■	■	■	■		■	■		
	Imperfect party discipline	■	■	■	■	■	■	■	■		■			
	Negative agenda-setting and imperfect party discipline	■	■	■	■	■	■	■	■		■			
	Positive agenda-setting	■									■			
	Positive agenda-setting and imperfect party discipline	■									■			

Note: Darkened cells indicate that the coefficient of the expected incentives for unilateral action in the model of the same row is statistically significant (95 percent significance level, one-tailed test), with expected sign. For each threshold, the darker the cell, the lower the Bayesian Information Criterion (BIC), and the better the model fit.

Table 5.3) are much higher than those for any models that assume the majority party median as a constraint. While the main coefficient for these models is always significant with the expected sign, the BIC scores for the models with negative agenda-setting, or with negative agenda-setting and imperfect party discipline, are weakly better than the other four models under the third discretion assumption. Therefore, overall, when we treat all EOs as significant, models assuming that discretion is directionally conditioned by the party median in the unilateral action stage and that there is either negative agenda-setting or negative agenda-setting and imperfect party discipline in the legislative stage do the best among the 18 competitors.[28]

As Table 5.5 indicates, increasing the threshold up until 1 produces a similar pattern with respect to model comparison. The primary difference is that a model assuming that discretion is directionally conditioned by the party median and that majority party medians exercise negative agenda-setting in the legislative stage weakly, positively or strongly dominates the rest of the models. For instance, with a threshold of -0.5, BIC comparisons indicate that such models are either weakly or strongly better fitted than the other models under the same discretion assumption. In general, models where the party median functions as a directional constraint on discretion in the unilateral action stage and where there is party-controlled negative agenda-setting in the legislative stage outperform other alternatives. Admittedly, they tend to do only slightly better than models with the same discretion constraint, but where it is assumed that only preferences matter,[29] there is imperfect discipline or there is negative agenda-setting and imperfect discipline, especially with increasing thresholds.[30]

Patterns of results start changing when the adopted threshold exceeds 1. With significance thresholds of 1.25 or 1.5, while models assuming either no directional discretion constraint in the unilateral action stage or that the chamber median acts as a directional constraint continue to be dominated by models assuming the majority party constrains discretion's direction, the preference-based model with this directional constraint no longer receives support, as its expected incentive variable's coefficient is not statistically significant. However, whether a legislative stage with negative agenda-setting, positive agenda-setting or imperfect party discipline gains the most support remains unclear.

This shift in which models better fit the data is borne out even more strongly when higher thresholds are adopted. When the significance threshold is set at 1.75 and 2, as shown in Table 5.4, the model where the chamber median is a directional constraint on discretion and where there is negative agenda-setting and imperfect party discipline outperforms the rest (both in terms of the main

---

[28] For a standard deviation increase from the mean of expected incentives, holding the other independent variables at their means, the President's expected mean EO issuance increases 19 percent.

[29] This directional discretion constraint assumption is not quite compatible with the only-preference assumption in the legislative stage, but for the sake of consistency we include it in our empirical analysis.

[30] Notice that the model where majority party medians act as a directional discretion constraint and exercise positive agenda-setting with or without discipline does as well as the best model, when the threshold is between 1 and 1.5. This is the only occasion where positive agenda-setting becomes prominent among party roles.

independent variable's coefficient significance tests and lower BIC scores),[31] trailed by the model with the same discretion assumption but assuming only imperfect discipline. By contrast, results when the party median is assumed to function as a directional discretion constraint are weaker, as the expected incentive coefficient is never significant and sometimes wrongly signed and BIC scores are higher. However, since the chamber median serving as the discretion constraint is not a chamber median with primitive preferences, but rather has majority party-induced preferences, finding that the chamber median is key is not tantamount to parties not constraining directional uses of discretion.

Overall, three key features stand out from our comparison of the 18 models across significance thresholds. First, changes in results are generally continuous: there are not large discontinuities in our findings that depend on which significance threshold is employed. Second, negative agenda-setting consistently plays a prominent role in influencing legislative outcomes and, therefore, shaping the President's anticipation of how his or her unilateral action, if any, will be countered in the legislature. Third, consistent with the intuition that parties should invest more political capital on high-stakes EOs, imperfect party discipline becomes more salient with increasing thresholds, i.e., the President must anticipate the parties being able to mobilize the rank and file when more important issues are under consideration.

In short, when we set the significance thresholds to be low or moderate, models where the party median functions as a directional discretion constraint in the unilateral action stage and where majority parties act as negative agenda-setters in the legislative stage best fit the data, although these models fit only weakly better than those with the same discretion direction assumption and where either negative agenda power, imperfect party discipline or no party role is assumed. Conversely, models assuming no directional discretion constraint always do worse (i.e., wrongly signed coefficients and higher BIC scores), while, for the same party roles, models where party medians are the directional discretion constraint tend to do better than those where the chamber median fulfills this role. When we set the significance threshold bar very high, the winning model is the one for which the party-induced chamber median functions as a directional constraint and there is negative agenda-setting and imperfect party discipline.

Our sensitivity analysis (results available from authors) where the standard deviation of the status quo distribution is 0.2, 0.3, 0.4 or 0.5 and the discretion upper bound is 0.1, 0.2, 0.3, 0.4 or 0.5 (i.e., there are 20 possible combinations) robustly uncovers the same the patterns with varying significance thresholds, especially with respect to which model ranks first. Interestingly, the difference in BIC scores between the two best-fitting models becomes larger with higher standard deviations or discretion upper bounds. In particular, with greater standard deviations, the model where the party median directionally constrains

---

[31] In this model, an increase in expected incentives from its mean to a standard deviation above it, while holding the other independent variable at its mean, leads to a 34 percent increase in the expected number of EOs issued.

discretion and negative agenda control significantly exists outperforms the rest of the models, especially for lower significance thresholds.[32]

DISCUSSION

By comparing each model with both a null alternative and myriad competing models, we produce a fuller picture of what roles parties play, and how discretion functions, with respect to unilateral action. Our results are striking, suggesting that parties are important in definable ways, discretion is directionally constrained and Presidents typically are more constrained than some think in exercising their will. All of this has considerable implications for presidential power, although some of the results might prove surprising.

Consider whether political parties play a role in the actions of the institutionalized presidency, at least with respect to the President's unilateral action. The upshot of our results is that majority parties play some role, especially when exercising negative agenda power, in the President's issuing of EOs, regardless of the thresholds adopted to distinguish significant from insignificant EOs, and they appear to influence the President's crucial EOs through negative agenda-setting and dealing with the rank and file via the ability to exercise party discipline. This is in line with the qualitative finding that the President often consults with party leaders and that these discussions do have real consequences (although, admittedly, this consultation might also apply to directional constraints that have bite in the unilateral stage as well as party roles in the legislative stage). As Figure 5.3 illustrates, some party roles (i.e., negative agenda-setting and imperfect party discipline) tend to strengthen gridlock incentives for unilateral action by expanding the gridlock interval.

Moreover, from the President's perspective or calculation, our results are consistent with the courts tending to act as if they are interpreting the majority party median as the will of the enacting coalition in judging whether the President uses discretion acceptably.[33] For highly significant EOs, our findings are in line with courts deferring more to the chamber median induced by parties (or, alternatively, with majority parties influencing presidential discretion). There is no evidence consistent with the courts simply interpreting discretion as having no directional constraints.

Conversely, our findings demonstrate that models without directional constraints on discretion are robustly rejected. This implies that presidential

---

[32] As in Chapter 4, although they are not derived from our theoretical analysis, we include two alternative variables to test the robustness of our analysis: presidential approval (again measured by average value by Congress, using Gallup data) and the so-called misery index (using inflation and unemployment levels). In both instances (findings available from authors), our main results regarding our primary independent variables (i.e., expected incentives and first-term) and the comparison of our competing models remain very similar.

[33] We emphasize that our results are only consistent and are not definitive proof; indeed, the relationship between Congress and the courts is generally recognized as amorphous and not particularly well understood (e.g., Bailey, Maltzman and Shipan 2012).

unilateral action is not tantamount to unilateral influence, confirming our findings in Chapter 4. The President can move the status quo only in the directions that bolster the interests of the majority median or the chamber median induced by parties. In other words, an inference that presidential unilateral action is a realization of the chief executive flexing his or her muscles is misleading; rather, our analysis implies that presidential action is tacitly guided or approved by Congress.

Note that our empirical results differ qualitatively from those produced in previous efforts. For example, while divided government is probably the most important independent variable examined in Mayer (2002), Howell (2003, 2005) and our analysis in Chapter 4, it fails to gain empirical support as a predictor of highly significant EOs.[34] By contrast, the models from our more-encompassing framework where the induced chamber median constrains the President's discretion in the unilateral action stage and the majority party influences legislation through negative agenda and party discipline can explain the variance of the number of highly significant EOs issued in each Congress. Put differently, we not only show that parties do seem to matter; we also capture the nuanced roles that they play in influencing presidential unilateral action.

As such, our empirical results actually demonstrate that, while parties reduce presidential power in the unilateral action stage, presidential influence is somewhat *larger* than we would infer if we did not account for partisan roles at the legislative stage. As discussed in the theoretical section, negative agenda-setting or imperfect party discipline generally augments presidential influence, while positive agenda-setting only does so under divided government. It might appear ironic that the President gains influence when parties become more active in Congress by exercising negative agenda-setting or by disciplining their members in ways that seem to help solve the collective action problems within parties that would seemingly constitute a legislative weakness in inter-branch bargaining. However, this seeming contradiction is easily resolved once one realizes that greater partisan cohesiveness or discipline and lesser collective action problems within parties actually makes Congress more fragmented, allowing the President to adjust policies somewhat closer to his or her ideal. Overcoming collective action problems as a means of reducing presidential power à la Moe and Howell would require the rather unlikely situation where Congress would act like a single actor, analogous to the way we conceptualize the chief executive.

Put differently, in conjunction with our results in Chapters 2 and 4, our analysis provides a much fuller picture of when the claims of scholars such as Moe and Howell, that collective action problems will undermine the legislature's influence to the President's advantage by weakening the former's

---

[34] We are specifically referring to EOs whose significance thresholds are higher than 1.5, as shown in Chapter 4.

ability to respond, actually hold.[35] While, if the legislature can function as a unitary actor, the President will be weakened, the strengthened party discipline that many find so attractive – which tends to have similar effects to negative agenda-setting – may both weaken *and* strengthen presidential power through different mechanisms. In Chapters 2 and 4 we found that the majority party's overcoming of collective action problems so that it can constrain how the President can directionally use discretion to move policy, as modeled in the unilateral action stage, can reduce the chief executive's ability to shift the status quo and reduce his or her power relative to what it would be otherwise. Conversely, when we build party roles into the legislative stage of our model, we find that the analogous ability to overcome intra-party collective action problems actually expands legislative gridlock and triggers more opportunities for the President to unilaterally act and be powerful. We should emphasize that this effect is less than that from parties in the unilateral action stage, so that our results from our analysis in this chapter should be seen as mitigating, but not eliminating, the overall ability of party collective action to reduce presidential authority and power.

To this we should add the one further caveat that the effect of a party's role in the legislature on presidential power depends upon the Senate majority's size relative to the filibuster rule. Increasing discipline will monotonically result in larger gridlock only if the Senate lacks a filibuster-proof majority (Chiou and Rothenberg 2009), at which point the effect will reverse, as increasing party discipline shrinks the EGI and undercuts what the President can accomplish through unilateral action. It also follows that strengthening filibuster rules (i.e., requiring a larger number of Senators for invocation of cloture and to bring a stuck proposal to the floor) will increase the chief executive's ability to shift policy closer to his or her ideal point through unilateral action (or, conversely, current efforts to relax filibuster rules will weaken the chief executive). All in all, these results indicate that institutional changes can have ramifications for presidential influence via unilateralism that are not typically recognized.

In summary, putting all these observations together, our empirical results demonstrate that presidential influence is somewhat larger than we would infer if we were to ignore partisan roles in the legislative stage and focus instead on the impact of parties in the unilateral action stage. As we discussed in the theoretical section, negative agenda-setting and imperfect party discipline generally augment presidential influence, while positive agenda-setting only does so under divided government. It might appear ironic that the President gains influence when parties become more active in Congress by exercising negative agenda control and disciplining their members in ways that seemingly help solve those collective

---

[35] Remember that Moe and Howell focus on collective action of the legislature as a whole, while party scholars concentrate on the ability of subgroups in each chamber, in the form of parties, to overcome collective inertia.

action problems that others have highlighted as reasons for legislative weakness in inter-branch bargaining. However, this seeming contradiction is easily resolved once one realizes that greater partisan cohesiveness or discipline and lesser collective action problems, while limiting the directional use of discretion to the President's disadvantage, actually make Congress more fragmented, allowing the President to adjust policies somewhat closer to his or her ideal.

CONCLUSION: PARTIES AND POWER

In our earlier analysis we followed the lead of modern presidential scholars, who have increasingly viewed the chief executive as an institutional actor. We did so because this research program has produced considerable insights into the role of the President in the policy process but could, nonetheless, be improved upon, theoretically and empirically, to shed light on issues of presidential power and the relationship between governmental branches. Hence, we linked theory and data by offering competing alternative models whose predictions could be directly compared with the relevant data to draw inferences about power. In doing so, we suggested that, with a variety of nuances, the President is not typically able to employ unilateral action as a means of exercising presidential power.

As part of this process, we examined whether parties impacted the exercise of discretion in what we have termed the unilateral action stage. We refrained from incorporating the myriad possible partisan roles that parties might play in the so-called legislative stage.

Now we have gone a step further afield by taking another logical step, integrating the potentially key roles of political parties. These roles have received far less attention than they likely should have, given the importance attributed to parties in other contemporary institutional research, although even such analyses have tended not to unpack the various means by which parties can impact outcomes. While bringing parties into the study of unilateral action and power in this way has involved a trade-off between a more-encompassing framework, theoretically, and a need to make some restrictive assumptions with respect to the distribution of status quos and to adopt a less intuitive and more cumbersome empirical analysis, the additional insights and the greater confidence we can have in some of our earlier inferences make it worthwhile.

Thus, in this chapter our encompassing framework allows us to generate a large series of competing, and empirically comparable, unilateral action models. In doing so, we integrate both party roles and alternative conceptualizations of direction constraints on presidential discretion.

Theoretically, our framework demonstrates how the systematic integration of myriad party roles, and building-in the interplay between such roles and assumptions regarding discretion, can produce competing predictions about when the President can successfully use gridlock and the ability to preempt as tools to garner influence. This framework, in turn, provides the foundation for estimating which model in our framework corresponds best with the observed data for EOs.

Empirically, and with the advantage of being able to compare our models directly, we find evidence that negative agenda-setting and party influence over members, particularly for more important concerns, both appear to be at work. In certain circumstances, this may actually suggest some increase in presidential influence beyond what our initial analysis in Chapter 4 suggests, although nothing along the lines of presidential imperialism or even leading to the conclusion that, on net, parties increase presidential power. We also uncover support for a judicial interpretation of acceptable presidential discretion that is not captured by a pivotal-politics-type approach.

Overall, our results provide additional evidence that the imagery of any unilateral action representing some raw form of presidential power needs to be tempered. Furthermore, we see that a key force behind the bargaining that we have suggested takes place between the chief executive and the legislature stems from the efforts of those controlling political parties. Certainly, our results indicate that parties are likely a key force in overcoming collective action problems. However, while this ability to overcome collective action has been suggested as essential for the legislature to check the chief executive's capacity for unilateral action, we make clear that partisan impacts can work at cross-purposes when contrasting limits on discretion's use with the ability of parties to control agendas or discipline members.

Also, we again demonstrate that results are sensitive to how we measure what the President is actually doing. While revealing the importance of negative agenda-setting, invariant of how we define significant EOs, our findings are somewhat conditioned by where we set our threshold level for separating significant, policy-relevant acts from other behaviors. This lesson is probably not unique to the analysis of executive orders or of unilateral action, and almost certainly can be helpful for understanding a variety of other phenomena in different contexts.

Finally, speaking to the larger issue of how we systematically examine the role of parties in presidential studies, our framework provides a good starting point for investigating whether and how various partisan roles in Congress may shape presidential incentives. As we have seen, for example, our analysis has important implications for how the role of parties might differ depending on the significance of the item under consideration and how changes in rules (e.g., the filibuster) might have different implications for policy outputs. Hence, we can improve the general understanding of the bargaining relationship between Congress and the President in various contexts by going beyond dichotomous characterization of parties in Congress (e.g., divided government or majority status), incorporating the role of parties into internal decision-making in the legislature and analyzing how it impacts the manner in which the President behaves strategically.

6

The Subtleties of Power: Assessing the Two Presidencies

INTRODUCTION: DELVING DEEPER INTO THE ANALYSIS
OF POWER

Recall that, in Chapter 1, we began by contrasting two different scenarios. In 1992, George H. W. Bush issued EO 12807, stipulating that the Coast Guard repatriate Haitian refugees picked up on the high seas. Despite opposition from Congress, the EO stood. In 1997, Bill Clinton held off on an EO stipulating the need for union-backed project labor agreements in return for allowing his nominee for Labor Department Secretary to receive a Senate vote.

In our previous two chapters, we conducted a variety of analyses, drawing a number of inferences designed to make sense of this seeming discrepancy, and to make the exercise of presidential power transparent rather than enigmatic. In Chapter 4 we found, after generally discovering that presidential power is mitigated (presumably due to the existence of extra-statutory legislative constraints), that there are considerable differences between which model (if any) best fits the data depending upon policy types. Hence, the relationship between unilateral action and power may be contingent upon policy area. Roughly speaking, we discovered relatively strong support for the partisan-compliance model for some issues (e.g., government operations and defense) and for the unilateralism model for others (i.e., international affairs and foreign aid), with sometimes no support for any of the three competing models (i.e., international trade). However, such distinctions were not as clear-cut as we might like, and our means of differentiating between policies could be critiqued as somewhat arbitrary. In Chapter 5, we expanded our theoretical and empirical investigations to the analysis of multifaceted partisan roles and discovered that, indeed, features such as agenda-setting and partisan influence of members actually seem to be quite germane. This indicates that understanding presidential power also means incorporating parties in more detail, despite the need to make some additional assumptions and the obvious loss of parsimony.

These two observations – that policy distinctions seem relevant but were not as clear as we might think that they might be (although there appears to be a difference roughly related to domestic versus foreign affairs) and that party roles matter for unilateral action production and presidential power – lead us naturally to the long-standing conjecture that has occupied presidential scholars of their being *two presidencies*, based on policy type.[1] As Wildavsky (1966) famously put it, these two presidencies comprise a powerful, autonomous foreign policy President and a weaker, more constrained domestic version. However, as we will discuss, this conjecture, while studied a great deal over the years, has neither been investigated with the kind of theoretical foundation that we have utilized in our analysis nor with parties integrated in a manner comparable to how we have done (principally focusing only on the difference between divided and unified governments). Doing so will not only shed light on whether there are, indeed, two presidencies, but will also provide additional insights into whether the chief executive is more free to use unilateral action to exercise power rather than to bargain more conventionally, for some issues compared to others.

This is exactly what we will now do.[2] We employ our competing theories (those found in both Chapters 2 and 5), our empirical measurement approach to significant actions developed in Chapter 3 and our means of estimating models utilized in Chapters 4 and 5 to examine the two presidencies empirically. In doing so, we show that, indeed, distinguishing between what subsets of EO data our models fit provides evidence both for the two presidencies and for the assertion that presidents enjoy greater influence and power over foreign policy. Building-in parties demonstrates that this inference continues to hold – although the ability to explain foreign EOs continues to be somewhat less strong than we might hope and reaffirms the inference from Chapter 5 that party roles in the legislative as well as the unilateral action stage are germane.

The reminder of this chapter proceeds in four stages. First, we review the past literature on the two-presidencies conjecture. We then reexamine the three models that we laid out theoretically in Chapter 2 and analyzed empirically in Chapter 4, in the context of the two presidencies. Before concluding, we integrate parties in a manner analogous to our approach in Chapter 5, studying whether parties have different roles in domestic and foreign policy areas as a means of making further sense of the two presidencies and its implications for presidential power.

---

[1] We employ the term "conjecture" here because there is not a theory with deductive components, whether informal or formal, in the manner that we offered in Chapters 2 and 5.

[2] One limitation of employing EOs to study the two presidencies is that some presidential directives, such as National Security Directives (also known as Presidential Decision Directives, which are issued with the advice and consent of the National Security Council, and only some of which are public), are not included here but exclusively cover foreign policy.

THE TWO PRESIDENCIES: RESEARCH TO DATE

Despite the prominence of Wildavsky's (1966) initial arguments, the two-presidencies conjecture is not a settled issue. One possible reason is that a connection between formal theoretical analysis and empirical work comparable to what we have conducted thus far is lacking. Theoretically, we have maintained throughout our analysis that a foundation for assessing the actual process of how presidents might be able to transform their institutional actions into policy that they prefer (and that others may not) is fundamental. The closest is Canes-Wrone, Howell and Lewis (2008) who, in elaborating on Wildavsky (1966), sketched an impressive verbal depiction of why presidents may influence foreign policy more than its domestic analog, focusing on legislators' having weaker electoral incentives and greater informational asymmetries vis-à-vis the President, and on the chief executive more commonly possessing a need and ability to move first (e.g., the President's need to move was much more urgent in our foreign policy motivating example than in its domestic counterpart), which forces the legislature to act or to accept the President's action. However, while providing more foundation for the two presidencies than its predecessors, this approach does not quite satisfy our needs for clearly distinguishable hypotheses. As Bond et al. (1991) pointed out earlier, while they are helpful and intuitive in motivating empirical work, such claims principally highlight different characteristics of domestic and foreign policies rather than precisely specifying how these differences generate the kinds of outcomes associated with the conjecture.

Regardless, the plethora of empirical work on the two-presidencies conjecture has generated no accepted empirical wisdom on the subject. We have often had difficulties in interpreting results and mixed evidence for the two-presidencies conjecture. As such, we cannot link the relationship between power on the one hand and the two-presidencies distinction on the other.

Existing empirical research is distinguishable in a number of respects. Most notable are differences in the actions studied. Earlier investigations largely centered on roll calls as well as, to a lesser extent, related considerations of presidential success in passing their prioritized legislative proposals. Most such research produced little evidence for the two presidencies or only uncovered support during certain periods (e.g., Sigelman 1979, Edwards 1986, Cohen 1992; but see Sullivan 1991) or for Republican presidents (Fleisher and Bond 1988, Fleisher et al. 2000; see also Zeidenstein 1981).[3] But after dissatisfaction with initial roll call analyses (e.g., Lindsay and Steger 1993), subsequent empirical efforts concentrated more directly on whether presidents are either getting policy or institutional outcomes closer to what they prefer with respect

---

[3] However, results from recent analyses by students of international relations (e.g., Milner and Tingley 2010, Marshall and Prins 2011) are more in the spirit of the two-presidencies conjecture.

to foreign policy issues. Choices studied included budget allocations relative to presidential requests (Canes-Wrone, Howell and Lewis 2008; for a related study, see Howell and Jackman 2013), the amount of discretion delegated to presidents and their bureaucratic allies (Canes-Wrone, Howell and Lewis 2008; for an earlier analysis, see Epstein and O'Hallaron 1999) and the issuance of EOs by presidents (Marshall and Pacelle 2005; see also Rudalevige 2002).

In this later stream of research, there are more results considered to suggest evidence for the two-presidencies conjecture, although these findings are often conditioned by whether there is divided government. For example, both in their analysis of agency appropriations and of agency creation, Canes-Wrone, Howell and Lewis (2008) uncovered significant evidence for the two-presidencies claims, but these results may not hold for unified government.[4] Additionally, Marshall and Pacelle (2005) claimed to discover evidence for the two-presidencies conjecture for the number of EOs produced – analyzing the universe of EOs without distinguishing whether actions were significant or not – and found that the effects of the resources possessed by a President and his or her political environment vary between foreign and domestic issues (note, however, that uncovering differential results is not equivalent to the two-presidencies claim that presidents are more free to act with respect to foreign policy). Also, interestingly, they reported negative effects for divided governments on foreign policy, contradicting the so-called evasion hypothesis (that EOs are employed when evading a fragmented Congress is possible), but no effects for domestic policy.

Overall, these works indicate that, particularly when we move away from roll call analyses, there are some differences between foreign and domestic issues. However, returning to the need to integrate theory and data, these results are best considered as suggestive, particularly for assessing presidential power. For example, analysis of appropriations requires that we model presidents' decisions for budgetary requests and their relationship with final passage; examining discretion demands that we account for the consequences of different means of allocating discretion and that we model bargaining between Congress and the President; and investigating EO production involves modeling precisely how such promulgations can translate into presidential power. Also, and consistent with our discussion in Chapter 5, while divided government has been incorporated, the multiplicity of partisan roles in the legislative stage has received short shrift; i.e., besides being the most common partisan variable used to predict presidential action, divided government is the main such variable employed to assess the two presidencies (e.g., Zeidenstein 1981, Fleisher and Bond 1988, Canes-Wrone, Howell and Lewis 2011).

Thus, it would seem that the apparatus we have constructed for analyzing unilateral action is ready-made for investigating the two presidencies in a new

---

[4] These findings about divided government were not explicitly stated, but can be inferred from the reported results.

and innovative manner. Conversely, results from investigating the two presidencies can shed additional insights on our core issue of whether, or when, unilateral action strongly buttresses presidential power or seems akin to bargaining between two competing branches, with the judiciary in the background.

THE TWO PRESIDENCIES: THEORETICAL AND EMPIRICAL ANALYSIS

As before, we start with theory, move to measurement and then advance to estimation. In many instances, we are brief, as we are recapping previous chapters' discussions. As mentioned in our introductory comments, we begin with the three models laid out in Chapter 2, leaving the introduction of parties à la Chapter 5 for the next section.

Theory[5]

Recall that Chapter 2 offers three coherent, competing models, each with an identical structure. The President, given the first-mover advantage, decides whether to issue an EO changing the status quo, anticipating legislative reactions and a potential judicial ruling. Then a legislative pivotal politics game, where Congress can reverse or revise presidential action through legislation (subject to a presidential veto and a possible override) or do nothing, takes place. Finally, a judicial stage, in which the court decides whether the President's action is within his or her level of discretion, occurs. The three competing models are distinguished exclusively by different discretion assumptions in the presidential unilateral action stage: in the unilateralism model, the President can move the status quo to the left or right; in the chamber-compliance model, the status quo can only be shifted in a direction consistent with the chamber median's ideal point; and in the partisan-compliance model, the status quo can exclusively be moved in the direction of the majority party medians.

These competing models imply different levels of presidential power, produce different expectations for the amount of presidential unilateral action and have distinct hypotheses, the latter two of which we recap in Figure 6.1 and Table 6.1, respectively. Recall that each model differs in predictions except for the common expectation that a new President whose party affiliation differs from his or her predecessor's will have more incentives to act unilaterally (the new incumbent will be more dissatisfied with status quos than a President from the same party): the first-term

---

[5] The reader may elect to skip this discussion of Chapter 2's models and move directly to the empirical discussion.

TABLE 6.1 *Summary of hypotheses for the unilateralism, chamber-compliance and partisan-compliance models*

	Unilateralism model	Chamber-compliance model	Partisan-compliance model
First-term	+	+	+
Filibuster-tail EGI	+	+	
Override-tail EGI	+		
Divided government			+

Notes: EGI indicates equilibrium gridlock interval; "+" indicates positive effects on unilateral action. Filibuster-tail EGI is the interval between the filibuster pivot and the midpoint of the two chamber medians; override-tail EGI is that between the override pivot and the midpoint.

hypothesis. While each EGI tail (to reiterate, the EGI is the equilibrium gridlock interval, constituting the set of status quos that a majority in the legislative process prefers to the existing policy but fails to alter in equilibrium) has positive impacts on unilateral action in the unilateralism model, only the tail for the filibuster pivot matters in the chamber-constraint model. Finally, divided government has a negative effect only for the partisan-compliance model.

As detailed in Chapter 2, in the unilateralism model the President is quite powerful, as he or she can circumvent legislative constraints and overstep congressional wills. By contrast, because the President can impact policy outcomes through unilateral action only with tacit congressional approval, given the possible application of extra-statutory means, the chief executive often fails to act unilaterally in the chamber-compliance model, and especially in the partisan-compliance model (particularly with divided government). As derived in Chapter 2, presidential influence or power is highest in the unilateralism model, trailed by the chamber- and partisan-compliance models, sequentially. Thus, if foreign EOs fit better with a model associated with more power than do domestic EOs, we would have initial evidence for the two presidencies. Otherwise, such support would be lacking.

As such, a feature distinguishing our analysis from previous studies is the stronger, more-deductive theoretical foundation regarding what domestic and foreign policy should look like if the President has greater or lesser discretion in unilateral movement of status quos. In particular, if foreign EO production is more consistent with the unilateralism model and domestic EO production corresponds more with the with partisan-compliance model, we can claim strong evidence for there being two presidencies. The starker this difference, the stronger the evidence for two presidencies.

(a) Unilateralism model

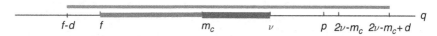

(b) Chamber-compliance model

(c) Partisan-compliance model (unified government)

(d) Partisan-compliance model (divided government)

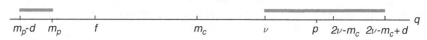

▬▬▬▬ Status quos where the president will take unilateral action

▬▬▬▬ The EGI filibuster-tail that affects presidential incentives for unilateral action

▬▬▬▬ The EGI override-tail that affects presidential incentives for unilateral action

FIGURE 6.1 Presidential unilateral action under three competing models.
Note: f, v, p, m_c, m_p, q and d denote the ideal points of the filibuster and override pivots, the President, the medians of the chamber and the majority party, the status quo and the level of discretion, respectively. The EGI denotes the equilibrium gridlock interval, which is bounded by the filibuster and override pivots.

Measurement

For assessing presidential influence or power in domestic and foreign policy areas, our dependent variable is the number of EOs on domestic and foreign affairs, respectively, issued over a two-year congressional session (spanning 1947–2002). This requires that we couple the measure of an EO's significance (developed in Chapter 3) with a measure distinguishing domestic from foreign actions. To accomplish the latter, we take two approaches, giving the first measure the most attention.

First, we employ the PAP (the Policy Agenda Project), which specifically differentiates between foreign and domestic EOs.[6] The PAP marks an EO as foreign if it has no domestic content, and as domestic otherwise. This code differs qualitatively from the related PAP measures for policy topics employed in Chapter 4. Specifically, most PAP-coded foreign EOs come from the policy topic labeled "international affairs and foreign aid" (61 percent from 1947 to 2002), but some fall under foreign trade (24 percent) and still others under defense (note that other issues under these latter topics, e.g., veteran affairs, are coded as domestic policy).[7]

Second, since EOs on foreign trade usually impact domestic interests, we narrow the PAP's set of foreign EOs by excluding those that deal with foreign trade.[8] Two examples of the kinds of actions we have in mind are EO 11052, issued by President Kennedy to assign the President's Cabinet Textile Advisory Committee new responsibilities for supervising the administration of cotton textiles, and EO 11651 from President Nixon, covering a textile trade agreement. Each of these presidential actions is coded as a foreign EO with our first measure, but both are closely related to domestic industries. While we will largely focus on the first measure, we will report our empirical results for this alternative coding for foreign EOs as well.

Figure 6.2 presents our significance estimates for our 3512 EOs, employing our first measure (there are 2911 domestic EOs and 601 foreign). Both policy types are characterized by similar distributions, although foreign EOs exhibit a higher peak for low significance EOs and a lower tail that is slightly less dense.

Also using this first measure, Figures 6.3 and 6.4 display the number of significant EOs per Congress for domestic policy and foreign policy, respectively. The pattern for domestic policy is quite similar to the overall pattern for EOs (recall Figure 3.4), where the peaks are centered on Truman's last two years and the first two years of Kennedy, Carter and Clinton. This is not surprising, given that domestic EOs make up 82.9 percent of the universe of EOs. The pattern for foreign policy looks quite different from the others in that the peak concentrates

---

[6] Note that, while we obtained the PAP data and codebook in 2008, subsequent EO data post-2004 is not coded an EO as domestic or foreign.

[7] This coding for domestic policy is much broader than Lapinski's (2008) categorization analyzed in Chapter 4. Recall that Lapinski defined four policy categories: (1) sovereignty, (2) organization and scope, (3) international relations and (4) domestic affairs. Lapinski's international relations grouping essentially encapsulates three PAP policy areas that we analyzed in Chapter 4 – defense, international affairs and foreign aid, and foreign trade. We believe that the PAP's coding for foreign EOs is more suitable for our purpose of assessing the two presidencies, as many defense EOs, such as those involving veterans' welfare and weapons production, as well as international trade, have substantial domestic impacts.

[8] The PAP tends to code to an EO involving trade as foreign if the germane trade concern does not target a specific country.

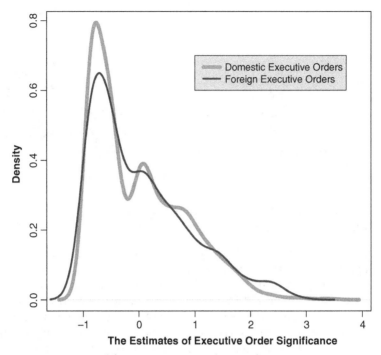

FIGURE 6.2 Domestic and foreign executive order significance

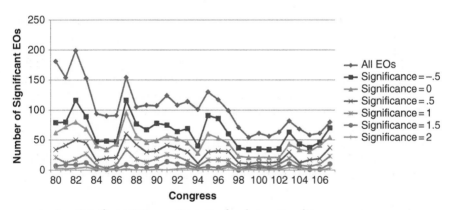

FIGURE 6.3 Significant EOs per Congress for domestic policy.
Note: Each curve corresponds to a threshold for determining a significant executive order.

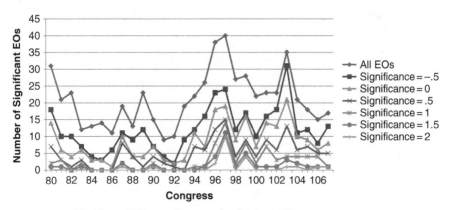

FIGURE 6.4 Significant EOs per Congress for foreign policy.
Note: Each curve corresponds to a threshold for determining a significant executive order.

on Carter's last two years and Reagan's first two years (which was the period of the Iran hostage crisis) and on Clinton's first two years.[10]

As in Chapter 4, we include independent variables suggested by each competing model (again, see Table 6.1).[9] Our dummy variable for first-term (scored one if a new President's party is different from his or her predecessor's in the first two years of his or her first term and zero otherwise) is incorporated in all models. For the unilateral and chamber median models, the length of the EGI filibuster- and override-tails, measured with common space scores (Poole 1998) to determine relevant ideal points, are included; for the partisan-compliance model, divided government, measured by a dummy variable, is specified.

Results

Analogous to Chapter 4, we estimate our models for foreign and domestic EOs with negative binomial regressions. While we estimate our analysis for a whole distribution of threshold significance scores, the results are once more roughly continuous and, hence, are presented at intervals of 0.5 on the significance scale, up to scores of 2.[11]

Table 6.2 presents our results comparing the unilateralism and the chamber-compliance specifications. The findings are striking. The unilateralism model does very poorly in explaining domestic EOs, regardless of significance thresholds, but

[9] Again, including other variables such as presidential popularity and the misery index (or war for foreign EOs; see Lewis, 2008) does not notably impact our results.

[10] The Iran hostage crisis refers to a 444-day period from 1979 through 1981 during which 52 American diplomats and citizens were held hostage. Presidents Carter and Reagan took considerable administrative actions in response to the crisis and in its aftermath.

[11] As we only have 41 domestic and 22 foreign EOs from 1947 through 2003 whose significance scores are higher than 2, we do not go beyond this threshold (as we will see, we do go up to 2.5 in examining foreign EOs, given the nature of our findings).

TABLE 6.2 *Determinants of number of significant executive orders (unilateralism and chamber-compliance models)*

(a) Domestic executive orders

	Expected sign	T = −1	T = −.5	T = 0	T = .5	T = 1.0	T = 1.5	T = 2.0
First-term	+	0.038	0.226*	0.255*	0.339**	0.576***	0.668***	0.979**
		(0.117)	(0.126)	(0.145)	(0.167)	(0.177)	(0.193)	(0.403)
Filibuster-tail EGI	+	−1.048	−0.174	0.389	1.324	0.917	1.613	−1.180
		(0.988)	(1.061)	(1.245)	(1.447)	(1.528)	(1.621)	(3.413)
Override-tail EGI	+	−3.313***	−2.574***	−2.261***	−2.824***	−2.554**	−2.533*	−1.636
		(0.662)	(0.716)	(0.816)	(0.974)	(1.077)	(1.308)	(2.597)
Constant		5.458***	4.642***	4.183***	3.628***	2.875***	1.815***	0.527
		(0.222)	(0.239)	(0.277)	(0.322)	(0.343)	(0.388)	(0.785)
Log-likelihood		−129.891	−118.507	−113.910	−102.887	−86.722	−66.409	−43.079

(b) Foreign executive orders

	Expected sign	T = −1	T = −.5	T = 0	T = .5	T = 1.0	T = 1.5	T = 2.0
First-term	+	0.126	0.443**	0.522**	0.941***	0.890*	1.440***	1.893**
		(0.157)	(0.224)	(0.264)	(0.335)	(0.497)	(0.525)	(0.864)
Filibuster-tail EGI	+	−3.100**	−3.816**	−5.435**	−7.833**	−12.671**	−10.812**	−10.578
		(1.35)	(1.902)	(2.324)	(3.088)	(5.431)	(5.462)	(8.293)
Override-tail EGI	+	−0.488	0.317	0.958	2.378†	3.834†	2.834	3.922
		(0.886)	(1.236)	(1.435)	(1.792)	(2.728)	(3.186)	(5.586)
Constant		3.527***	2.789***	2.486***	1.804***	1.388†	0.530	−0.571
		(0.309)	(0.426)	(0.505)	(0.633)	(1.069)	(1.141)	(1.83)
Log-likelihood		−93.952	−86.787	−80.006	−69.427	−55.010	−40.472	−28.841

Notes: $N = 28$. Negative binomial regression coefficients with standard errors in parentheses. T indicates the significance threshold for determining a significant EO. Likelihood ratio tests for each regression that alpha equals zero all strongly suggest the existence of overdispersion. Two-tailed tests are conducted for all parameters. $***p$-value $< .01$ $**.01 < p$-value $< .05$ $*.05 < p$-value $< .1$ †$.1 < p$-value $< .2$

gains some empirical support for foreign orders with moderate significance thresholds. In Table 6.2(a) we see that, for domestic EOs, the model's three hypotheses are never supported (i.e., when the coefficients are statistically significant, their signs are contradictory to theoretical expectations), except for first-term with very high significance thresholds. Conversely, results for foreign EOs are better, as seen in Table 6.2(b). While the first-term hypothesis gains strong empirical support, that for the EGI override tail is marginally supported only when the significance thresholds are set between 0.2 and 1.[12] Hence, overall, the unilateralism model seems to apply for foreign EOs for some significance thresholds, but does poorly for domestic actions for all thresholds.

By contrast, the chamber-compliance model does not explain EO production for domestic and foreign policies well. The variable for the EGI's filibuster tail, which is the key variable for the model, is not always statistically significant and is wrongly signed when it is. Since the EGI's override tail is key for distinguishing between the unilateralism and chamber-compliance models, these results indicate that the unilateralism model explains foreign EOs better than the chamber-compliance model. However, neither model explains the variance of domestic EOs well.

Results for the partisan-compliance model provide a much greater contrast – they are good for domestic actions and poor for foreign actions (Table 6.3). Recall that the main variables in testing the partisan-compliance model are first-term and divided government. The domestic EO results (Table 6.3[a]) indicate that divided government's coefficient is always statistically significant and correctly signed (except for extremely high significance thresholds),[13] while first-term is significant with almost all significance thresholds. Divided government decreases the expected number of EOs by around 40 percent for significance thresholds lower than 1.5 and by roughly 20 percent for higher thresholds. By contrast, Table 6.3(b)'s findings for foreign EOs indicate that first-term is statistically significant and correctly signed only for highly significant foreign EOs, while divided government is usually insignificant and is wrongly signed.

For our alternative coding of foreign versus domestic actions, while the findings for domestic EOs are essentially unchanged, there is stronger support regarding foreign actions (results available from the authors).[14] Specifically, in contrast to the result for the EGI override tail shown in Table 6.2(b), the

---

[12] For presentational consistency, we employ two-tailed tests. However, as our theory predicts a clear sign, we should employ one-tailed tests for this variable, which would suggest a *p*-value between 0.05 and 0.1 when the significance thresholds are set to be 0.5 or 1 (see Table 6.2).

[13] As mentioned several times, the model suggests interaction terms between unified government and the EGI override-tail and the EGI filibuster-tail. Divided government's coefficient is insignificant with inclusion of these terms, but joint tests show strong evidence of multicollinearity.

[14] In other words, foreign EOs mainly include all of the PAP's international affairs and foreign aid EOs and some of its defense EOs.

TABLE 6.3 *Determinants of number of significant domestic executive orders (partisan-compliance model)*

(a) Domestic executive orders

	Expected sign	T = −1	T = −.5	T = 0	T = .5	T = 1.0	T = 1.5	T = 2.0
First-term	+	0.083	0.227**	0.259**	0.386**	0.623***	0.752***	1.034***
		(0.133)	(0.103)	(0.128)	(0.149)	(0.171)	(0.204)	(0.397)
Divided govt.	−	−0.387***	−0.501***	−0.460***	−0.538***	−0.401**	−0.306†	−0.053
		(0.120)	(0.094)	(0.116)	(0.136)	(0.161)	(0.200)	(0.397)
Constant		4.842***	4.368***	4.028***	3.518***	2.690***	1.670**	0.038
		(0.106)	(0.082)	(0.102)	(0.118)	(0.141)	(0.177)	(0.371)
Alpha		0.079	0.039	0.063	0.083	0.092	0.074	0.243
		(0.023)	(0.015)	(0.023)	(0.033)	(0.047)	(0.077)	(0.323)
Log-likelihood		−134.199	−113.850	−111.229	−101.018	−86.848	−67.684	−43.324

(b) Foreign executive orders

	Expected sign	T = −1	T = −.5	T = 0	T = .5	T = 1.0	T = 1.5	T = 2.0
First-term	+	0.072	0.289	0.320	0.556†	0.417	1.093**	1.440*
		(0.167)	(0.231)	(0.280)	(0.365)	(0.528)	(0.501)	(0.811)
Divided govt.	−	−0.093	−0.133	0.053	0.020	0.334	0.283	0.558
		(0.151)	(0.212)	(0.258)	(0.340)	(0.493)	(0.505)	(0.849)
Constant		3.085***	2.483***	2.017***	1.441***	.628†	−0.251	−1.233†
		(0.134)	(0.189)	(0.233)	(0.307)	(0.440)	(0.467)	(0.761)
Alpha		0.091	0.186	0.272	0.488	1.099	0.732	2.419
		(0.037)	(0.074)	(0.105)	(0.212)	(0.463)	(0.413)	(1.510)
Log-likelihood		−96.203	−88.691	−83.174	−73.840	−59.404	−43.268	−29.840

Notes: $N = 28$. Negative binomial regression coefficients with standard errors in parentheses. T indicates the significance threshold for determining a significant EO. Likelihood ratio tests for each regression that alpha equals zero all strongly suggest the existence of overdispersion. Two-tailed tests are conducted for all parameters. *** p-value < .01 ** .01 < p-value < .05 * .05 < p-value < .1 † .1 < p-value < .2

166 The Subtleties of Power: Assessing the Two Presidencies

coefficient is correctly signed and statistically significant for more important foreign EOs (when thresholds are set to 1 or 1.25).

Regardless, overall the unilateralism model explains foreign EOs better than the two alternatives. By contrast, the partisan-compliance model is quite suitable for explaining domestic EOs.

Returning to presidential power, this juxtaposition between what subsets of EO data the unilateralism and the partisan-compliance models fit provides considerable evidence for two presidencies. Presidents enjoy great influence and power over foreign policy, as is evidenced by the support for the unilateralism model, where the President has the ultimate directional latitude for discretion. Conversely, presidents are substantially undercut in domestic policy, as reflected by how well the partisan-compliance model, where the direction of discretion is conditioned by the majority party, corresponds to the data. These results are consistent with a world where legislators, and particularly those in the majority party, have opportunities and incentives to act collectively and wield extra-statutory means to influence the President for domestic affairs, but not for foreign policies.

LEGISLATIVE PARTIES AND THE TWO PRESIDENCIES

Analogous to our analyses in previous chapters, having established evidence for the two presidencies when we examine the possibility that political parties play a role in constraining the directional use of discretion in the unilateral action stage, we turn to the more complicated world where parties may play various roles in the legislative stage that can, in turn, shape presidential calculations regarding unilateral action decisions. We do so by, essentially, transporting Chapter 5's framework, where we build party roles into the legislative action stage of our model, to the study of the two presidencies. This allows us to see whether parties play qualitatively different roles in each policy domain and to assess the degree to which differences are seemingly a function of partisan efforts.

As we have discussed elsewhere, most of our attention in contrasting the unilateralism, chamber-compliance and partisan-compliance models with respect to the two presidencies focuses on the unilateral action stage's assumption about specifically how the President can shift policy via discretion. We nevertheless went beyond previous analyses of the two presidencies (which have principally focused on divided government) in considering what parties can do, by examining whether majority parties can directionally constrain the use of presidential discretion. However, Chapter 5 showed that, while considerably more complicated to examine, parties also matter for the production of all EOs in ways not captured by the kind of analysis that we just conducted. As such, we wish to integrate additional partisan roles in the legislative process, as they are potentially key for fully distinguishing between foreign and domestic actions and assessing the two presidencies.

Thus, we integrate legislative parties into our examination of the two presidencies. In doing so, we examine how presidential power is conditioned by whether policy is domestic or foreign in a manner corresponding to the analysis in Chapter 5.

Theory[15]

Recall that there are three principal roles ascribed to parties in the legislative parties literature: (1) negative agenda control, where parties are gatekeepers and can block a bill that would be preferred to the status quo at the floor stage; (2) positive agenda-setting, by which the majority party can control what goes to a floor vote; and (3) party discipline, by which members may tend to vote according to their party's wishes rather than their own personal preferences. This results in six possible combinations of party roles in the legislative politics subgame: (1) pure preference, (2) negative agenda-setting, (3) imperfect party discipline, (4) negative agenda-setting and imperfect party discipline, (5) positive agenda-setting and (6) positive agenda-setting and imperfect party discipline.[16]

Therefore, while our initial analysis focused mostly on directional constraints on how the President can employ discretion, the chief executive's incentives for unilateral action in this world may come from the amount of discretion, gridlock and a desire to preempt. As the latter two are shaped by the EGI and the agenda-setter's location relative to the boundaries of EGI, they may be impacted by various partisan roles (as illustrated by Chapter 5's Figure 5.3).

Figure 6.5 briefly illustrates the impacts of various party roles in the legislative stage on unilateral action under the unilateralism model, where the President is able to exercise his or her discretion without any directional constraints. Figures 6.5(b) and (c) demonstrate that negative agenda-setting or party discipline expands the EGI, triggering more gridlock incentives for unilateral action. The effects of positive agenda-setting hinge on whether government is unified or divided. Under divided government, per Figure 6.5(d), positive agenda-setting not only generates more gridlock incentives but also substantially boosts preemption incentives. While not shown in Figure 6.5, positive agenda-setting under unified government largely eliminates preemption incentives.[17] These results show how party roles in the legislative stage can structure presidential decisions about unilateral action.

---

[15] Again, the reader for whom this is familiar may wish to skip to the empirical analysis.

[16] Remember that our positive agenda-setting role also incorporates negative agenda-setting under the conditions specified in Chapter 5.

[17] Rather, this is found in Figure 5.3, as part of Chapter 5's detailed analysis of the effects of party roles under the alternative discretion constraint assumptions.

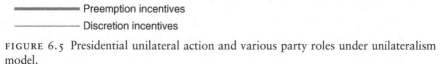

(a) Pure-preference equilibrium gridlock interval

(b) Equilibrium gridlock interval with negative agenda-setting

(c) Equilibrium gridlock interval with party-induced preferences

(d) Equilibrium gridlock interval with positive agenda-setting

━ ━ ━ ━ Status quos where *P* will take unilateral action
▬▬▬▬▬ Gridlock incentives (also equilibrium gridlock interval)
▬▬▬▬▬ Preemption incentives
───────── Discretion incentives

FIGURE 6.5 Presidential unilateral action and various party roles under unilateralism model.
Note: *f, v, p, m$_c$, m$_p$, q* and *d* denote the ideal points of the filibuster and override pivots, the President, the medians of the chamber and the majority party, the status quo and the level of discretion, respectively. *f′* and *v′* are party-induced preferences of *f* and *v*. The three types of incentives compose presidential incentives for unilateral action.

As discussed in Chapter 5, the six partisan alternatives in the legislative political subgame, combined with the three alternative assumptions from the unilateral action stage about the direction in which the President can exercise discretion to alter the status quo, yield 18 competing models, 6 each associated with unilateralism, chamber-compliance, and partisan-compliance. Every model has different empirical predictions, making comparative model testing possible.

Measurement

In comparing how each model performs empirically, we follow Chapter 5 by applying a predictor analogous to the gridlock interval, expected incentives for unilateral action, for the number of foreign and domestic EOs issued in a Congress, for all of the competing models.[18] To reiterate, this measure captures presidential incentives for unilateral action, weighing presidential decisions with regard to status quos located more within the EGI. We can then compare our prediction to the actual number of EOs produced in the two policy areas to see which model does best.

Once more, we incorporate a variable for first-term. This is, of course, based on the idea that new presidents from a different party will have more to change.

Results

We again employ negative binomial regression to estimate our models. We present results for all domestic EOs in our data in Table 6.5, with a summary for alternative significance thresholds in Table 6.4 showing essential patterns of interest. Tables 6.6 and 6.7 provide analogous findings for foreign EOs.[19] Models are again compared, both by looking at the signs and the significance of coefficients and by using the BIC (Bayesian Information Criterion, with lower scores constituting better fits; Raftery 1995).

Five important findings emerge from our analysis. First, even with the addition of these different party roles, the results in the last section – that the unilateralism model is better for foreign EOs (although it does not do a particularly wonderful job for certain significance thresholds) and that the

---

[18] As mentioned in Chapter 5, technically expected incentives are obtained by integrating the occurrence of presidential action over distributions of status quo and discretion. We do so while assuming that status quos are normally distributed with the chamber median of the previous Congress as the mean and various standard deviation values (such that at least a majority of status quos locate within the EGI). Also, discretion is uniformly distributed between zero and a reasonable level. While for results presented in the present analysis the average EGI size is 0.37, the standard deviation of the status quo distribution equals 0.4, and the upper bound of discretion is 0.3, sensitivity analysis shows that our findings are quite robust.

Also, as discussed earlier, empirically we measure party discipline using Snyder and Groseclose's (2000) measure, with the induced preferences of members and pivots calculated employing Volden and Bergman's (2006) approach.

[19] Note that Table 6.6 is somewhat different than the similar tables that we have employed containing empirical results. First, we employ significance thresholds up to 2.5. Second, while we show significance level of 90 percent for one-tailed tests, we also include those for 80 percent here. We make these changes because they are helpful for indicating which models best explain foreign EOs.

TABLE 6.4 *Domestic executive orders: Alternative models, significant executive orders, and model fit (negative binomial estimates with increasing significance thresholds [T])*

Competing models/threshold	-1	-0.75	-0.5	-0.25	0	0.25	0.5	0.75	1	1.25	1.5	1.75	2
No additional constraints on discretion — Preference													
Negative agenda-setting													
Imperfect party discipline													
Negative agenda-setting and imperfect party discipline													
Positive agenda-setting													
Positive agenda-setting and imperfect party discipline													
Discretion constrained by chamber median — Preference													
Negative agenda-setting													
Imperfect party discipline													
Negative agenda-setting and imperfect party discipline													
Positive agenda-setting													
Positive agenda-setting and imperfect party discipline													
Discretion constrained by party median — Preference													
Negative agenda-setting													
Imperfect party discipline													
Negative agenda-setting and imperfect party discipline													
Positive agenda-setting													
Positive agenda-setting and imperfect party discipline													

Notes: Darkened cells indicate that the coefficient of the expected incentives for unilateral action in the model of the same row is statistically significant (95 percent significance level, one-tailed test), with expected sign. For each threshold, the darker the cell, the lower the Bayesian Information Criterion (BIC), and the better the model fit.

partisan-compliance model is superior for domestic EOs – are confirmed, as seen when we contrast Table 6.4 with Table 6.6. This, again, implies that presidents enjoy more power in their foreign policy activities than in their domestic policy actions. Note that, similar to our results in the last section when we examined our initial three models, when we adopt our alternative definition of foreign EOs (i.e., excluding foreign trade EOs from this category), empirical support for the unilateralism model is stronger.

Second, party roles in the legislative subgame differ for domestic and foreign EOs. For domestic EOs, negative agenda-setting in the legislative process is crucial for how Congress responds to presidential unilateral action – and, hence, for shaping how the President's anticipation of how any unilateral action will be responded to in the legislature – when lower or moderate significance thresholds are adopted (Table 6.4). Taking the lowest threshold as an example, as seen in Table 6.5, we find that the main predictor for all of the partisan-compliance models and the chamber-compliance models with positive agenda-setting is correctly signed with statistical significance. However, the partisan-compliance model with negative agenda-setting has the lowest BIC scores, suggesting a better fit. As such, this model is the proverbial winner among the 18 competing models. When higher thresholds are adopted so that we examine only more-significant EOs, the partisan-compliance model with positive agenda-setting and imperfect party discipline does best, as is also seen in Table 6.4. The latter result again suggests that parties mobilize when the issue is deemed important to the party and its members.

Conversely, when the significance threshold is set low (i.e., below 0.5), none of the 18 competing models can explain foreign EOs (Table 6.6). For thresholds at or above 0.5, the unilateralism model with negative agenda-setting performs the best among the competing models, as its main predictor at least has the correct sign while the other models tend to have the wrong sign (and it receives the most support among the models examined).[20] When the significance threshold is 1.25, as seen in Table 6.7, the unilateralism model with negative agenda-setting gains stronger empirical support (the p-value for a one-tailed test is 0.08), while the other models' main predictor is wrongly signed or insignificant.[21] When we move the threshold to 2.5, the same model gains marginal support (the p-value for a one-tailed test is 0.05), while the others receive none.

Similar to our results in the last section, when we adopt the alternative definition of foreign EOs (i.e., by excluding foreign trade from this category), the empirical support for the unilateralism model with negative agenda-setting (which is, again, the winner among the 18 competing models) is stronger. When we set the significance threshold higher than 1, the main predictor is correctly signed and the p-value for the one-tailed test is within 0.15.

---

[20] For the unilateralism model with majority parties engaging in negative agenda-setting, when the significance threshold is higher than 0.25, the coefficient of the main predictor is correctly signed, with a p-value for a one-tailed test ranging from 0.07 to 0.4. The other models' main predictors tend to be wrongly signed, with p-values for one-tailed tests much higher than that for the unilateralism model with negative agenda-setting.

[21] Only the predictor of the unilateralism models with different party roles is correctly signed.

TABLE 6.5 *Determinants of domestic executive orders (negative binomial estimates with significance threshold equaling −1)*

Model		Constant	First-term	Expected incentives for unilateralism	2*log-likelihood	BIC
No additional constraints on discretion	Preference	6.291***	0.071	−2.729***	−267.744	281.072
	Negative agenda-setting	6.416***	0.073	−2.696**	−264.777	278.105
	Imperfect party discipline	5.835***	0.079	−1.956**	−269.643	282.971
	Negative agenda-setting and imperfect party discipline	5.815***	0.082	−1.827**	−269.952	283.28
	Positive agenda-setting	5.289***	0.066	−1.034**	−270.176	283.504
	Positive agenda-setting and imperfect party discipline	5.213***	0.096	−0.957*	−271.486	284.814
Discretion constrained by chamber median	Preference	4.205***	0.183	0.909	−277.111	290.439
	Negative agenda-setting	5.553***	0.173	−2.110‡	−274.600	287.928
	Imperfect party discipline	4.024***	0.133	1.394	−275.642	288.97
	Negative agenda-setting and imperfect party discipline	4.340***	0.160	0.575	−277.152	290.48
	Positive agenda-setting	3.276***	0.136	3.179**	−269.760	283.088
	Positive agenda-setting and imperfect party discipline	3.890***	0.101	1.829*	−273.520	286.848
Discretion constrained by party median	Preference	4.203***	0.144	1.107**	−269.081	282.409
	Negative agenda-setting	4.108***	0.128	1.224***	−266.270	279.598
	Imperfect party discipline	4.178***	0.136	1.179**	−268.600	281.928
	Negative agenda-setting and imperfect party discipline	4.106***	0.123	1.277***	−266.562	279.89
	Positive agenda-setting	3.648***	0.257*	2.449***	−263.994	277.322
	Positive agenda-setting and imperfect party discipline	3.794***	0.174	2.247***	−266.020	279.348

Notes: N = 28. T indicates the significance threshold for determining a significant EO. Likelihood ratio tests for each regression that alpha equals zero all strongly suggest the existence of overdispersion. Two-tailed tests are conducted for all parameters. ***p-value < .001 **.001 < p-value < .01 *.01 < p-value < .05 ‡.05 < p-value < .1 †.1 < p-value < .2

TABLE 6.6 *Alternative models, significant foreign executive orders, and model fit (negative binomial estimates with increasing significance thresholds [T])*

Competing models/threshold		-1	-0.75	-0.5	-0.25	0	0.25	0.5	0.75	1	1.25	1.5	1.75	2	2.25	2.5
No additional constraints on discretion	Preference															
	Negative agenda-setting										■		□	▨		■
	Imperfect party discipline															
	Negative agenda-setting and imperfect party discipline															
	Positive agenda-setting															
	Positive agenda-setting and imperfect party discipline															
Discretion constrained by chamber median	Preference															
	Negative agenda-setting															
	Imperfect party discipline															
	Negative agenda-setting and imperfect party discipline															
	Positive agenda-setting															
	Positive agenda-setting and imperfect party discipline															
Discretion constrained by party median	Preference															
	Negative agenda-setting															
	Imperfect party discipline															
	Negative agenda-setting and imperfect party discipline															
	Positive agenda-setting															
	Positive agenda-setting and imperfect party discipline															

Notes: Darkened cells indicate that the coefficient of the expected incentives for unilateral action in the model of the same row is with expected theoretical sign and statistically significant (■ indicating 90 percent significance level, one-tailed test; ▨ indicating 85 percent significance level, one-tailed test; □ indicating 80 percent significance level, one-tailed test). Only darkened cells are empirically supported with corresponding *p*-values.

TABLE 6.7 *Determinants of foreign executive orders (negative binomial estimates with significance threshold equaling 1.25)*

Model		Constant	First-term	Expected incentives for unilateralism	2*log-likelihood	BIC
No additional constraints on discretion	Preference	0.785	0.547	-0.339	-107.928	121.256
	Negative agenda-setting	-2.395	0.812†	4.212†	-106.063	119.391
	Imperfect party discipline	0.017	0.643	0.837	-107.840	121.168
	Negative agenda-setting and imperfect party discipline	-0.647	0.674	1.764	-107.483	120.811
	Positive agenda-setting	0.143	0.647	0.603	-107.793	121.121
	Positive agenda-setting and imperfect party discipline	0.221	0.621	0.514	-107.837	121.165
Discretion constrained by chamber median	Preference	6.175***	0.472	-13.893**	-98.830	112.158
	Negative agenda-setting	2.601	0.623	-4.485	-107.360	120.688
	Imperfect party discipline	2.729*	0.918‡	-5.691‡	-104.835	118.163
	Negative agenda-setting and imperfect party discipline	2.320‡	0.903‡	-4.314†	-106.233	119.561
	Positive agenda-setting	3.062‡	0.796†	-6.348†	-105.789	119.117
	Positive agenda-setting and imperfect party discipline	1.539	0.754†	-2.681	-107.217	120.545
Discretion constrained by party median	Preference	1.255*	0.570	-2.223†	-105.423	118.751
	Negative agenda-setting	1.337*	0.618	-2.191†	-105.639	118.967
	Imperfect party discipline	1.274*	0.589	-2.286†	-105.309	118.637
	Negative agenda-setting and imperfect party discipline	1.338*	0.627	-2.288†	-105.495	118.823
	Positive agenda-setting	2.822***	0.282	-6.504**	-99.147	112.475
	Positive agenda-setting and imperfect party discipline	2.315**	0.530	-5.520*	-101.235	114.563

Notes: N = 28. T indicates the significance threshold for determining a significant EO. Likelihood ratio tests for each regression that alpha equals zero all strongly suggest the existence of overdispersion. Two-tailed tests are conducted for all parameters. ***p-value < .001 **.001 < p-value < .01 *.01 < p-value < .05 ‡ .05 < p-value < .1 † .1 < p-value < .2

Third, incorporating partisan roles in the legislative process improves our ability to predict foreign and domestic EOs compared to the relatively party-less analysis in the previous section, and this underscores the importance of separating the two types of policies. As the previous discussion implies, in explaining more-significant domestic EOs we find that positive agenda-setting and party discipline are more relevant in the partisan-compliance model than negative agenda-setting, the role that parties are assumed to have in Chapter 2's partisan-compliance model. Because of this, the partisan-compliance model with positive agenda-setting and party discipline can still explain domestic EOs with significance scores that exceed 2 (Table 6.4), whereas the partisan-compliance model in Table 6.3 cannot. The unilateralism model with negative agenda-setting explains significant foreign EOs relatively well and performs better than with no party or other partisan roles.

Fourth, once we empirically distinguish domestic and foreign policy and the seemingly fundamentally different structures that characterize them, our results differ somewhat from Chapter 5's empirical analysis of pooled EOs. While these earlier findings indicate that negative agenda-setting is consistently more relevant in explaining all EOs, regardless of significance threshold, positive agenda-setting is more important in explaining domestic EOs for higher-significance thresholds, perhaps because negative agenda-setting is relevant for more-significant foreign EOs. Thus, adding the roughly 17 percent of foreign policy EOs into an analysis undermines the drawing of proper inferences about how parties affect presidential incentives for issuing domestic EOs.

Finally, while we find that evidence for the two presidencies is robust even after controlling for various party roles, our results confirm that the combination of fragmented congressional preferences and party roles impacts presidential incentives for unilateral action, presidential power and the extent to which there are two presidencies. In particular, to some extent, a majority party exercising negative agenda-setting in the legislative stage undercuts congressional responses to unilateral action addressing foreign affairs (i.e., in the unilateralism model), providing the chief executive with additional strategic opportunities. On the other hand, under the partisan-compliance model, a majority party's positive agenda-setting strengthens presidential incentives to some degree with divided government and reduces them with unified government, leaving presidential unilateral action incentives in domestic policy largely unchanged. In total, these effects from fragmentation and party activities further deepen the presidential power gap between foreign and domestic policies.

DISCUSSION AND CONCLUSIONS

We started our analysis in this chapter by recognizing both that we had found in Chapter 4 that policy distinctions seem relevant and that we had documented in Chapter 5 that party roles and extra-statutory mechanisms appear to matter for unilateral action production and presidential power. This directed our attention to the long-standing conjecture that there are two presidencies – a powerful foreign policy President and a constrained one for domestic affairs. Previous studies assessing the two presidencies tend to be without deductive theoretical guidance about how, precisely, domestic and foreign policies should differ empirically, and our theoretical approach provides an excellent opportunity to more rigorously examine the conjecture. Thus, we employed our theoretical, measurement and empirical apparatus to shed light on the two presidencies and to investigate whether focusing on the foreign/domestic distinction is a means of further clarifying the enigma of presidential power, as highlighted by the two motivating examples that we recounted in our introductory remarks.

Our analysis has largely accomplished these goals. Per the two-presidencies conjecture, analyzing unilateral actions using our approach suggests that presidents not only act differently depending on policy type, but that they are more constrained and less powerful in domestic issues than in foreign policy. In the first part of our analysis, we produce evidence that a unilateralism model consistent with a strong, powerful foreign affairs President, and a partisan-compliance model associated with a weaker, more limited domestic policy chief best fit the data. We also uncover markedly different effects for key factors, notably for divided government, which are routinely included in analyses, depending on whether foreign or domestic issues are being considered. When we incorporate a multitude of party effects at the legislative stage into the mix, we discover additional distinctions (although, once again, the explanation for foreign EOs could be better). For domestic issues, negative agenda-setting in the legislative process is crucial for Congress in responding to presidential unilateral action when lower or moderate significance thresholds are adopted, while the partisan-compliance model with positive agenda-setting and imperfect party discipline does best when only higher-significance actions are being considered.[22] When foreign EOs are analyzed, there does seem to be a partisan effect through negative agenda-setting, although – consistent with what we might expect when we consider the incentives of legislators, the time-sensitive nature of foreign affairs issues and the potential importance to politicians of having a nation not appearing to be divided on foreign affairs considerations – parties seem to play less of a role, overall.

Taken jointly, our analysis also indicates that we might want to exercise caution in pooling all EOs. Particularly given that foreign EOs constitute less than 20 percent of EOs, their distinctive features might easily be missed and incorrect inferences drawn about domestic EOs if all EOs were pooled.

---

[22] Recall that negative agenda-setting and imperfect party discipline do generally somewhat *augment* presidential influence, while positive agenda-setting only does so under divided government. Hence, we cannot say in this situation whether the chief executive is better off with lower or higher salience EOs.

As for solving the enigma of power, our final analysis buttresses our previous results. Overall, on significant domestic issues the President seems to have to bargain, given the ability of the legislature to brandish extra-statutory tools, and the legislature appears able to significantly overcome obstacles to collective action through the organization of political parties (specifically, a majority party). Foreign policy appears to represent a different kettle of fish and, overall, for intuitive reasons, the chief executive may be better positioned to flex his or her muscles and be less concerned with constraints from legislators and their partisan organizations.

7

Conclusions: Solving the Enigma of Presidential Power

We commenced our analysis with what we characterized as the seeming enigma of presidential power: there appear to be instances where the chief executive can brandish unilateral action as a weapon; conversely, there are other times where the President comes across as extremely sensitive to the preferences of those in the majority in Congress and the legislative parties to which they belong. We pointed to various instances that jointly epitomized the enigma. We discussed George H. W. Bush acting without much regard to legislative considerations with respect to Haiti, juxtaposed against Bill Clinton's backing down to congressional pressures despite the urgings of his organized labor allies. In one instance, the chief executive appeared quite powerful – by either of the definitions that we proffered – and in the other he seemed extremely weak-kneed.

In delving further into the enigma of power, we reviewed circumstances where party leaders in Congress seemed to be key as compared to those where the chief executive came across as being more sensitive to the chamber median – each with different implications for how much power the President possessed – and emphasized that such leaders not only engage in direct bargaining with the executive branch but appear to control or impact many extra-statutory features, such as the legislative agenda, Senate-approval of appointments, agency budgets and legislative riders. The effectiveness of these extra-statutory considerations would appear to be crucial for the legislature, placing significant breaks on the presidential use of any discretion contrary to congressional or partisan wishes. Related impacts could include whether a unilateral action such as an EO is issued at all, exactly where a policy is changed to in an ideological space as a result of a presidential action and the direction in which presidential discretion is employed. In addition, we investigated how the exercise of executive power might be conditioned, typically intuitively, both by the significance of the actions that are being considered and by the policy area.

We believe that, when taken *in toto*, our theoretical and empirical analyses by and large solve the enigma of presidential power in a manner heretofore not recognized by social scientists. Simply put, claims of the imperial presidency are misguided and incorrect, and need to be replaced by a more nuanced appreciation of how the institutions of government and politics interact. This includes integrating the potential impacts of Congress's extra-statutory mechanisms and the multiplicity of roles that political parties might take on in the legislative process.

For most significant issues, the relationship between the chief executive and the legislature and its parties is roughly akin to how we conceptualize the fashion by which the chief executive deals with Congress more generally: there is a back-and-forth between the President and the legislature – often led by the majority party interests – that involves strategic bargaining and interactions. The Congress and its legislative parties do not typically sit with their hands tied merely because they lack the ability to directly override a unilateral presidential action, and the chief executive does not anticipate that such lethargy will be the case, should he or she act. In contrast to previous claims, the legislature is often able to substantially overcome the collective action problems that it confronts, many times, seemingly, with the help of organized political parties, to wield a variety of tools at its control to make the chief executive care. The courts, despite the rarity of their need to overturn a unilateral action, may reinforce inter-branch bargains and the use of features such as party pressure from sitting legislators and agenda-setting for what does and does not get taken up on the chamber floor.

As a consequence, we see that significant unilateral actions are not necessarily, to use a phrase that we have often employed, tantamount to power. Rather, the underlying politics tends to be far less one-sided, as the separation of powers operates in a way that is considerably more balanced than the assumption that significant unilateral action is equivalent to the flexing of executive muscle would imply. This is not equivalent to asserting that the President can never exercise the kind of authority that would seem consistent with strong, Dahlian power. Not only can we pinpoint anecdotes that appear contradictory to the President being circumscribed in his or her employment of unilateral action, perhaps due to considerations not captured by our models and/or a propensity of the media to cover cases that are unusual or off the proverbial equilibrium path; we can also provide evidence that the type of issues that are considered and the way they impact legislative incentives can be key, so that some variant of our unilateral action model actually captures well what is observed. For example, the unilateralism model gains some support when foreign EOs are analyzed separately, indicating that there is more to such an exercise of Dahlian power than mere anecdote. Nonetheless, in the larger scheme, what we discover are more limits on the President's power derived from unilateral action than we might be led to believe given a perspective that focuses only on the legislature's ability to pass overriding legislation, especially in light of collective action problems, or the court's willingness to rule a presidential action out of bounds.

Our remaining discussion consists of three parts. First, we summarize the joint findings of our chapters and link them together with respect to what they imply about presidential power. We then overview the implications of our analysis for a number of issues relevant for those who care about political processes and policy outcomes, and follow by including suggestions for future research. To conclude, we offer some final thoughts about what our investigation says about how best to think normatively about the American political system.

PUTTING OUR FINDINGS TOGETHER

We began with the puzzle that we referenced above: What is the explanation for why presidents sometimes appear able to employ unilateral actions, of which executive orders are the most prominent but certainly not the sole example, to great effect, while at other times this option appears far more restricted? More specifically, in certain instances the chief executive acts as if he or she requires legislative acquiescence – even when the Congress will not be able to pass a bill that would reverse a presidential action and the courts will not throw the action out – and sometimes he or she appears not to, and still backs down in line with the wishes of the legislative and/or the partisan majorities. How can this set of observations be reconciled?

Making sense of this world, we emphasized, has become particularly important because of the seeming increasing prominence of unilateral actions in the United States today, where we live in a world of widespread government intervention in society, on the one hand, and in one of legislative gridlock and judicial acquiescence, on the other. Myriad major policies of our day, and of the last few decades, have involved the executive use of unilateral authority. Furthermore, when we surveyed how scholars reacted to the variety of unilateral tools that the chief executive can potentially wield, we saw that these analysts generally viewed presidential unilateral actions as direct reflections of presidential power (which, to reiterate, can be conceptualized as the President using unilateral actions to get what he or she wants in opposition to legislative majorities [the Dahlian view] or using these actions to change an existing status quo to one he or she prefers). From this conception, the only constraints on the President were the ability of the legislature to pass a statute overturning the chief executive's initial move or of the courts to rule the President's action to be beyond his or her delegated discretion – either of which hardly ever happens in the real world. And, to reiterate, if these were the only two obstacles that the President faces, he or she might, indeed, be far more powerful than is a textbook version of a separation of powers system would suggest.

However, we suggested that there may be other, extra-statutory constraints – something that is talked about with respect to Congress in general terms, but only rarely with reference to unilateral actions – and that the implications of these for presidential power and influence could be substantial. Situations where legislators possess incentives to exercise such constraints, whether actually realized by congressional actions or having their impact due to an understanding of the potential for such actions, could limit the one-sided nature of unilateral action and the accrual of presidential power. Indeed, we discover that such constraints go a long way in helping to explain the puzzle with which we began, suggesting that inferences that unilateral actions always equal presidential power are off base.

After laying out the fundamental unresolved issue of whether unilateral action represents a tool disrupting the institutional balance of power or is a reflection of the congressional-presidential back-and-forth (with courts looming in the background) that we see elsewhere, and carefully offering alternative definitions of power, we provided a roadmap for producing an answer to our quandary. Such an answer involved developing a new theoretical framework that would be suitable for examining the nature or extent of presidential power arising from unilateral action and employing variants of it to test data (one incorporating political parties more comprehensively than the other), specifying advanced measurement techniques and applying modern statistical analysis. Previous studies have not integrated theory, measurement and data in this way. In addition, we supplemented this theoretical and empirical approach with case studies highlighting the processes that we observe.

As a first step to accomplishing our goals, we presented three models that, in contrast to earlier work, had both directly comparable empirical predictions and different, corresponding implications for the amount of presidential power (whichever definition was adopted) that the chief executive could accrue from unilateral action. The only distinguishing aspect of these models involved the chief executive's directional use of his or her discretion. The unilateralism model assumed that discretion could be exercised in either ideological direction, while the chamber- and partisan-compliance models assumed that the direction of the President's discretion was constrained by the chamber median or the majority party median, respectively. Directional constraints on discretion, whether by the chamber or party median, would be expected if extra-statutory features were effective; otherwise they should not be relevant. Indeed, assumptions about directional use of discretion are far more important in the overall scheme than those about the amount or size of discretion, on which scholars have traditionally focused. Interestingly, which directional assumption is selected has considerable and nuanced implications for presidential power, with the unilateralism model generally implying the most and the partisan-compliance model the least.

Having laid out a clear set of competing models with associated predictions that we could employ to assess presidential power, we then spent the next two chapters addressing empirical considerations in two steps. First, motivated by the possibility that evaluation of models may be contingent on the significance of the actions under consideration, we measured EO significance and showed how it varies by type of policy. Subsequently, we tested our competing models for all EOs and for subsets, by significance and by policy area, to draw inferences about presidential power and the processes underlying it.

Regarding the first task, we demonstrated that while, in some sense, it has been common knowledge that unilateral actions differ greatly in their significance – however we conceptualize that term – in practice there has been a considerable gap between the recognition of this state of affairs and the measurement of the latent concept. Although there have been previous steps that moved in the direction of creating more informative measures (and even more progress with respect to the measurement of legislative outputs), our investigation, besides utilizing far more data than did past efforts, is the first that employs a new, rigorous statistical measurement model and generates a continuous measure of EO significance. Depending on the thresholds employed, the ultimate estimates regarding the number of significant EOs per Congress vary across time and with respect to specific types of policy. Recall, for instance, that we discovered that the patterns of how many significant EOs were issued per Congress for certain policy areas, such as for government operations, are similar to the pattern for the entire universe of EOs, in that more significant EOs were issued during the first administrations of Presidents Kennedy, Carter and Clinton. Conversely, we found qualitatively different patterns when we examined other policy areas, such as international trade. In short, measurement really does matter.

When we examined our models' competing hypotheses, we found that unilateral action and presidential power are not identical and that a variety of processes are important enough to merit recognition.[1] When we pooled all the EOs in our data set, we demonstrated that our partisan-compliance model, under which the discretion of the President is conditioned by the wishes of the leaders of the majority party in Congress, received strong support, essentially without regard to which significance thresholds we stipulated. As such, our initial inference, and one that continued to receive considerable support throughout much of our latter analysis, was that we must be quite cautious in ascribing power to presidential unilateral acts. Rather, the underlying process generating executive orders is generally more akin to separation-of-powers, bargaining with a Congress able to employ threats beyond just statutory overrides, than to a President acting with great hubris and daring others to respond – with a Congress unable to mobilize due to collective action problems or stymied by policy gridlock, and generally compliant courts – and winning the great majority of the time.

---

[1] To reiterate a point we made earlier, our inferences about power generally are not conditioned by which of the definitions of power we employ and, so, we usually just talk about power generically.

When we dug deeper to ascertain whether pooling by policy area was obscuring different political processes that vary for understandable reasons, such as by how much elected legislators care about the issues in question, we uncovered nuanced, intuitive relationships. Production of many EOs, such as those involving government operations, defense, public lands, civil rights or labor and unemployment, is consistent with the partisan-compliance model, implying weaker presidential power; however, others, such as EOs for international affairs and foreign aid, are well-explained by the unilateralism model, suggesting stronger power; and still others, notably foreign trade EOs, are inconsistent with any alternative model. These results underscore how the relationship between presidential unilateral action and power reflects differences in the varying degrees of statutory and extra-statutory influence that Congress likely possesses across policies. The more forcefully Congress can, and is incentivized to, exercise such influence, the more likely the President will have to account for legislative preferences in deciding whether and how he or she takes unilateral action. As such, our findings provide a much fuller picture than previously furnished for understanding just when the President is particularly powerful and can triumph with unilateral action despite congressional opposition. In doing so, and returning to the enigma of power, we showed why we might witness both instances, where the President sometimes seemingly oversteps congressional will and at other times appears to succumb to congressional pressure.

Through the first four chapters, we focused principally on the interplay between the chief executive, legislators and judges, and its relevance for understanding political power. In some sense, this follows past research. But in the background of our models are political parties, particularly in the partisan-compliance model, where it is stipulated that the majority party constrains the directional exercise of discretion in the unilateral action stage. This contrasts with previous works on the institutionalized presidency, which, other than acknowledging the potential importance of divided government and partisan support of presidents in the legislative arena, have generally ignored the alternative roles that parties might play and their potential effects.[2]

As the partisan-compliance model receives considerable support, one of our important findings is that majority parties play an important role in overcoming the collective action problems stressed in previous studies, such as Moe and Howell (1999a), although for subsets of legislators rather than for the entire chamber. Particularly, given that the chamber-compliance model receives little support, our results are consistent with a world where solving collective action problems is generally challenging for the chamber or its median and, in the spirit of Cox and McCubbins (2007), where majority parties exercise extra-statutory means to constrain the directional use of discretion in presidential unilateral

---

[2] To reiterate, there are studies of the importance of the President for parties in terms of voting and elections.

action. That legislative influence seems to rest with majority parties is unsurprising, as it is typically believed that extra-statutory mechanisms are principally controlled by parties and their leaders. Intriguingly, with the caveat that we will return to this issue when we discuss the results of Chapter 5, our findings indicate that solving collective action as a whole, à la Moe and Howell (1999a), is not a requirement for limiting presidential power, since a majority party's own collective action will suffice. Congress is found to be neither weak nor handicapped by collective action problems with respect to unilateral action, at least in most policy areas, and can much more substantially shape presidential unilateral action in most policy areas than previous studies would lead us to expect, and a good deal of the ability can be ascribed to the influence of majority parties.

However, we obviously did not stop by looking at partisan influence generating constraints on the direction of discretion. Rather, we then turned to the legislative arena itself. Following the lead of many of those who have studied institutions more broadly, in Chapter 5 we built in the myriad roles that political parties can take on in the Congress. We did so not just because legislative scholars have spilled a great deal of ink discussing whether and how parties matter, but also because our careful reading of the qualitative literature and of discussions of individual EOs led us to believe that such partisan influences needed to be taken quite seriously. This is particularly the case if one believes that parties can pressure members or control legislative calendars in a variety of ways that impact the agenda. While in a rarified universe, all that may matter is whether or not key pivots overturn a unilateral action, *realpolitiks* appear considerably messier and more nuanced.

Just as the actual world is more complicated than we might like, our theoretical framework was necessarily more intricate as well. Rather than laying out models with a fully specified game sequence and players, we produced a framework into which we could fit a large number of alternative models. This allowed us to incorporate situations where parties are irrelevant to the legislative process, where parties can exercise negative or positive agenda control and where parties can pressure their members to behave differently than they otherwise would. The key technical insight generated from analyzing this framework is that, to varying degrees, incorporation of different party roles at the legislative stage substantially determines the size of the gridlock interval where presidents can move policy without concerns of their actions being overturned, while alternative assumptions about presidential discretion can dramatically shape how much leverage the chief executive has with respect to unilateral action for a given gridlock interval.

Estimating these models in a straightforward way required a qualitatively new approach in which we generated a prediction in a comparable way for each of our 18 models (admittedly, at the expense of a need to make somewhat more restrictive assumptions). Implementing this, we found that, indeed, majority parties take on various roles in influencing unilateral actions and impact the

President's crucial EOs through negative agenda control and party discipline. Furthermore, we again documented that the President's discretion is more constrained than is often claimed, with either the majority party median or the party-induced chamber median, depending on an EO's significance, playing a key role. Finally, while previous theoretical models (including our own in Chapter 2) cannot explain the empirical variance of highly significant orders, the integration of parties allows us to do so.

Thus, Chapter 5 provided additional insights into how presidential power is actually conditioned and mitigated by political actors, even when neither the legislature directly overrules the chief executive nor the courts find that a unilateral action exceeds discretionary authority. Our results also built upon those in Chapter 2 in demonstrating that parties matter for unilateral behavior, and demonstrating how they do it. Intriguingly, we actually found that presidential influence is somewhat greater than we would have concluded had we *not* accounted for partisan roles at the legislative stage, since negative agenda-setting or imperfect party discipline generally heightens presidential influence, and such forces were found empirically to be rather prominent. As such, the effects of collective action by parties that reduced presidential power at the unilateral action stage were partially mitigated by countervailing impacts in the legislative stage. In addition, we established how our results may be sensitive to the significance levels of the actions being studied, demonstrating the crucial importance of measuring the importance of an action.

Finally, we concluded by applying our theoretical, measurement and empirical approaches to the long-standing conjecture that there are two presidencies, both to add clarity to this debate and to further delve into the enigma of presidential power. Corresponding to the idea of two presidencies, we found that presidents not only behave differently depending on the type of policy being considered, but that they are more constrained and less powerful when the issue is domestic. A model associated with strong presidential power (the unilateralism model) better explains foreign affairs EOs, and one with weaker, more constrained, executive power (the partisan-compliance model) is superior for understanding domestic EOs. When party effects are built into the legislative stage of our models, we again discover instances where negative agenda-setting is crucial for Congress (at least for low and moderate significance thresholds), while in other circumstances (with high thresholds), positive agenda-setting and imperfect party discipline are more relevant. For foreign EOs, negative agenda-setting (which, to reiterate, somewhat increases presidential power) is relevant, but, consistent with the underpinning of the two-presidencies argument, the overall importance of parties seem to play less of a role, overall.

In general, our analysis of the two-presidencies conjecture reinforced many of the inferences drawn from the previous chapters. For domestic issues, the President appears to behave strategically in a manner that weighs extra-statutory considerations and, depending on the significance of the issue, the ability of parties to set the legislative agenda and to discipline members. For foreign policy issues, the chief executive is less constrained by formal political institutions or partisan organizations.

In summary, our analysis sheds considerable light on the unilateral action process, so that presidential power is, rather than enigmatic, clearly understandable. The President is not nearly as powerful as one might be led to believe, based on past scholarship. With theoretical models that can be compared, measures of significant actions that have strong foundations, parties well-integrated and policies carefully distinguished, we have shown that most of the time the actions of the chief executive are consistent with inter-branch bargaining where the relationship between the legislature and the executive is relatively balanced, with the courts in the background and legislative parties, particularly those in the majority, acting collectively and playing a key role. Parties can then have an effect on the strategic conditions that the chief executive faces and the power that he or she has, as well as the importance of features such as legislative rules. It would appear that models that include a premise that extra-statutory factors matter, alongside statutory and judicial overrides, and where different party effects on the legislative process are at work, generally do better in illuminating the unilateral action process and the resulting distribution of power. In a minority of instances, such as with respect to certain subsets of EOs as broken out by policy or significance, the effectiveness of extra-statutory forces or agenda control and party member pressure abates, and something akin to the unilateralism model is more appropriate. Thus, the enigma of power is no more when we consider these different forces that can condition the exercise of unilateral action.

FURTHER IMPLICATIONS

Although our principal goal in our analysis has been to solve the puzzle that we have termed the "enigma of presidential power" with respect to unilateral action, our analysis has ramifications for a variety of other, related considerations of interest to students, scholars and observers of the modern political process. These include approaches to the study of unilateral action generally, means to gauge the importance of government outputs empirically, the testing of models of inter-branch bargaining, the impacts of divided government, the integration of political parties into the analysis of the presidency specifically and into political institutions generally and the conceptualization of legislative collective action.

First, we have demonstrated a new approach for analyzing presidential unilateral actions. Although we employed this approach to investigate executive orders, it could be productively utilized to study a range of presidential dictums of the sort that we surveyed in Chapter 1. In other words, one could take our theoretical approaches, measurement techniques and means of empirically executing comparative model testing and apply them to presidential unilateral actions besides EOs, such as proclamations or other presidential directives. It would also be possible, with some theoretical adjustments related to their issuance after the legislature moves, to apply this means of analysis to presidential signing statements.

Along these lines, we have also both documented the key role of measurement – as evidenced by different findings that depend on significance thresholds – and provided a new, more comprehensive means of measuring important concepts. Not only has this approach and our EO measure the potential to be employed to answer questions about EOs that we have not addressed in our study and to examine other unilateral actions, including determining to what degree empirical results are contingent on level of significance being investigated, given that actions vary from routine to important policy initiatives, but it also offers ways of improving the measurement of a variety of other features of interest to us as institutional scholars. Per unilateral actions, we could take our new measure of EO significance (or comparable measures of other unilateral actions) and analyze previously proffered empirical questions, such as the effect of the last 100 days of a presidential administration (Howell and Mayer 2005) or of a political environment (Krause and Cohen 2000), including how results hinge on what significance threshold we adopt. Similarly, our measure or analogous measures using the same methodology will facilitate rich empirical studies on any new research questions or agendas pertaining to unilateral actions.

As for other concerns of interest to institutional scholars, our approach could, for example, be employed to gauge the significance of regulations (where, for example, the importance of some social regulations, such as those governing abortion or access to healthy meals for the underprivileged, may be more difficult to quantify than other regulations, such as those that stipulate pollution controls, where more standard cost–benefit analyses can be applied).[3] Hence, we could develop an estimate of the importance of individual regulations or of regulations issued at a given time that goes beyond something such as a count of the number of new pages in the *Federal Register* employed in the past (e.g., Carey 2015). This, in turn, would allow us to examine questions with respect to regulation and interest group influence, delegated agency discretion and judicial decision-making in ways heretofore unimaginable.

Third, we have shown that the kinds of issues that garner the interest of many institutional scholars, and indeed of many scholars generally, require the careful integration of theory, measurement and empirical testing. Most notably, for myriad concerns that capture the attention of those studying inter-branch bargaining, where numerous actors are involved in complicated games, analysis benefits greatly from theoretically founded comparative model testing. In our investigation, this EITM approach, which results in such careful comparative

---

[3] Even when cost-benefit analysis can be applied, there is much debate about what a proper cost-benefit assessment looks like (e.g., Hahn and Dudley 2007).

model testing, allows us to draw the inferences that we desire about presidential power generally and more specific questions about the importance of delegated discretion and of political parties, even for a very large number of alternative models, as is the case in Chapter 5. Without such a systematic approach, as we have seen, inferences drawn about issues such as presidential power necessarily have a somewhat ad hoc quality.

For example, in the future, we could imagine expanding our analysis theoretically and empirically to more comprehensively assess the role of the courts. In our analysis, for parsimony and because we were constrained by an inability to place the courts, the President, and legislators in the same ideological common space, we did not fully explore the theoretical and empirical implications of how the judiciary might impact presidential calculations regarding unilateral action, although they are implicitly factored in some of our theoretical results (e.g., in Chapter 5). Yet there are certainly examples where the courts have played a key role, such as in response to Barak Obama's recent immigration actions (not technically EOs), where the appellate court ruled them beyond presidential discretion and the deadlocked Supreme Court left the lower court's decision unchanged. The possibility of the courts invalidating Obama's actions also may have conditioned the Republican Congress's response to the EOs, as it could hope that judges would reinstate the previous status quo. Such instances suggest that we could benefit from a theoretically richer approach that, for example, would model legislative expectations about the courts. Furthermore, recent empirical efforts (e.g., Bonica 2013) suggest that in the future we will have an ability to put the President, legislators and the courts on a single dimension for a sufficiently long time period to accommodate the type of empirical analyses required for comparative model testing.[4]

Fourth, along these lines, our analysis has ramifications for thinking about divided government. In much work, be it on unilateral actions, legislative productivity or presidential appointments, divided government has been included in empirical work as a kind of catch-all, without much attention to the exact underlying mechanisms. Not surprisingly, results tended to be positive, negative and null depending on the specification and research design. In our analysis, we present a different way to examine divided government, in that we emphasize isolating the underlying mechanisms at work. Most notably, we suggest that divided government will impact presidential actions in those instances where legislators who make up the majority party in Congress are incentivized, perhaps as a function of policy, and are able to employ extra-

---

[4] Bonica's (2013) approach uses campaign finance contributions (available since the late 1970s to develop common ideological scores (i.e., the scores do not go back nearly as far in time as the EO data that we analyze). Another future possibility that is the subject of much current scholarship and that may be less time constrained is using text analysis (e.g., Benoit and Herzog 2017) to develop such ideological scores.

statutory tools. In the future, this means of examining the effects of divided government could be expanded by focusing on other mechanisms, such as party roles in the legislature that we have theoretically suggested should matter, or alternative outputs.

Fifth, our study underscores how presidential or legislative actions may vary by policy types and, therefore, that disaggregation is important as part of the research process. In our analysis of EOs we found that pooling data with all policy types sometimes obscured our understanding of unilateral actions' dynamics, as presidents acted differently in some policy arenas, such as international trade or foreign policies, than in others. Similarly, we discovered that policy areas (along with EO significance) condition the roles that parties play in the legislative process with respect to the patterns of EOs that are promulgated. Broadly, our results suggest that analyses of presidential policy-making or the legislative process should take the conditioning effects of policy type very seriously.

Sixth, we have demonstrated the importance for scholars of the institutionalized presidency that they think about political parties and the multifaceted ways in which they might have an impact on outcomes as carefully as they think about the legislature, the judiciary or the voters themselves. While the various roles of political parties have been systematically addressed in studies outside of the presidency (for example, with respect to legislative productivity; e.g., Chiou and Rothenberg 2003, 2009), our analyses in Chapters 2 through 6 are the first in the context of studying the chief executive. As we saw, parties may have a variety of implications for how the President behaves strategically, the amount of the power that he or she can garner from unilateral action and the impact of changing rules for outcomes. To reiterate a point made in earlier chapters, this is not to suggest that presidential scholars have been oblivious to the importance of political parties. Rather, we only wish to emphasize that parties have not been given the emphasis and the systematic treatment that we believe yields the greatest intellectual payoff. Hopefully, our analysis provides an impetus for work on the presidency, especially anything where legislative cooperation is required, that carefully synthesizes party roles with presidential incentives and authorities.

Seventh, and related to our discussion of parties and how they shape presidential power, our analysis has important implications for the presence and impact of legislative collective action problems. As we have discussed at length, Moe and Howell (1999a) argued that Congress cannot overcome collective action problems as a whole and that, as a consequence, the legislature is even further weakened in effectively responding to the chief executive when he or she moves first. Cox and McCubbins (2007), while not focusing on unilateral actions per se, maintained that parties generally have mechanisms to overcome intra-party collective action problems. Our analysis finds that the ability of the majority party to overcome collective action problems is widespread and, although the effects are numerous and subtle, overall they tend to reduce presidential power in favor of the Congress. Our initial analyses in Chapters 2 through 4 corresponded to a world where the majority party overcomes collective action problems in a manner that allows it to use extra-statutory mechanisms (which is intuitive, given that the control of such mechanisms largely rests with the majority party) that limit the direction in which the chief executive can employ delegated discretion and limit his or her power. In Chapter 5, we found additional evidence that majority parties solve collective action problems, this time in the legislative stage via agenda-setting and pressuring members to act in ways that differ somewhat from their primitive preferences. Intriguingly, solving collective action problems in the legislative stage actually expands legislative gridlock, leading to some increase in presidential power and influence relative to a world without such agenda-setting or membership pressure effects. However, since the impacts of parties on presidential power in the unilateral action stage are much larger than in the legislative stage, majority party members, acting collectively, on net reduce the extent to which Congress is weakened by an inability to overcome collective action problems.

Put differently, we take the notion of collective action seriously and, rather than assume it, we specify models and examine the data. We find that Howell and Moe are largely right in asserting that the chamber as a whole is not able to effectively overcome collective action problems. Conversely, we find that the related inference, that Congress is highly disadvantaged, needs to be tempered because the ability of subsets of legislators, in the form of political parties, to overcome their own collective action problems substantially mitigates presidential power and leads to something much more akin to separation-of-powers bargaining. This would be consistent with why, for example, we have found little support for the evasion hypothesis, that the chief executive will act more, given unified government, in an effort to move before Congress does, the lack of support for which has been a puzzle (e.g., Mayer 2009); because so often majority parties in the legislature, in some combination, exercise extra-statutory authority, pressure party members or control agendas, the ability of presidents to evade Congress in this way is likely extremely limited.

FINAL THOUGHTS

Throughout our lengthy analysis, we have principally adopted a positivist's stance, trying to explain how the world actually works, about the concerns at hand. Do presidents typically exercise power in a more-or-less fettered manner and, if not, under what conditions does this not hold? While we have touched on more normative considerations, regarding what state of the world is actually better for society, this consideration has not preoccupied our analysis.

However, one cannot help but offer some passing comments about the normative consequences of what we have uncovered. The very idea of an *imperial presidency* typically receives a negative normative response and has motivated many discussions of unilateral actions, such as by those in the legal community who have debated the desirability of a unitary executive. Indeed, as a candidate, Barack Obama himself decried George W. Bush's efforts to act without paying attention to Congress, only to be accused of comparable abuses himself once elected (e.g., Douthat 2014). If one takes such accusations at face value, they would suggest that anything that limits imperial behavior, particularly choices that are substantially opposed by those in the legislative branch, might be cause for rejoicing. Certainly, one could applaud that (if our results are to be believed) we do seem to inhabit a world where checks and balances function to a considerable degree, albeit perhaps not in a manner that the American Founding Fathers could ever quite envision.

Alternatively, for those who bemoan either the parochialism of the legislative branch generally (e.g., Moe 1987, Moe and Wilson 1994) – where social welfare is seemingly sacrificed to the pursuit of narrow interests of legislators and their organized supporters – or the debilitating effects of political polarization (e.g., McCarty, Poole and Rosenthal 2008) – where real public policy problems are not addressed due to the conflicting preferences of key actors – our findings may prove less comforting. Simply put, unilateral action does not even begin to furnish a "way out" for rationalizing policy or for overcoming the deadlock that frustrates so many. Nor is it consistent with the unitary executive that certain legal scholars advocate. Regardless, if we are relying on decisive executive actions to solve American policy problems, unilateral action offers only a very small glimpse of hope at best.

Put differently, hoping that a public-minded chief executive will be able to carry the day through unilateral action, daring the inert and gridlocked legislature and the quiescent courts to take him or her on, is not realistic. Instead, barring dramatic changes in rules governing the branches, if public problems are to be dealt with in an effective manner, our analysis would indicate that changes in preferences of the relevant actors, be they primitive preferences or those promulgated by partisan leadership, is likely a requirement. Whether such changes would be enough to overcome parochial concerns and organized pressures would still be a considerable issue, but without them, stalemate, rather than effective executive solutions, is likely to be the rule of the day.

Statements of Probability of Unilateral Action, Propositions 1–4 and Their Proofs

$\Pr(Act)$, the expected probability of unilateral action in equilibrium in the game, can be formally defined as $\Pr(Act) = \int_{-\infty}^{\infty} \int_{0}^{\gamma} \Pr(Act \,|\, t, q) g(q) g(t) dt \, dq$, where $g(q)$ and $g(t)$ represent the probability density functions of status quos and discretion, respectively, and $\Pr(Act \,|\, t, q)$ denotes the equilibrium probability of unilateral action, given a certain level of discretion and a certain status quo, which are drawn from their respective distributions. In words, we obtain $\Pr(Act)$ by integrating $\Pr(Act \,|\, t, q)$ over the distributions of status quos and discretions.

Proposition 1 (Unilateralism Model): Given our assumptions in this model,

$$(1)\ \Pr(Act) = \int_{f}^{m_c} g(q)dq + \int_{m_c}^{2v-m_c} g(q)dq + \int_{f-.5\gamma}^{f} \left(\frac{\gamma - 2f + 2q}{\gamma} \right) g(q)dq$$
$$+ \int_{2v-m_c}^{2v-m_c+\gamma} \left(\frac{\gamma + 2v - m_c - q}{\gamma} \right) g(q)dq.$$

$$(2)\ \frac{\partial \Pr(Act)}{\partial v} > 0 > \frac{\partial \Pr(Act)}{\partial f}.$$

PROOF OF PROPOSITION 1

(1) We first solve for $\Pr(Act \,|\, t, q)$ for all possible status quos and discretion levels in the unilateralism model. By backward induction, the court will overturn only those unilateral actions where the president overuses the given discretion level t. The chamber median will only introduce a new bill when the policy outcome after presidential action $p(q, t)$, denoted by q', which equals $q + p(q, t)$, falls outside the equilibrium gridlock interval between f and v, assuming that the chamber median is indifferent to q' and the final policy

outcome and will not introduce a new bill. Define $q'' \equiv q$ if $|p(q,t)| > t$; $q'' \equiv q'$ otherwise. The chamber median will move q'' to m_c if $q'' \leq 2f - m_c$ or $q'' \geq 2v - m_c$, to $2f - q''$ if $2f - m_c < q'' \leq f$ and to $2v - q''$ if $v < q'' \leq 2v - m_c$.

Given the players' responses in the legislative and judicial stages, equilibrium presidential unilateral action will depend on q and t as selected by *Nature*. For $q \in [f,v)$, the President will, regardless of the discretion level, definitely move q closer to v, because the pivots in Congress cannot reverse any policies within the equilibrium gridlock interval. Similarly, regardless of the discretion level, $q \in (v, 2c - m_c]$, the President will move q closer to v to preempt the chamber median's attempt to move q closer to m_c in the legislative stage. By contrast, for $q < f - \gamma/2$, regardless of the discretion level, the President is better off not taking any unilateral action and letting the median move q, as all he or she can do is move q to $q + t$, which is to the left of $2f - q$ (the final policy outcome without presidential action). Similar logic applies to $q > 2v - m_c + \gamma$.

Finally, for $f - \gamma/2 \leq q < f$, the President can choose to move q to $q + t$, which is to the left of what the chamber would select without presidential unilateral action (i.e., $2f - q$) if and only if $t < 2f - 2q$. This implies that the President will act unilaterally if and only if $t > 2f - 2q$ for this range of q. For $2v - m_c \leq q < 2v - m_c + \gamma$, the President will prefer to move q to the left of $2v - m_c$ (and closer to v) to prevent the chamber median from moving q closer to m_c. This attempt will prevail if and only if $t > q - (2v - m_c)$.

Given the results above and our assumptions about the distributions of q and t, we can determine the probability of presidential unilateral action for all possible q and its *ex ante* equilibrium probability, $\Pr(Act)$, i.e.,

$$\Pr(Act) = \int_f^{m_c} g(q)dq + \int_{m_c}^{2v-m_c} g(q)dq + \int_{f-.5\gamma}^{f} \left(\frac{\gamma - 2f + 2q}{\gamma}\right)g(q)dq$$

$$+ \int_{2v-m_c}^{2v-m_c+\gamma} \left(\frac{\gamma + 2v - m_c - q}{\gamma}\right)g(q)dq.$$

(2) To obtain $\frac{\partial \Pr(Act)}{\partial v}$, we take the derivative of the relevant arguments on the right-hand side of the above equation (i.e., on the second and fourth arguments) with respect to v with the fundamental theorem of calculus and the Leibniz integral rule:

$$\frac{\partial \Pr(Act)}{\partial v} = 2g(2v - m_c) + 2 \cdot 0 \cdot g(2v - m_c + \gamma) - 2 \cdot 1 \cdot g(2v - m_c)$$

$$+ \frac{2}{\gamma} \int_{2v-m_c}^{2v-m_c+\gamma} g(q)dq.$$

$$= \frac{2}{\gamma} \int_{2v-m_c}^{2v-m_c+\gamma} g(q)dq > 0$$

(because the probability density is positive, by definition).

Similarly, we take the derivative of the first and the third arguments on the right-hand side of the equation with respect to f:

$$\frac{\partial \text{Pr}(Act)}{\partial f} = -g(f) + g(f) - 0 \cdot g(f - .5\gamma) - \frac{2}{\gamma}\int_{f-.5\gamma}^{f} g(q)dq.$$

$$= -\frac{2}{\gamma}\int_{f-.5\gamma}^{f} g(q)dq < 0.$$

Proposition 2 (Chamber-compliance Model): Given our assumptions in this model,

$(1)\ \text{Pr}(Act) = \displaystyle\int_{f}^{m_c} g(q)dq + \int_{v}^{2v-m_c} g(q)dq + \int_{f-.5\gamma}^{f} \left(\frac{\gamma - 2f + 2q}{\gamma}\right)g(q)dq$

$\qquad\qquad + \displaystyle\int_{2v-m_c}^{2v-m_c+\gamma} \left(\frac{\gamma + 2v - m_c - q}{\gamma}\right)g(q)dq.$

$(2)\ \dfrac{\partial \text{Pr}(Act)}{\partial f} < 0 \text{ and } \dfrac{\partial \text{Pr}(Act)}{\partial v} = \dfrac{2}{\gamma}\displaystyle\int_{2v-m_c}^{2v-m_c+\gamma} g(q)dq - g(v).$

PROOF OF PROPOSITION 2

The equilibrium behavior in this model is very similar to that in the model for Proposition 1, except that the President will not act unilaterally for status quos locating between m_c and v. This is because of the assumption that the President is allowed to use discretion to move policy only in the direction of the chamber median. Therefore, the $\text{Pr}(Act)$ for this proposition is established. The proof of the comparative statics in this proposition is very similar to that in the last proposition as well.

Proposition 3 (Partisan-compliance Model): Given our assumptions in this model,[1]

$(1)\ \text{Pr}(Act) = \displaystyle\int_{f}^{2m_p-m_c} g(q)dq + \int_{f-.5\gamma}^{f} \left(\frac{\gamma - 2f + 2q}{\gamma}\right)g(q)dq$

$\qquad\qquad + \displaystyle\int_{2m_p-m_c}^{2m_p-m_c+\gamma} \left(\frac{\gamma + 2v - m_c - q}{\gamma}\right)g(q)dq, \text{ if the government is unified;}$

$\qquad = \displaystyle\int_{v}^{2v-m_c} g(q)dq + \int_{m_p-.5\gamma}^{m_p} \left(\frac{\gamma - 2m_p + 2q}{\gamma}\right)g(q)dq$

$\qquad\qquad + \displaystyle\int_{2v-m_c}^{2v-m_c+\gamma} \left(\frac{\gamma + 2v - m_c - q}{\gamma}\right)g(q)dq, \text{ if the government is divided}$

with unifed Congress.

[1] We assume that $v < m_p < p$ under unified government and that $m_c < f$ under divided government in order to make our results concise, and that the minimized distance between m_c and m_p among Congresses with unified government is at least as large as that between m_c and v, given divided government.

(2) The *ex ante* probability of presidential unilateral action is higher under unified government than under divided government.

(3) Under unified government, $\frac{\partial \Pr(Act)}{\partial m_p} > 0 > \frac{\partial \Pr(Act)}{\partial f}$.

PROOF OF PROPOSITION 3

(1) Under unified government, since we assume that $f < m_c < v < m_p < p$, as displayed in Figure 2(c), the resulting EGI is now bounded by f and m_p. The proof for $\Pr(Act \,|\, Unified\ Government)$ is identical to that in (1) of Proposition 1 except that m_p replaces v.

Under divided government with a unified Congress, given the assumption of $m_p < f < m_c < v < p$ (illustrated in Figure 2[d]), the resulting EGI is bounded by m_p and v. Again, the proof for $\Pr(Act \,|\, Divided\ Government)$ is identical to that in (1) of Proposition 1, except that f replaces m_p and that presidential unilateral action is absent for $m_p < q \leq v$. The reason for the latter is that, while the President has incentives to act unilaterally to move the status quo closer to his or her ideal point, this attempt is not viable, given the court's or majority party's opposition.

(2) The effect of unified government:

Suppose that there are two sets of pivots, one of which is under divided government (i.e., $f^D, m_c, v^D, p^D, m_p^D$) and the other of which is under unified government (i.e., $f^U, m_c, v^U, p^U, m_p^U$). To facilitate comparison, we rescale the location of the chamber median so that it is identical under the two government regimes. Given the assumptions in the model and Proposition 3, the net difference, denoted as ND, is

$$\Pr(Act \,|\, Unified\ Government) - \Pr(Act \,|\, Divided\ Government)$$

$$= \int_{f^U}^{2m_p^U - m_c} g(q)dq + \int_{f^U - .5\gamma}^{f^U} \left(\frac{\gamma - 2f^U + 2q}{\gamma} \right) g(q)dq$$

$$+ \int_{2m_p^U - m_c}^{2m_p^U - m_c + \gamma} \left(\frac{\gamma + 2v - m_c - q}{\gamma} \right) g(q)dq - \int_{v^D}^{2v^D - m_c} g(q)dq$$

$$- \int_{m_p^D - .5\gamma}^{m_p^D} \left(\frac{\gamma - 2m_p^D + 2q}{\gamma} \right) g(q)dq - \int_{2v^D - m_c}^{2v^D - m_c + \gamma} \left(\frac{\gamma + 2v - m_c - q}{\gamma} \right) g(q)dq$$

$$= \left[\int_{f^U}^{m_c} g(q)dq - \int_{2v^D - m_c}^{2v^D - m_c + \gamma} \left(\frac{\gamma + 2v - m_c - q}{\gamma} \right) g(q)dq \right]$$

$$+ \left[\int_{f^U - .5\gamma}^{f^U} \left(\frac{\gamma - 2f^U + 2q}{\gamma} \right) g(q)dq - \int_{m_p^D - .5\gamma}^{m_p^D} \left(\frac{\gamma - 2m_p^D + 2q}{\gamma} \right) g(q)dq \right]$$

$$+\left[\int_{m_c}^{2m_p^U-m_c}g(q)dq-\int_{v^D}^{2v^D-m_c}g(q)dq\right]+\int_{2m_p^U-m_c}^{2m_p^U-m_c+\gamma}\left(\frac{\gamma+2v-m_c-q}{\gamma}\right)g(q)dq>0$$

where the first bracket is positive because $g(q)$ is symmetric, $m_c-f^U>\gamma$ and $\frac{\gamma-2f^U+2q}{\gamma}<1$ for $2v^D-m_c<q<2v^D-m+\gamma$, the second is positive because $m_p^D<f$ and $g(q)$ is decreasing and the third is positive because $g(q)$ is decreasing and $v^D<m_p^U$.

(3) The proof for the effects of moving f and m_p is identical to that in (2) of Proposition 1.

Define $EU_p^k\equiv\int_{-\infty}^{\infty}\int_0^y u(y;p)g(d)g(t)dtdq$, $k=U,M,PU,PD$, as the *ex ante* expected utility of the President in the unilateralism, chamber-compliance, partisan-compliance under unified government and partisan-compliance under divided government models where $u(y;p)$ represents the President's utility function for any final policy y, given a presidential ideal point p, which is symmetric and single-peaked. Denote EU_p as the *ex ante* expected utility of the President in the corresponding model where only the pivotal politics game is played (i.e., the President lacks the right to act unilaterally). Finally, define $G_p^k\equiv(EU_p^k-EU_p)$ as the President's gain from having an opportunity to act unilaterally and as a first mover in model k. We now can compare how presidents gain from the possibility of unilateral action in each of the models.

Proposition 4:   Given   the   assumptions   in   each   model, $\min\{G_p^U,G_p^{PU}\}>G_p^M>G_p^{PD}$. With a more restrictive assumption of the President's utility function, $G_p^{PU}>G_p^U$.

PROOF OF PROPOSITION 4

We can compare the *ex ante* expected utility of the President under different models piecewise with symmetric single-peaked preferences. First, we can easily show that $G_p^U>G_p^M$. Since the pivotal politics game is identical in the unilateralism and chamber-compliance models, we only need to show that $EU_p^U>EU_p^C$. Moreover, the final policy outcome in these two models is identical for all discretion levels and all status quos except for when $q\in[m_c-t,v]$, during which the final policy outcome in the unilateralism model is, for all possible discretion levels, always closer to the President than that in the chamber-compliance model.

Second, we show that $G_p^{PU}>G_p^M$. The President's gains from unilateral action in the chamber-compliance model and partisan-compliance model with unified government are identical, except for when $q\in[m_c-t,2m_p-m_c+t]$, so we only need to focus on these status quos. For all possible discretion levels t, the President's gain in the chamber-compliance model is positive only for $q\in[v,2v-m_c+t]$, but the total expected gain for this range under this model is smaller than that for $q\in[m-t,v]$ under the partisan-compliance model with unified government, given the assumption that the density probability of status quo distribution is weakly decreasing as q moves away from the chamber median. Additionally, the President can gain for $q \in [v, 2m_p - m_c + t]$ under the partisan-compliance model with unified government. This establishes the result.

Third, we can show that $G_p^M > G_p^{PD}$. Given our assumption that $m_p < f$ in the partisan-compliance model with divided government, the final policy outcomes under this model and its corresponding pivotal politics game, for all possible discretion levels, differ only for $q \in [v, 2v - m_c - t]$ (i.e., the President will take unilateral action for this range). For the chamber-compliance model, the differences occur not only for this range of status quos (the magnitude of differences are identical for these two models), but also when $q \in [f - .5t, m_c]$. Given that the President's incentives in utilizing unilateral action only involve improving his or her welfare, the result that $G_p^M > G_p^{PD}$ is established.

Finally, we want to show that $G_p^{PU} > G_p^U$ if we make a more restrictive assumption for the President's utility function, i.e., $-|y - p|$. For all possible discretion levels, the President's gains in the partisan-compliance model with unified government and the unilateralism model are identical, except for when $q \in [v - t, 2m_p - m_c + t]$. Under this range of status quos, the President's gain

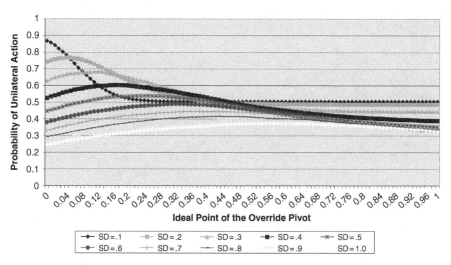

FIGURE A.1 Effects of varying override pivots on presidential unilateral action.
Note: It is assumed that the ideal points of the filibuster pivot and chamber medians are −0.4 and 0, respectively, that the President is to the right of the override pivot, that discretion is distributed uniformly between 0 and 0.3, and that the status quo is distributed normally with a mean of 0 and a standard deviation represented by SD. Each curve represents the *ex ante* probability of presidential unilateral action with the specific standard deviation of the status quo distribution, while varying the location of the override pivot (i.e., the left boundary of equilibrium gridlock interval).

in the latter model occurs for only a subset, i.e., for $q \in [v - t, 2v - m_c + t]$, but occurs for this entire range in the former model. Given our assumption that the probability density of status quos is weakly decreasing from their mean, the total of this expected gain for $q \in [v - t, 2v - m_c + t]$ is smaller in the latter model than that for the same set in the former model. Additionally, the President also gains from unilateral action for $q \in [2v - m_c + t, 2m_p - m_c + t]$ in the partisan-compliance model with unified government. Therefore, $G_p^{PU} > G_p^{U}$.

APPENDIX 2

An Item-Response Model Incorporating Rater Attributes

Having provided the conceptual rationale for adopting a Bayesian IRT approach to measurement in our text, we now formally specify our model for estimating significance. Specifically, as discussed, we develop an IRT model that, in contrast to past works, also controls for rater attributes that might otherwise create error in our significance measure.

As foreshadowed, political scientists have increasingly applied item response theory, particularly so-called two-parameter IRT, in the last decade.[1] Such models have been employed to measure the latent ability of graduate student applicants (Jackman 2004), the ideal points of judges and legislators (e.g., Martin and Quinn 2002, Poole and Rosenthal 1997, Londregan 1999, Clinton, Jackman and Rivers 2004), party pressure (Chiou 2005) and legislative significance (Clinton and Lapinski 2006).

In this spirit, our starting point is Johnson and Albert's (1991) Bayesian hierarchical IRT model that Clinton and Lapinski (2006) creatively apply to measure legislative significance. As the latter articulate, a hierarchical IRT is useful for measuring significance because additional exogenous information for objects can be incorporated into the estimation of latent traits. This is especially beneficial when a majority of objects, such as legislation, may be mentioned by few raters if the distribution of raters' thresholds is skewed toward a high level. Provided that the information included is correlated with the latent traits of objects, introduction of additional information can substantially help distinguish such underlying traits. The same situation that

---

[1] There are three typical item response models: one-parameter, two-parameter and three-parameter models. One-parameter IRT models (i.e., the Rasch model) contain only a difficulty parameter (how easy or difficult an item is); two-parameter models add a discrimination parameter (how effectively an item can discriminate, e.g., between significant and insignificant EOs); and three-parameter IRT models include a guessing parameter (how often the "right answer" is produced by guessing). For reviews of item response theory, see Hambleton, Swaminathan and Rogers (1991), Johnson and Albert (1999) and Baker and Kim (2004).

Clinton and Lapinski (2006) underscore occurs in our EO data, justifying the need for hierarchical structures for estimating significance. Most EOs will fly under the radar of raters, so it is helpful to provide additional trait data.

However, one shortfall of this approach, as previously specified, is that it does not take into account that each rater may possess attributes that impact its evaluation of the object, such as ability or significance, whose latent traits are to be estimated. This is critical as, without controlling for raters' potential biases toward certain characteristics of objects, estimates of the underlying latent traits will be biased in a manner akin to the problems caused by omitted variables. Thus, as discussed in the main body of Chapter 3, if the *Wall Street Journal* tends to focus on macroeconomic or labor issues, it will use a lower threshold for including related EOs than for EOs covering other concerns, and not building such predilections into the model can lead to bias.

To deal with such possibilities, we extend Johnson and Albert's model by allowing for additional exogenous explanatory variables to control for the attributes of each rater. This approach, we should note, is similar to that developed in Chiou (2005) to disentangle the effects of ideological preferences and of party discipline on roll-call decisions, where the goal was to know to what degree a legislator's votes reflected the member's ideological disposition, as compared to reflecting pressure applied by the party.[2]

Hence, first assume that there are n individual objects (e.g., pieces of successful legislation or issued executive orders) the latent traits of which are to be estimated, and there are m raters who independently evaluate some or all of these objects. While, of course, the latent trait in question can be interpreted as something other than the significance of either legislation or an EO, given our application we refer to it as the significance of EOs.

Assume that EO i, $i = 1, ..., n$, has a "true" level of significance, and denote it by $z_i \in \mathbb{R}$. Rater j, $j = 1, ..., m$, perceives the significance of each individual object with $x_{ij} \in \mathbb{R}$. Assume, also, that $x_{ij} = z_i + \varepsilon_{ij}$, where ε_{ij} is the error of rater j in assessing the ith EO and is normally distributed with mean of 0 and variance δ_j^2, implying that the variance (i.e., precision) differs among raters. Let Y be an $n \times m$ matrix of ratings, with element y_{ij} indicating rater j's observed dichotomous choices of the EO i. In rating, rater j classifies EO i as either 0 or 1, with $y_{ij} = 1$ when $y_{ij}^* = z_i + \pi_j^T S_{ij} + \varepsilon_{ij} > \gamma_j$, where γ_j, S_{ij}, and π_j denote rater j's threshold, the exogenous variables other than significance that affect rater j's rating, and their coefficients, respectively.[3] If there are no additional explanatory variables for rater j, $S_{ij} = 0$ and $\pi_j = 0$. Otherwise, S_{ij} and π_j are both a $d_j \times 1$ vector, where $d_j \geq 1$ denotes the number of explanatory

---

[2] The difference between our model and Chiou's model is that the latter does not contain a hierarchical structure but, rather, employs a more general structure for specifying how exogenous variables impact dichotomous decisions.

[3] We treat the situation of a rater not rating an EO as random missing data. Such data are easily dealt with, given our Bayesian approach.

variables for rater j. It is this innovation of adding S_{ij} and π_j, enabling us to control for idiosyncratic factors of each rater in classifying EOs, which represents a new extension of Johnson and Albert's (1999) hierarchical IRT model.

Given the rating rule, the probability of rater j's classifying one is given by

$$
\begin{aligned}
\Pr(y_{ij} = 1) &= \Pr(y_{ij}^* > \gamma_j) \\
&= \Pr(z_i + \pi_j^T S_{ij} + \varepsilon_{ij} > \gamma_j) \\
&= \Pr(\varepsilon_{ij} > \gamma_j - z_i - \pi_j^T S_{ij}) \\
&= 1 - F((\gamma_j - z_i - \pi_j^T S_{ij})/\delta_j) \\
&= F(z_i \beta_j - \alpha_j + \lambda_j^T S_{ij}),
\end{aligned}
\tag{1}
$$

where $\beta_j \equiv 1/\delta_j$, $\alpha_j \equiv \gamma_j/\delta_j$, $\lambda_j^T = \pi_j^T/\delta_j$, and $F(\cdot)$ is the cumulative density function of the normal distribution. β_j is the typical discrimination parameter used in IRT, measuring the extent to which rater j distinguishes the latent traits of object i. When rater j is more precise in rating, the associated error standard deviation, δ_j, is smaller and, therefore, the relevant discrimination parameter, β_j, is larger. α_j, representing rater j's difficulty parameter, is larger either when its threshold is higher or when its error variance is smaller. Finally, λ_j recovers the effects of rater j's explanatory variables divided by rater j's error standard deviation.

With the structure laid out above, and the assumption that each rating is independent across objects and raters, the likelihood of the underlying parameters is

$$
L(z, \beta, \alpha, \lambda) = \prod_{i=1}^{n} \prod_{j=1}^{m} F(z_i \beta_j - \alpha_j + \lambda_j^T S_{ij})^{y_{ij}} (1 - F(z_i \beta_j - \alpha_j + \lambda_j^T S_{ij}))^{1-y_{ij}}.
\tag{2}
$$

While this model's likelihood is similar to Chiou's (2005), given the inclusion of exogenous variables for each rater, it differs notably from typical IRT models employed in political science, such as in Clinton, Jackman and Rivers (2004) and Clinton and Lapinski (2006).

Given our Bayesian approach, we need to specify prior distributions for each parameter in the likelihood. In particular, specifying the prior for the significance parameter, z_i, provides a handy means of incorporating additional information for estimating the significance of EOs rarely classified by all raters as 1 (i.e., mentioned by all raters). Specifically, we assume that z_i is normally distributed with mean $\kappa^T W_i$ and variance τ^2, where W_i is a $k \times 1$ vector of exogenous variables potentially correlated with z_i, and κ is the coefficients of these variables.[4] κ and τ^2, so-called "hyper priors," are given with their own prior distributions. In estimation, we can also include a number of variables

---

[4] The first element of W_i is a constant of one.

that may be correlated with an EO's significance, such as the issuing President's party affiliation, whether the EO creates a new government organization and whether the EO is policy oriented. As mentioned, this hierarchical structure will help distinguish the significance of those EOs less frequently mentioned by the raters.

Finally, we need to specify the prior distribution for $\beta, \alpha, \lambda, \kappa$ and τ^2. For the former four, we assume normal priors while, for the latter, we assume inverse-gamma. To generate the underlying Bayesian estimation procedure, we first derive full conditionals of the joint posterior distribution for Markov Chain Monte Carlo (MCMC) and then write C codes to sample the values of all parameters from the full conditionals.

APPENDIX 3

Formal Presentation of Framework with Party Roles in Legislative Stage, Proposition 1 and Expected Incentives of Unilateral Action

Assume that every player except the court has a symmetric, single-peaked preference with an ideal point whose notation coincides with that of the player. So, in step (5) of the game sequence, each legislative pivot will not veto if and only if the new status quo established by the agenda-setter in Congress makes him or her better off than the status quo generated from the presidential unilateral action (i.e., if the former is closer to his or her ideal point than the latter). Given these decisions made by legislative pivots, we can obtain the set of status quos unaltered in the legislative stage comprising the EGI (Krehbiel 1998). By Chiou and Rothenberg (2009), $G_L = \min\{A, L\}$ and $G_R = \max\{A, L\}$, where G_L and G_R are denoted as the EGI's left and right bounds, respectively, and where A and L denote the agenda-setter and the set of legislative pivots in a given game. Furthermore, denote y as the status quo in the beginning of the legislative stage (i.e., at the start of step [3]). The agenda-setter A's proposal z is a function of y, as given below:[1]

$$z \begin{cases} = \max\{A, 2G_R - y\} & \text{if } y > G_R \\ = y & \text{if } G_L < y \le G_R \\ = \min\{A, 2G_L - y\} & \text{if } y \le G_L. \end{cases} \quad (1)$$

Note that we include the same three assumptions in the unilateral action stage that we laid out and justified in Chapter 2: (1) the President's action is always within the boundary of delegated discretion (i.e., the President can move policy in a manner that makes Congress worse off, as long as it is within the range of t); (2) the President can move the status quo only in the direction consistent with the interests of the chamber median; or (3) the interests of the majority party

---

[1] The congressional agenda-setter will not introduce a bill to override presidential unilateral action in step (4) if and only if $z = y$ (i.e., if the status quo at the beginning of legislative stage is within the EGI).

median, rather than of the chamber median, serve as a *de facto* directional constraint on discretion.

We formally express these alternative assumptions about directional constraints on presidential discretion's use as follows. Let $M = \min\{M_H, M_S\}$ be the chamber median further away from the President. $MP = \min\{MP_H, MP_S\}$ under divided government and $MP = \max\{MP_H, MP_S\}$ under unified government. For the President's unilateral action x, we can state the following three rules, each of which corresponds to the alternative discretion assumptions mentioned above, sequentially:

> C1: Presidential unilateral action will be sustained if and only if $|x - q| \leq t$.
> C2: Presidential unilateral action will be sustained if and only if $|x - q| \leq t$ and $(x - q)(M - q) \geq 0$ for $q \neq M$.
> C3: Presidential unilateral action will be sustained if and only if $|x - q| \leq t$ and $(x - q)(MP - q) \geq 0$ for $q \neq MP$.

In words, rule C1 means that the President's unilateral action cannot move the status quo more than t. Rule C2 (C3) implies that, in addition to the constraint in C1, the President's action is permissible only for those moves that go in the direction of the chamber medians (majority party medians) in both legislative chambers.

Given the results above, we can now state the equilibrium unilateral action, denoted by x^*, with unilateral action occurring when $x^* \neq q$.[2]

Proposition 1: Given that *Nature* draws t and q,

(1) Under rule C1, when $A < G_R$,

$$x^* \begin{cases} = q, & \text{if } q \leq \min\{G_L - t/2, A - t\} \text{ or } q > 2G_R - A + t \\ = \min\{q + t, G_R\}, & \text{if } \min\{G_L - t/2, A - t\} < q \leq G_R \\ = \max\{q - t, G_R\}, & \text{if } G_R < q \leq 2G_R - A + t. \end{cases}$$

When $A = G_R$,

$$x^* \begin{cases} = q, & \text{if } q < \max\{G_L - t/2, 2G_L - A\} \text{ or } q > G_R \\ = \min\{q + t, G_R\}, & \text{if } \max\{G_L - t/2, 2G_L - A\} < q \leq G_R. \end{cases}$$

(2) Under rule C2 (C3), x^* is the same as under rule C1, except that $x^* = q$ for $q \in (M, G_R)$ (q locating between MP and G_R).[3]

---

[2] Consistent with the literature, throughout our theoretical framework we assume that the President will neither take a unilateral action that will be overridden by Congress or the court nor that will move the status quo further away from the EGI (the latter assumption ruling out some inconceivable presidential actions that would damage the chief executive's reputation).

[3] Here we assume a unified Congress. Under a divided Congress, $x = q$ for those status quos between the majority party medians in the House and Senate. Our empirical results also account for the divided Congress case. Note that if we were to integrate the court as a strategic actor constraining presidential discretion's direction, our theoretical results would be the same as under rule C2 except that the court's ideal point would replace the chamber median's.

PROOF OF PROPOSITION I

Given the result shown in the text and the model's assumptions, we know that $G_L \leq A \leq G_R < P$.

I. RULE C I

We first prove the President's equilibrium unilateral action under rule C_1, which permits the President to move the status quo q in any direction, as long as he does not overuse the discretion t. In contemplating whether to take unilateral action, the President compares the relative benefits of acting unilaterally and of taking no unilateral action, while anticipating possible policy changes that might occur in the legislative stage. Two situations need to be considered: $A < G_R$ and $A = G_R$.

(1) **Suppose** $A < G_R$. Given q and t drawn at the very beginning of the game, we discuss how the President will behave in equilibrium for different ranges of q and t.

Case 1: $q \geq 2G_R - A + t$. Note that whenever q is to the right of $2G_R - A + t$ in the beginning of the legislative stage, the agenda-setter can move q to his or her ideal point. Without unilateral action, the agenda-setter would move q to his or her ideal point (i.e., the final policy outcome would be his or her ideal point), according to equation (1) in the text. Even when the President fully takes advantage of t and moves q to $q - t$, it is still to the right of $2G_R - A$. In other words, no unilateral action will alter the final policy outcome. Therefore, the President will not act unilaterally for this range of q.

Case 2: $G_R \leq q < 2G_R - A + t$. For this range of q, the President has a chance to preempt the agenda-setter by undermining her ability to move q to be closer to his or her ideal point. For $q \in [2G_R - A, 2G_R - A + t)$, according to equation (1), without unilateral action the agenda-setter can move q to be A. The President can preempt the agenda-setter by moving q to somewhere between G_R and $2G_R - A$ (precisely, $\max\{G_R, q - t\}$) so that the agenda-setter can sequentially move it only to somewhere between A and G_R (i.e., $\min\{G_R, 2G_R - (q - t)\}$), which is to the right of A and definitely closer to the President's ideal point. Similarly, for $q \in [G_R, 2G_R - A)$, the President can preempt the agenda-setter by moving q to be closer to G_R so that the agenda-setter's ability to move q further away from the President's ideal point is undercut.

Case 3: $G_L \leq q < G_R$. Since the status quo is within the gridlock interval, it will be the final policy outcome in the game without any unilateral action. Clearly, the President can benefit from unilateral action by moving q to be as close to G_R as possible (i.e., $\min\{q + t, G_R\}$). Note that the President has no incentive to move q to the right of G_R, as the agenda-setter will then, sequentially, move it to the left of G_R. As long as the President sets the policy within the gridlock interval without overusing discretion, it will also be the final policy outcome in the game.

Case 4: $q < G_L$. Given this range of q, we want to show that the President will unilaterally act only for $q \in [\min(G_L - t/2, A - t,), G_L]$. Note that $G_L - t/2 \le A - t$ if $t \le 2(A - G_L)$. First, suppose that $t \le 2(A - G_L)$. For $q \in [G_L - t/2, G_L]$, without unilateral action the agenda-setter will move q to $\min\{2G_L - q, A\}$, according to equation (1), which is $2G_L - q$ since $t \le 2(A - G_L)$. The President will move q to be as close to G_R as possible, i.e., $\min\{q + t, G_R\}$, which locates it within the gridlock interval and therefore would be the final policy. Furthermore, $\min\{q + t, G_R\} \ge 2G_L - q$, since $q \ge G_L - t/2$ (which implies $2G_L - q \le G_L + t/2$ and $q + t \ge G_L + t/2$) and $2G_L - q \le A < G_R$. This establishes the result that the President prefers to take unilateral action $\min\{q + t, G_R\}$ for this range of q.

For $q \in [2G_L - A, G_L - t/2]$, we want to show that the President prefers to take no unilateral action. Without any unilateral action, the agenda-setter will move q to $2G_L - q$. The question is whether the President can accomplish more with unilateral action. The only scenario for this possibility is to move q to the right of $2G_L - q$. However, $q + t \le 2G_L - q$, as $q \le G_L - t/2$.

Similarly, for $q \in (-\infty, 2G_L - A]$, any unilateral action will lead to $q + t'$ or $2G_L - (q + t')$ for any $t' \in [0, t]$, which is always to the left of A, while a lack of unilateral action gives the agenda-setter more leverage to move q to be A. The outcome is that the President prefers to take no unilateral action for this range of q.

Now suppose $t > 2(A - G_L)$. This implies that $A - t \le G_L - t/2 \le 2G_L - A \le G_L$. For $q \in [A - t, G_L]$, without presidential unilateral action, the final policy outcome would be $\min\{2G_L - q, A\}$, which locates either on A or to his or her left. Given this, the President prefers to take unilateral action by moving q to $\min\{q + t, G_R\}$, which is to the right of A, because $q \ge A - t$. For $q \in (-\infty, A - t]$, a lack of unilateral action enables the agenda-setter to move q to his or her ideal point A, as $A - t \le 2G_L - A$. As q is too extreme for the President to move it to the right of A, even with the full use of discretion t, the President would instead prefer to hold off and let the agenda-setter move q to his or her idea point in the legislative stage.

(2) **Suppose** $A = G_R$. The equilibrium behavior for $A = G_R$ is identical to that for $A < G_R$, except for some of the status quos outside the gridlock interval. For $q \in (G_R, 2G_R - A + t)$, the President now has no incentive to take unilateral action, as he can use discretion at most to move q to be closer to, and to the right of, G_R (i.e., $\max(q - t, G_R)$). However, with or without unilateral action, the agenda-setter will be able to move any q to the right of G_R to his or her ideal point because $A = G_R$. In other words, there is no point in the President's taking unilateral action.

Also, for $q < G_L$, the President's equilibrium behavior is slightly different. When $t < 2(A - G_L)$, which is almost always the case because discretion's upper bound, $2(A - G_L)$, is extremely large, the President, as in the previous situations, will unilaterally act only for $q > G_L - t/2$. However, when $t \geq 2(A - G_L)$, $G_L - t/2 < 2G_L - A$. For $q \in [2G_L - A, G_L]$, without presidential unilateral action, the agenda-setter would move q only to $2G_L - q$ because of the constraint G_L. Given the ample discretion delegated to the President, he can do better than $2G_L - q$ by moving q to $\min\{q + t, G_R\}$. For $q \in [-\infty, 2G_L - A]$, the agenda-setter, without prior presidential unilateral action, can always move q to his or her ideal point A, which is the right bound of the gridlock interval, and is the best outcome that the President can accomplish even with unilateral action. Therefore, the President will not unilaterally act for this range of q.

II. RULE C2

According to this rule, the President cannot move the status quo in a direction inconsistent with the chamber medians' ideal points. The proof for the results under rule C1 remains valid, except that the President now cannot move those status quos between M and G_R. Moving these status quos to their right is not the direction permitted by the rule, while shifting them to the left will only make the President worse off.

III. RULE C3

Rule C3 is identical to rule C2, except that majority party medians replace the role of chamber medians in constraining presidential discretion. Here we assume a unified Congress. Under unified government, majority party medians are assumed to be more extreme than override pivots but more moderate than the President, so MP, which is defined as $\max\{MP_H, MP_S\}$ under unified government, is either the right bound of the gridlock interval or is to the right of this right bound. The result is that the President now cannot preempt the agenda-setter for those status quos between the left bound and MP, as any attempt to move them will either violate this rule or undermine the President's own interests. Similarly, under divided government, the President prefers not to exercise any unilateral action for the status quos between MP and G_R, where now MP, defined as $\min\{MP_H, MP_S\}$ under divided government, is assumed to be more extreme than the filibuster pivot and therefore locates to the left of G_L.

EXPECTED INCENTIVES OF UNILATERAL ACTION

We calculate the expected incentives for unilateral action by integrating possible unilateral action over the distributions of discretion and status quos, i.e., $\Pr(x^* \neq q) = \iint \Pr(x^* \neq q \mid t, q) g(t) g(q) dt dq$, where $g(t)$ and $g(q)$ are the distributions of discretion and the status quos, respectively, and $\Pr(x^* \neq q \mid t, q)$ represents the probability of unilateral action given t and q being drawn. To reiterate, and as seen in Proposition 1, $\Pr(x^* \neq q \mid t, q) = 1$ for some

q regardless of the values of t, but $\Pr(x^* \neq q \mid t, q) = 0$ for some others. Therefore, $\Pr(Act) = \Pr(x^* \neq q)$ formally defines the unconditional expected incentive for unilateral action. As mentioned, this implies that a higher $\Pr(Act)$ is associated with more significant EOs being issued during a given Congress, a hypothesis that we can examine empirically for each of our 18 models.

Results with Party Roles in Legislative Stage for Alternative
Threshold Levels

TABLE A.1 *Alternative models and the production of significant executive orders (negative binomial estimates with significance threshold equaling −0.5)*

Model		Constant	First-term	Expected incentives for unilateral action	2* log-likelihood	BIC
No additional constraints on discretion	Preference	5.27*** (0.46)	0.27** (0.12)	−1.68 (0.72)	−243.0	256.3
	Negative agenda-setting	5.61*** (0.38)	0.24*** (0.10)	−2.03 (0.54)	−236.5	249.8
	Imperfect party discipline	5.23*** (0.34)	0.25** (0.11)	−1.59 (0.52)	−239.6	252.9
	Negative agenda-Setting and imperfect party discipline	5.36*** (0.31)	0.25** (0.10)	−1.71 (0.45)	−236.6	249.9
	Positive agenda-setting	5.08*** (0.16)	0.18** (0.09)	−1.28 (0.23)	−226.4	239.7
	Positive agenda-setting and imperfect party discipline	5.02*** (0.16)	0.22** (0.09)	−1.23 (0.23)	−228.6	241.9
Discretion constrained by chamber median	Preference	4.01*** (0.48)	0.33*** (0.12)	0.51 (1.15)	−248.1	261.4
	Negative agenda-setting	5.40*** (0.44)	0.32*** (0.11)	−2.58 (0.96)	−241.7	255.0
	Imperfect party discipline	3.88*** (0.32)	0.29** (0.13)	0.85 (0.78)	−247.2	260.5
	Negative agenda-setting and imperfect party discipline	4.17*** (0.33)	0.32*** (0.13)	0.12 (0.77)	−248.2	261.5
	Positive agenda-setting	4.69*** (0.13)	0.26*** (0.10)	−1.10 (0.28)	−235.2	248.5
	Positive agenda-setting and imperfect party discipline	4.61*** (0.16)	0.32*** (0.11)	−1.04 (0.38)	−241.3	254.6
Discretion constrained by party median	Preference	3.77*** (0.09)	0.28*** (0.08)	1.29*** (0.22)	−225.5	238.8
	Negative agenda-setting	3.68*** (0.09)	0.27*** (0.07)	1.36*** (0.20)	−220.8	234.1
	Imperfect party discipline	3.75*** (0.09)	0.27*** (0.08)	1.35*** (0.24)	−225.9	239.2
	Negative agenda-setting and imperfect party discipline	3.70*** (0.09)	0.26*** (0.08)	1.39*** (0.22)	−223.6	236.9
	Positive agenda-setting	3.63*** (0.20)	0.37*** (0.11)	1.56*** (0.51)	−240.2	253.5
	Positive agenda-setting and imperfect party discipline	3.71*** (0.18)	0.31*** (0.11)	1.47*** (0.50)	−240.8	254.1

Note: $N = 28$. One-tailed tests are used for first-term and expected incentives for unilateral action and standard errors are in parentheses. *** $p < .01$, ** $.01 < p < .05$, * $.05 < p < .10$

TABLE A.2 *Alternative models and the production of significant executive orders (negative binomial estimates with significance threshold equaling 0)*

Scenario		Constant	First-term	Expected incentives for unilateral action	2* log-likelihood	BIC
No additional constraints on discretion	Preference	4.87*** (0.46)	0.28*** (0.12)	−1.54 (0.73)	−226.3	239.6
	Negative agenda-setting	5.11*** (0.40)	0.27*** (0.11)	−1.78 (0.58)	−222.2	235.5
	Imperfect party discipline	4.85*** (0.35)	0.27*** (0.11)	−1.49 (0.53)	−223.3	236.6
	Negative agenda-setting and imperfect party discipline	4.95*** (0.33)	0.27*** (0.10)	−1.58 (0.48)	−221.2	234.5
	Positive agenda-setting	4.61*** (0.19)	0.22** (0.10)	−1.04 (0.27)	−218.4	231.7
	Positive agenda-setting and imperfect party discipline	4.59*** (0.18)	0.24*** (0.10)	−1.05 (0.27)	−218.1	231.4
Discretion constrained by chamber median	Preference	3.77*** (0.48)	0.34*** (0.12)	0.32 (1.15)	−230.6	243.9
	Negative agenda-setting	4.91*** (0.46)	0.34*** (0.11)	−2.21 (0.99)	−226.0	239.3
	Imperfect party discipline	3.72*** (0.32)	0.32*** (0.13)	0.44 (0.80)	−230.4	243.7
	Negative agenda-setting and imperfect party discipline	3.96*** (0.33)	0.35*** (0.13)	−0.13 (0.76)	−230.7	244.0
	Positive agenda-setting	4.27*** (0.15)	0.28*** (0.11)	−0.86 (0.31)	−223.4	236.7
	Positive agenda-setting and imperfect party discipline	4.21*** (0.16)	0.33*** (0.11)	−0.80 (0.40)	−226.8	240.1
Discretion constrained by party median	Preference	3.51*** (0.10)	0.29*** (0.09)	1.13*** (0.25)	−215.4	228.7
	Negative agenda-setting	3.43*** (0.10)	0.28*** (0.09)	1.20*** (0.24)	−212.3	225.6
	Imperfect party discipline	3.50*** (0.10)	0.28*** (0.09)	1.17*** (0.27)	−216.0	229.3
	Negative agenda-setting and imperfect party discipline	3.45*** (0.11)	0.28*** (0.09)	1.21*** (0.26)	−214.4	227.7
	Positive agenda-setting	3.29*** (0.20)	0.38*** (0.10)	1.61*** (0.50)	−221.9	235.2
	Positive agenda-setting and imperfect party discipline	3.41*** (0.18)	0.32*** (0.11)	1.42*** (0.50)	−223.7	237.0

Note: N = 28. One-tailed tests are used for first-term and expected incentives for unilateral action and standard errors are in parentheses. *** $p < .01$, ** .01 < p < .05, * .05 < p < .10

TABLE A.3 *Alternative models and the production of significant executive orders (negative binomial estimates with significance threshold equaling 0.5)*

Scenario		Constant	First-term	Expected incentives for unilateral action	2* log-likelihood	BIC
No additional constraints on discretion	Preference	4.46***(0.57)	0.41***(0.14)	-1.78(0.90)	-208.1	221.4
	Negative agenda-setting	4.78***(0.49)	0.40***(0.13)	-2.11(0.71)	-204.1	217.4
	Imperfect party discipline	4.68***(0.41)	0.38***(0.13)	-2.10(0.63)	-201.8	215.1
	Negative agenda-setting and imperfect party discipline	4.75***(0.38)	0.39***(0.12)	-2.12(0.57)	-200.0	213.3
	Positive agenda-setting	4.21***(0.23)	0.34***(0.12)	-1.29(0.32)	-198.9	212.2
	Positive agenda-setting and imperfect party discipline	4.19***(0.21)	0.37***(0.12)	-1.31(0.32)	-198.1	211.4
Discretion constrained by chamber median	Preference	3.19***(0.58)	0.47***(0.15)	0.36(1.39)	-211.9	225.2
	Negative agenda-setting	4.53***(0.56)	0.48***(0.14)	-2.60(1.22)	-207.7	221.0
	Imperfect party discipline	3.17***(0.39)	0.45***(0.16)	0.43(0.97)	-211.8	225.1
	Negative agenda-setting and imperfect party discipline	3.44***(0.40)	0.48***(0.15)	-0.22(0.92)	-211.9	225.2
	Positive agenda-setting	3.82***(0.17)	0.41***(0.13)	-1.14(0.37)	-203.2	216.5
	Positive agenda-setting and imperfect party discipline	3.74***(0.20)	0.47***(0.13)	-1.04(0.48)	-207.5	220.8
Discretion constrained by party median	Preference	2.88***(0.12)	0.43***(0.11)	1.32***(0.31)	-197.6	210.9
	Negative agenda-setting	2.79***(0.13)	0.42***(0.11)	1.40***(0.29)	-194.7	208.0
	Imperfect party discipline	2.89***(0.13)	0.42***(0.12)	1.30***(0.34)	-199.8	213.1
	Negative agenda-setting and imperfect party discipline	2.84**(0.14)	0.41***(0.12)	1.35***(0.33)	-198.4	211.7
	Positive agenda-setting	2.68***(0.25)	0.51***(0.13)	1.74***(0.63)	-205.2	218.5
	Positive agenda-setting and imperfect party discipline	2.83***(0.23)	0.45***(0.13)	1.47***(0.63)	-207.1	220.4

Note: N = 28. One-tailed tests are used for first-term and expected incentives for unilateral action and standard errors are in parentheses. *** $p < .01$, ** $.01 < p < .05$, * $.05 < p < .10$

TABLE A.4 *Alternative models and the production of significant executive orders (negative binomial estimates with significance threshold equaling 1)*

Scenario		Constant	First-term	Expected incentives for unilateral action	2* log-likelihood	BIC
No additional constraints on discretion	Preference	3.36*** (0.63)	0.57*** (0.16)	−1.18 (0.98)	−177.6	190.9
	Negative agenda-setting	3.53*** (0.57)	0.56*** (0.15)	−1.33 (0.82)	−176.5	189.8
	Imperfect party discipline	3.47*** (0.48)	0.55*** (0.15)	−1.33 (0.74)	−175.9	189.2
	Negative agenda-setting and imperfect party discipline	3.55*** (0.47)	0.55*** (0.14)	−1.40 (0.69)	−175.1	188.4
	Positive agenda-setting	3.21*** (0.28)	0.52*** (0.15)	−0.87 (0.40)	−174.6	187.9
	Positive agenda-setting and imperfect party discipline	3.21*** (0.27)	0.54*** (0.14)	−0.90 (0.39)	−174.2	187.5
Discretion constrained by chamber median	Preference	2.61*** (0.62)	0.61*** (0.15)	0.02 (1.48)	−179.1	192.4
	Negative agenda-setting	3.34*** (0.63)	0.61*** (0.15)	−1.57 (1.36)	−177.8	191.1
	Imperfect party discipline	2.75*** (0.42)	0.63*** (0.16)	−0.33 (1.03)	−179.0	192.3
	Negative agenda-setting and imperfect party discipline	2.89*** (0.42)	0.64*** (0.16)	−0.63 (0.98)	−178.7	192.0
	Positive agenda-setting	2.96*** (0.20)	0.57*** (0.15)	−0.80 (0.44)	−175.8	189.1
	Positive agenda-setting and imperfect party discipline	2.94*** (0.22)	0.61*** (0.14)	−0.86 (0.54)	−176.6	189.9
Discretion constrained by party median	Preference	2.31*** (0.15)	0.58*** (0.14)	0.90** (0.39)	−174.1	187.4
	Negative agenda-setting	2.24*** (0.17)	0.57*** (0.13)	0.97** (0.38)	−173.1	186.4
	Imperfect party discipline	2.33*** (0.16)	0.57*** (0.14)	0.86** (0.42)	−175.1	188.4
	Negative agenda-setting and imperfect party discipline	2.28*** (0.17)	0.57*** (0.14)	0.91** (0.42)	−174.6	187.9
	Positive agenda-setting	2.17*** (0.28)	0.64*** (0.14)	1.20** (0.71)	−176.3	189.6
	Positive agenda-setting and imperfect party discipline	2.32*** (0.25)	0.60*** (0.15)	0.87 (0.70)	−177.6	190.9

Note: $N = 28$. One-tailed tests are used for first-term and expected incentives for unilateral action and standard errors are in parentheses. *** $p < .01$, ** $.01 < p < .05$, * $.05 < p < .10$

TABLE A.5 *Alternative models and the production of significant executive orders (negative binomial estimates with significance threshold equaling 1.5)*

Model		Constant	First-term	Expected incentives for unilateral action	2* log-likelihood	BIC
No additional constraints on discretion	Preference	2.27*** (0.74)	0.72*** (0.18)	-0.96 (1.16)	-140.4	153.7
	Negative agenda-setting	2.36*** (0.69)	0.71*** (0.18)	-1.01 (1.00)	-140.1	153.4
	Imperfect party discipline	2.00*** (0.60)	0.73*** (0.18)	-0.52 (0.92)	-140.8	154.1
	Negative agenda-setting and imperfect party discipline	2.06*** (0.60)	0.73*** (0.18)	-0.59 (0.87)	-140.7	154.0
	Positive agenda-setting	2.13*** (0.36)	0.68*** (0.18)	-0.68 (0.51)	-139.4	152.7
	Positive agenda-setting and imperfect party discipline	1.98*** (0.36)	0.72*** (0.18)	-0.48 (0.52)	-140.3	153.6
Discretion constrained by chamber median	Preference	1.35** (0.71)	0.75*** (0.17)	0.76 (1.70)	-141.0	154.3
	Negative agenda-setting	1.98*** (0.76)	0.76*** (0.17)	-0.69 (1.65)	-141.0	154.3
	Imperfect party discipline	0.88** (0.51)	0.65*** (0.18)	1.95** (1.23)	-138.7	152.0
	Negative agenda-setting and imperfect party discipline	0.97** (0.53)	0.67*** (0.18)	1.62** (1.21)	-139.4	152.7
	Positive agenda-setting	1.93*** (0.26)	0.72*** (0.18)	-0.62 (0.56)	-139.9	153.2
	Positive agenda-setting and imperfect party discipline	1.71*** (0.28)	0.76*** (0.17)	-0.11 (0.67)	-141.1	154.4
Discretion constrained by party median	Preference	1.41*** (0.20)	0.73*** (0.17)	0.75* (0.49)	-138.8	152.1
	Negative agenda-setting	1.33*** (0.22)	0.72*** (0.17)	0.88** (0.48)	-137.9	151.2
	Imperfect party discipline	1.36*** (0.20)	0.71*** (0.17)	0.91** (0.51)	-138.0	151.3
	Negative agenda-setting and imperfect party discipline	1.29*** (0.21)	0.70*** (0.16)	1.01** (0.50)	-137.3	150.6
	Positive agenda-setting	1.23*** (0.33)	0.78*** (0.16)	1.15* (0.83)	-139.2	152.5
	Positive agenda-setting and imperfect party discipline	1.18*** (0.29)	0.73*** (0.16)	1.41** (0.78)	-137.9	151.2

Note: N = 28. One-tailed tests are used for first-term and expected incentives for unilateral action and standard errors are in parentheses. *** $p < .01$, ** $.01 < p < .05$, * $.05 < p < .10$

References

Aldrich, John, and James Alt. 2003. "Introduction to the Special Issue," *Political Analysis* 11(4): 309–315.

Aldrich, John, James Alt and Arthur Lupia. 2008. "The EITM Approach: Origins and Interpretations," in *The Oxford Handbook of Political Methodology*, Janet M. Box-Steffensmeier, Henry E. Brady and David Collier, eds. New York: Oxford University Press.

Bailey, Brian E. 2000. "Federalism: An Antidote to Congress's Separation of Powers Anxiety and Executive Order 13,083," *Indiana Law Journal* 75(1), Article 17.

Bailey, Michael A., Forrest Maltzman and Charles R. Shipan. 2012. "The Amorphous Relationship between Congress and the Courts," in *The Handbook of Political Economy*, George C. Edwards, Frances E. Lee and Eric Schickler, eds. New York: Oxford University Press.

Baker, Frank B., and Seock-Ho Kim. 2004. *Item Response Theory: Parameter Estimation Techniques*. New York: Marcel Dekker.

Baker, Peter. 1997. "Clinton Assails GOP Delay on Herman Vote," *Washington Post*, April 21, 1997, p. A10.

Beckmann, Matthew N. 2010. *Pushing the Agenda: Presidential Leadership in US Lawmaking, 1953–2004*. New York: Cambridge University Press.

Bennet, James. 1998. "True to Form, Clinton Shifts Energies Back to US Focus," *New York Times*, July 5, 1998, p. 10.

Benoit, Kenneth, and Alexander Herzog. 2017. "Text Analysis: Estimating Policy Preferences from Written and Spoken Words," in *Analytics, Policy and Governance*, Jennifer Bachner, Kathryn Wagner Hill and Benjamin Ginsberg, eds. New Haven, CT: Yale University Press.

Berry, Christopher R., Barry C. Burden and William G. Howell. 2010. "The President and the Distribution of Federal Spending," *American Political Science Review* 104(4): 783–799.

Berry, Michael John. 2008. Beyond Chadha: The Modern Legislative Veto as Macropolitical Conflict. PhD dissertation, University of Colorado, Department of Political Science.

Binder, Sarah A. 1999. "The Dynamics of Legislative Gridlock, 1947–96," *American Political Science Review* 93(3): 519–33.

Binder, Sarah A. 2003. *Stalemate: Causes and Consequences of Legislative Gridlock.* Washington, DC: Brookings Institution Press.

Bjerre-Poulsen, Niels. 2012. "The Bush Administration and the Theory of 'The Unitary Executive,'" in *Projections of Power in the Americas*, Niels Bjerre-Poulsen, Helene Balslev Paulson and Jan Gustafsson, eds. New York: Routledge.

Bond, Jon R., Gary W. Copeland, Lance T. LeLoup, Russell D. Renka and Steven A. Shull. 1991. "Implications for Research in Studying Presidential-Congressional Relations: Conclusions," in *The Two Presidencies: A Quarter Century Assessment*, Steven A. Shull, ed. Chicago, IL: Nelson-Hall.

Bond, Jon R., and Richard Fleisher. 1990. *The President in the Legislative Arena.* Chicago, IL: University of Chicago Press.

Bonica, Adam. 2013. "Mapping the Ideological Marketplace," *American Journal of Political Science* 58(2): 367–386.

Boyle, Stephen Charles. 2007. Consultation, Cooperation, and Delegation: Presidential Power in the Twenty-First Century. PhD dissertation, University of Florida, Department of Political Science.

Brady, David W., Joseph Cooper and Patricia A. Hurley. 1979. "The Decline of Party in the US House of Representatives, 1887–1968," *Legislative Studies Quarterly* 4(3): 381–407.

Brady, David W., and Craig Volden. 2005. *Revolving Gridlock: Politics and Policy from Carter to Clinton*, 2nd edn. New York: Westview.

Broder, David S. 1983. "Old Debate Revived: Latin Unit Gets Mixed Reviews," *Washington Post*, July 19, 1983, p. A1.

Burnham, David. 1985. "Budget Office Role in Reviewing New Rules Expanded by Reagan," *New York Times*, January 5, 1985, p. 7.

Calabresi, Steven G., and Christopher S. Yoo. 2008. *The Unitary Executive.* New Haven, CT: Yale University Press.

Cameron, Charles M. 2000. *Veto Bargaining: Presidents and the Politics of Negative Power.* Cambridge: Cambridge University Press.

Cameron, Charles M. 2006. "The Political Economy of the US Presidency," in *The Handbook of Political Economy*, Barry Weingast and Donald Wittman, eds. New York: Oxford University Press.

Cameron, Charles M. 2009. "The Presidential Veto," in *The Oxford Handbook of the American Presidency*, George C. Edwards III and William G. Howell, eds. New York: Oxford University Press.

Cameron, Charles, and Nolan McCarty. 2004. "Models of Vetoes and Veto Bargaining," *Annual Review of Political Science* 7: 409–435.

Canes-Wrone, Brandice. 2005. *Who Leads Whom?: Presidents, Policy and the Public.* Chicago, IL: University of Chicago Press.

Canes-Wrone, Brandice, William G. Howell, and David E. Lewis. 2008. "Toward a Broader Understanding of Presidential Power: A Re-evaluation of the Two Presidencies Thesis," *Journal of Politics* 70(1): 1–16.

Carey, Maeve P. 2015. "Counting Regulations: An Overview of Rulemaking, Types of Federal Regulations and Pages in the *Federal Register*." Washington, DC, Congressional Research Report R43056.

Chiou, Fang-Yi. 2005. "A New Approach for Jointly Measuring Party Pressure, Party Effects and Preferences." Unpublished manuscript.

Chiou, Fang-Yi, and Lawrence S. Rothenberg. 2003. "When Pivotal Politics Meets Partisan Politics," *American Journal of Political Science* 47(3): 503–522.

Chiou, Fang-Yi, and Lawrence S. Rothenberg. 2006. "Preferences, Parties and Legislative Productivity," *American Politics Research* 34(6): 705–731.

Chiou, Fang-Yi, and Lawrence S. Rothenberg. 2009. "A Unified Theory of US Lawmaking," *Journal of Politics* 71(4): 1257–1272.

Chiou, Fang-Yi, and Lawrence S. Rothenberg. 2014. "Executive Appointments: Duration, Ideology and Hierarchy," *Journal of Theoretical Politics* 26(3): 496–517.

Christenson, Dino P., and Douglas Kriner. 2015. "Political Constraints on Unilateral Executive Action," *Case Western Law Review* 65(4): 897–931.

Clarke, Kevin A. 2001. "Testing Non-nested Models of International Relations: Re-evaluating Realism," *American Journal of Political Science* 45(3): 724–744.

Clinton, Joshua, Simon Jackman and Douglas Rivers. 2004. "The Statistical Analysis of Roll Call Data," *American Political Science Review* 98(2): 355–370.

Clinton, Joshua D., and John T. Lapinski. 2006. "Measuring Legislative Accomplishment, 1977–1994," *American Journal of Political Science* 50(1): 232–249.

Cohen, Jeffrey E. 1992. "A Historical Reassessment of Wildavsky's 'Two Presidencies' Thesis," *Social Science Quarterly* 63(3): 549–55.

Cooper, Joseph, and William F. West. 1988. "Presidential Power and Republican Government: The Theory and Practice of OMB Review of Agency Rules," *Journal of Politics* 50(4): 864–895.

Cooper, Phillip J. 1986. "By Order of the President: Administration by Executive Order and Proclamation," *Administration & Society* 18(2): 233–262.

Cooper, Phillip J. 2001. "The Law: Presidential Memoranda and Executive Orders: Of Patchwork Quilts, Trump Cards and Shell Games," *Presidential Studies Quarterly* 31(1): 126–141.

Cooper, Phillip J. 2002. *By Order of the President: The Use and Abuse of Executive Direct Action*. Lawrence, KS: University of Kansas Press.

Cooper, Phillip J. 2005. "George W. Bush, Edgar Allan Poe and the Use and Abuse of Presidential Signing Statements," *Presidential Studies Quarterly* 35(3): 515–532.

Čopič, Jernej, and Jonathan N. Katz. 2014. "Scheduling Auctions and Proto-Parties in Legislatures." Working paper, California Institute of Technology.

Cox, Gary W. 2006. "The Legislative Calendar," in *The Oxford Handbook of Political Economy*, Barry G. Weingast and Donald A. Wittman, eds. New York: Oxford University Press.

Cox, Gary W., and Mathew D. McCubbins. 2005. *Setting the Agenda: Responsible Party Government in the US House of Representatives*. New York: Cambridge University Press.

Cox, Gary W., and Mathew D. McCubbins. 2007. *Legislative Leviathan: Party Government in the House*, 2nd edn. New York: Cambridge University Press.

Cox, Gary W., and Mathew D. McCubbins. 2011. "Managing Plenary Time: The US Congress in Comparative Context," in *The Oxford Handbook of the American Congress*, George C. Edwards, Frances E. Lee and Eric Schickler, eds. New York: Oxford University Press.

Cox, Gary W., and Keith T. Poole. 2002. "On Measuring Partisanship in Roll-Call Voting: The US House of Representatives, 1877–1999," *American Journal of Political Science* 46(3): 477–489.

Crombez, Christophe, Tim Groseclose and Keith Krehbiel. 2006. "Gatekeeping," *Journal of Politics* 68(2): 322–334.

Dahl, Robert A. 1957. "The Concept of Power," *Behavioral Scientist* 2(3): 201–215.

Deering, Christopher J., and Forrest Maltzman. 1999. "The Politics of Executive Orders: Legislative Constraints on Presidential Power," *Political Research Quarterly* 52(4): 767–83.

Dodds, Graham G. 2006. "Executive Orders from Nixon to Now," in *Executing the Constitution: Putting the President Back into the Constitution*, Christopher S. Kelley, ed. Albany, NY: SUNY Press.

Dodds, Graham G. 2013. *Take Up Your Pen: Unilateral Presidential Directives in American Politics*. Philadelphia, PA: University of Pennsylvania Press.

Douthat, Ross. 2014. "The Making of an Imperial President," *New York Times*, November 23, 2014, p. SR9.

Edwards, George C. 1986. "The Two Presidencies: A Re-evaluation," *American Politics Quarterly* 14(2): 247–263.

Epstein, David, and Sharyn O'Halloran. 1999. *Delegating Powers: A Transaction Cost Politics Approach to Policy Making under Separate Powers*. New York: Cambridge University Press.

Evans, C. Lawrence, and Claire E. Grandy. 2009. "The Whip Systems in Congress," in *Congress* Reconsidered, 9th edn., Lawrence C. Dodd and Bruce I. Oppenheimer, eds. Washington, DC: Congressional Quarterly Press.

Fine, Jeffrey A., and Adam L. Warber. 2012. "Circumventing Adversity: Executive Orders and Divided Government," *Presidential Studies Quarterly* 42(2): 256–274.

Fisher, Louis. 2005. "Legislative Vetoes after *Chadha*," Washington, DC, Congressional Research Service Report RS22132.

Fleisher, Richard, and Jon R. Bond. 1988. "Are There Two Presidencies? Yes, But Only for Republicans," *Journal of Politics* 50(3): 747–767.

Fleisher, Richard, Jon R. Bond, Glen S. Krutz, and Stephen Hanna. 2000. "The Demise of the Two Presidencies," *American Politics Quarterly* 28(1): 3–25.

Gentzkow, Matthew, and Jesse Shapiro. 2010. "What Drives Media Slant? Evidence from U.S. Daily Newspapers," *Econometrica* 78(1): 35–71.

Gleiber, Dennis W., and Steven A. Shull. 1992. "Presidential Influence in the Policy-Making Process," *Western Political Quarterly* 45(2): 441–468.

Grant, J. Tobin, and Nathan J. Kelly. 2008. "Legislative Productivity of the U.S. Congress, 1789–2004," *Political Analysis* 16(3): 303–323.

Groseclose, Tim, and Jeffrey Milyo. 2005. "A Measure of Media Bias," *Quarterly Journal of Economics* 120(4): 1191–1237.

Hahn, Robert W., and Patrick M. Dudley. 2007. "How Well Does the U.S. Government Do Benefit–Cost Analysis?," *Review of Environmental Economics and Policy* 1(2): 192–211.

Hahn, Robert W., and Cass R. Sunstein. 2002. "A New Executive Order for Improving Federal Regulation? Deeper and Wider Cost-Benefit Analysis," AEI-Brookings Joint Center for Regulatory Studies Working Paper No. 02–4.

Hambleton, Ronald K., H. Swaminathan and H. Jane Rogers. 1991. *Fundamentals of Item Response Theory*. Newbury Park, CA: Sage Publications.

Hassell, Hans J. G., and Samuel Kernell. 2016. "Veto Rhetoric and Legislative Riders," *American Journal of Political Science*, 60(4): 845–859.

Holland, Steve. 2014. "Obama's Executive Actions: The Power of Taking Small Steps," Washington, DC: *Reuters*.

Hollibaugh, Gary E., Jr. 2015. "Vacancies, Vetting and Votes: A Unified Dynamic Model of the Appointments Process," *Journal of Theoretical Politics* 27(2): 206–236.

Howell, William G. 2003. *Power without Persuasion: The Politics of Direct Political Action*. Chicago, IL: University of Chicago Press.

Howell, William G. 2005. "Unilateral Powers: A Brief Overview," *Presidential Studies Quarterly* 35(3): 417–439.

Howell, William, Scott Adler, Charles Cameron and Charles Riemann. 2000. "Divided Government and the Legislative Productivity of Congress, 1945–94," *Legislative Studies Quarterly* 25(2): 285–312.

Howell, William G., and Saul P. Jackman. 2013. "Interbranch Negotiations over Policies with Multiple Outcomes," *American Journal of Political Science* 57(4): 956–970.

Howell, William G., and Kenneth R. Mayer. 2005. "The Last One Hundred Days," *Presidential Studies Quarterly* 35(3): 533–553.

Hudak, John. 2014. *Presidential Pork: White House Influence over the Distribution of Federal Grants*. Washington, DC: Brookings Institution Press.

Jackman, Simon. 2004. "What Do We Learn from Graduate Admissions Committees? A Multiple-Rater, Latent Variable Model, with Incomplete Discrete and Continuous Indicators," *Political Analysis* 12(4): 400–424.

Johnson, Valen E., and James H. Albert. 1999. *Ordinal Data Modeling*. New York: Springer-Verlag.

Kelly, Sean Q. 1993. "Divided We Govern? A Reassessment," *Polity* 25(3): 475–484.

King, Gary, and Lyn Ragsdale. 1988. *The Elusive Executive: Statistical Patterns in the Presidency*. Washington, DC: Congressional Quarterly Press.

Kosterlitz, Julie. 1997. "Labor's Along for the Ride," *National Journal*, May 3, 1997, p. 896.

Krause, George A., and Jeffrey E. Cohen. 1997. "Presidential Use of Executive Orders, 1953–1994," *American Politics Quarterly* 25(4): 458–481.

Krause, George, and David Cohen. 2000. "Opportunity, Constraints, and the Development of the Institutional Presidency: The Case of Executive Orders Issuance, 1939–1996," *Journal of Politics* 62(1): 88–1114.

Krehbiel, Keith. 1993. "Where's the Party?" *British Journal of Political Science* 23(2): 235–266.

Krehbiel, Keith. 1998. *Pivotal Politics: A Theory of U.S. Lawmaking*. Chicago, IL: University of Chicago Press.

Krehbiel, Keith, Adam Meirowitz and Thomas Romer. 2005. "Parties in Elections, Parties in Government, and Partisan Bias," *Political Analysis* 13(2): 113–138.

Kriner, Douglas L., and Andrew Reeves. 2012. "The Influence of Federal Spending on Presidential Elections," *American Political Science Review* 106(2): 348–366.

Lapinski, John S. 2008. "Policy Substance and Performance in American Lawmaking, 1877–1994," *American Journal of Political Science* 52(2): 235–251.

LeoGrande, William M. 1984. "Through the Looking Glass: The Kissinger Report on Central America," *World Policy Journal* 1(2): 251–284.

Lessig, Lawrence, and Cass R. Sunstein. 1994. "The President and the Administration," *Columbia Law Review* 94(1): 1–123.

Lewis, David E. 2008. *The Politics of Presidential Appointments: Political Control and Bureaucratic Performance.* Princeton, NJ: Princeton University Press.

Lewis, David E., and Terry M. Moe. 2010. "The Presidency and the Bureaucracy: The Levers of Bureaucratic Control," in *The Presidency and the Political System,* 9th edn., Michael Nelson, ed. Washington, DC: Congressional Quarterly Press.

Light, Paul C. 1982. *The President's Agenda: Domestic Policy Choice from Kennedy to Carter.* Baltimore, MD: Johns Hopkins University Press.

Lindsay, James M., and Wayne P. Steger. 1993. "The 'Two Presidencies' in Future Research: Moving beyond Roll-Call Analysis," *Congress & the Presidency* 20(2): 103–117.

Londregan, John. 1999. "Estimating Legislators' Preferred Points," *Political Analysis* 8(1): 35–56.

Lowande, Kenneth S. 2014. "*The Contemporary Presidency* after the Orders: Presidential Memoranda and Unilateral Action," *Presidential Studies Quarterly* 44(4): 724–741.

Lowi, Theodore J. 1964. "American Business, Public Policy, Case Studies and Political Theory," *World Politics* 16(4): 677–715.

Macey, Jonathan. 2006. "Executive Branch Usurpation of Power: Corporations and Capital Markets," *Yale Law Journal* 115(9): 2416–2444.

Maisel, L. Sandy, and Jeffrey M. Berry, eds. 2010. *The Oxford Handbook of American Political Parties and Interest Groups.* New York: Oxford University Press.

Marcus, Maeva, and Louis Fisher. 1994. *Truman and the Steel Seizure Case: The Limits of Presidential Power.* Durham, NC: Duke University Press.

Marshall, Bryan W., and Richard L. Pacelle, Jr. 2005. "Revisiting the Two Presidencies: The Strategic Use of Executive Orders," *American Politics Research* 33(1): 81–105.

Marshall, Bryan W., and Brandon C. Prins. 2011. "Power or Posturing? Policy Availability and Congressional Influence on U.S. Presidential Decisions to Use Force," *Presidential Studies Quarterly* 41(3): 521–545.

Martin, Andrew D., and Kevin M. Quinn. 2002. "Dynamic Ideal Point Estimation via Markov Chain Monte Carlo for the U.S. Supreme Court, 1953–1999," *Political Analysis* 10(2): 134–153.

Martin, Lisa L. 2000. *Democratic Commitments: Legislatures and International Cooperation.* Princeton, NJ: Princeton University Press.

Martin, Lisa L. 2005. "The President and International Commitments: Treaties as Signaling Devices," *Presidential Studies Quarterly* 35(3): 440–65.

Mayer, Kenneth R. 1999. "Executive Orders and Presidential Power," *Journal of Politics* 61(2): 445–466.

Mayer, Kenneth R. 2002. *With the Stroke of a Pen: Executive Orders and Presidential Power.* Princeton, NJ: Princeton University Press.

Mayer, Kenneth R. 2009. "Going Alone: The Presidential Power of Unilateral Action," in *The Oxford Handbook of the American Presidency,* George C. Edwards III and William G. Howell, eds. New York: Oxford University Press.

Mayer, Kenneth R., and Kevin Price. 2002. "Unilateral Presidential Powers: Significant Executive Orders, 1949–1999," *Presidential Studies Quarterly* 32(2): 367–386.

Mayhew, David. 2005. *Divided We Govern: Party Control, Lawmaking, and Investigations, 1946–2002,* 2nd edn. New Haven, CT: Yale University Press.

McCarty, Nolan. 1997. "Presidential Reputation and the Veto," *Economics and Politics* 9(1): 1–26.

McCarty, Nolan. 2000a. "Proposal Rights, Veto Rights, and Political Bargaining," *American Journal of Political Science* 44(3): 506–522.

McCarty, Nolan. 2000b. "Presidential Pork: Executive Veto Power and Distributive Politics," *American Political Science Review* 94(1): 117–129.

McCarty, Nolan. 2004. "The Appointments Dilemma," *American Journal of Political Science* 48(3): 413–428.

McCarty, Nolan, Keith T. Poole and Howard Rosenthal. 2008. *Polarized America: The Dance of Ideology and Unequal Riches.* Cambridge, MA: MIT Press.

McCarty, Nolan, and Rose Razaghian. 1999. "Advice and Consent: Senate Responses to Executive Branch Nominations 1885–1996," *American Journal of Political Science* 43(4): 1122–1143.

McDonald, Jason A. 2010. "Limitation Riders and Congressional Influence over Bureaucratic Policy Decisions," *American Political Science Review* 104(4): 766–782.

Milkis, Sidney M., and Jesse H. Rhodes. 2010. "The President, Party Politics, and Constitutional Development," in *The Oxford Handbook of American Political Parties and Interest Groups*, L. Sandy Maisel and Jeffrey M. Berry, eds. New York: Oxford University Press.

Miller, Gary. 1993. "Formal Theory and the Presidency," in *Research the Presidency: Vital Questions, New Approaches*, George C. Edwards II, John H. Kessel, and Bert A. Rockman, eds. Pittsburgh, PA: University of Pittsburgh Press.

Milner, Helner, and Dustin Tingley. 2011. "Who Supports Global Economic Engagement? The Sources of Preferences in American Foreign Economic Policy," *International Organization* 65(1): 37–68.

Moe, Terry M. 1987. "An Assessment of the Positive Theory of 'Congressional Dominance'," *Legislative Studies Quarterly* 12(4): 475–520.

Moe, Terry M. 2009. "The Revolution in Presidential Studies," *Presidential Studies Quarterly* 39(4): 701–724.

Moe, Terry M., and William G. Howell. 1999a. "The Presidential Power of Unilateral Action," *Journal of Law, Economics, and Organization* 15(1): 132–179.

Moe, Terry M., and William G. Howell. 1999b. "Unilateral Action and Presidential Power: A Theory," *Presidential Studies Quarterly* 24(4): 850–873.

Moe, Terry M., and Scott A. Wilson. 1994. "Presidents and the Politics of Structure," *Law and Contemporary Problems* 59(2): 1–44.

Monroe, Nathan W., Jason M. Roberts and David W. Rohde. 2008. "Electoral Accountability, Party Loyalty, and Roll-Call Voting in the U.S. Senate," in *Why Not Parties? Party Effects in the United States Senate*, Nathan W. Monroe, Jason M. Roberts, and David W. Rohde, eds. Chicago, IL: University of Chicago Press.

Morgan, Ruth P. 1970. *The President and Civil Rights: Policy-Making by Executive Order.* New York: St. Martin's.

National Bipartisan Commission on Central America. 1984. *Report of the President's Bipartisan Commission on Central America.* New York: Macmillan.

Neustadt, Richard E. 1991. *Presidential Power and the Modern Presidents: The Politics of Leadership from Roosevelt to Reagan.* New York: Free Press.

O'Connell, Anne Joseph. 2015. "Shortening Agency and Judicial Vacancies through Filibuster Reform? An Examination of Confirmation Rates and Delays from 1981 to 2014," *Duke Law Journal* 64(8): 1645–1715.

Palmer, Maxwell. 2013. "Time and Political Power: Setting the Calendar in a Busy Legislature." Working paper, Harvard University.

Patterson, Samuel C., and Gregory A. Calderia. 1988. "Party Voting in the United States Congress," *British Journal of Political Science* 18(1): 111–131.

Patty, John W., and Elizabeth Maggie Penn. 2008. "The Legislative Calendar," *Mathematical and Computer Modeling* 48(9–10): 1590–1601.

Poole, Keith T., and Howard Rosenthal. 1997. *Congress: A Political-Economic History of Roll Call Voting*. New York: Oxford University Press.

Primo, David, Sarah Binder and Forrest Maltzman. 2008. "Who Consents? Competing Pivots in Federal Judicial Selection," *American Journal of Political Science* 52(3): 471–489.

Raftery, Adrian E. 1995. "Bayesian Model Selection in Social Research," *Sociological Methodology* 25: 111–163.

Relyea, Harold C. 2008. "Presidential Directives: Background and Overview," Washington, DC, Congressional Research Service Report 980–611.

Ripley, Randall B., and Grace A. Franklin. 1984. *Congress, the Bureaucracy, and Public Policy*, 3rd edn. Homewood, IL: Dorsey Press.

Rodriguez, Daniel B., Edward H. Stiglitz, and Barry R. Weingast. 2016. "Executive Opportunism, Presidential Signing Statements, and the Separation of Powers," *Journal of Legal Analysis* 8(1): 95–119.

Rohde, David W. 1991. *Parties and Leaders in the Postreform House*. Chicago, IL: University of Chicago Press.

Rohde, David W. 2010. "What a Difference Twenty-Five Years Makes: Changing Perspectives on Parties and Leaders in the U.S. House," in *The Oxford Handbook of American Political Parties and Interest Groups*, L. Sandy Maisel and Jeffrey M. Berry, eds. New York: Oxford University Press.

Rottinghaus, Brandon, and Jason Maier. 2007. "The Power of Decree: Presidential Use of Executive Proclamations, 1977–2005," *Political Research Quarterly* 60(2): 338–343.

Rudalevige, Andrew. 2002. *Managing the President's Program: Presidential Leadership and Legislative Policy Formulation*. Princeton, NJ: Princeton University Press.

Rudalevige, Andrew. 2012. "The Contemporary Presidency: Executive Orders and Presidential Unilateralism," *Presidential Studies Quarterly* 42(1): 138–160.

Schlesinger, Arthur M., Jr. 1973. *The Imperial Presidency*. Boston, MA: Houghton Mifflin.

Shipan, Charles R. 2004. "Regulatory Regimes, Agency Actions, and the Conditional Nature of Political Influence," *American Political Science Review* 98(3): 467–480.

Shull, Steven A., and Brad T. Gomez. 1997. "Presidential Executive Action," in *Presidential-Congressional Relations: Policy and Time Approaches*, Steven A. Shull, ed. Ann Arbor, MI: University of Michigan Press.

Sigelman, Lee. 1979. "A Reassessment of the Two Presidencies Thesis," *Journal of Politics* 41(4): 1195–1205.

Singh, Robert. 2009. "George W. Bush and the U.S. Congress," in *Assessing the George W. Bush Presidency: A Tale of Two Terms*, Andrew Wroe and Jon Herbert, eds. Edinburgh, Scotland: Edinburgh University Press.

Smith, Steven S. 2007. *Partisan Influence in Congress*. New York: Cambridge University Press.

Smith, Steven S., Jason M. Roberts, and Ryan J. Vander Wielen. 2013. *The American Congress*, 7th edn. New York: Cambridge University Press.

Snyder, James M., Jr., and Tim Groseclose. 2000. "Estimating Party Influence in Congressional Roll-Call Voting," *American Journal of Political Science* 44(2): 193–211.

Sullivan, Terry. 1991. "A Matter of Fact: The 'Two Presidencies' Thesis Revitalized," in *The Two Presidencies: A Quarter Century Assessment*, Steven A. Shull, ed. Chicago, IL: Nelson-Hall.

Sundquist, James. 1989. "Needed: A Political Theory for the New Era of Coalition Government in the United States," *Political Science Quarterly* 103(4): 613–635.

Turner, Ronald. 1996. "Banning the Permanent Replacement of Strikers by Executive Order: The Conflict between Executive Order 12954 and the NLRA," *Journal of Law & Politics* 12(1): 1–61.

Volden, Craig. 2002. "A Formal Model of the Politics of Delegation in a Separation of Powers System," *American Journal of Political Science* 46(1): 111–133.

Volden, Craig, and Elizabeth Bergman. 2006. "How Strong Should Our Party Be? Party Member Preferences over Party Cohesion," *Legislative Studies Quarterly* 31(1): 71–104.

Warber, Adam L. 2006. *Executive Orders and the Modern Presidency: Legislating from the Oval Office*. Boulder, CO: Lynne Reinner.

Wasitis, Dennis E. 1993–94. "Sale v. Haitian Centers Council, Inc: Closing the Golden Door," *Akron Law Review* 27(2): 237–252.

Waterman, Richard W. 2009. "Assessing the Unilateral Presidency," in *The Oxford Handbook of the American Presidency*, George C. Edwards III and William G. Howell, eds. New York: Oxford University Press.

Wells, Robert Marshall. 1997. "Labor: Herman is Confirmed Easily after Clinton-GOP Accord," *Congressional Quarterly Weekly Report*, May 3, 1997, p. 1026.

West, William F. and Joseph Cooper. 1985. "The Rise of Administrative Clearance," in George Edwards, Norman Thomas, and Steven Schull, eds. *The President and Public Policy Making*. Pittsburgh, PA: University of Pittsburgh Press.

Wicker, Tom. 1983. "Hiding Behind Henry," *New York Times*, July 19, 1983, p. A21.

Wigton, Robert C. 1996. "Recent Presidential Experience with Executive Orders," *Presidential Studies Quarterly* 26(2): 473–484.

Wildavsky, Aaron. 1966. "The Two Presidencies," *Trans-action* 4(2): 162–173.

Wilson, James Q. 1973. *Political Organizations*. New York: Basic Books.

Yoo, Christopher S. 2010. "Symposium: Presidential Power in Historical Perspective: Reflections on Calabresi and Yoo's *The Unitary Executive*: Foreword," *University of Pennsylvania Journal of Constitutional Law* 12(2): 241–250.

Zeidenstein, Harvey G. 1981. "The Two Presidencies Thesis Is Alive and Well and Has Been Living in the U.S. Senate Since 1973," *Presidential Studies Quarterly* 11(4): 511–552.

Index